Disclaimer:

The information within this book was gathered from various sources and is for reference purposes only as issues could arise due to problems with the original source of information or through translation. Therefore, though all efforts have been made to provide the most reliable source of data possible, all information taken from within this book should be verified from other independent external sources before applying such information to ensure safety, quality and efficiency when performing tasks which require information on the many aspects discussed herein. The author and publisher takes no responsibility for any damage to equipment or bodily harm to personnel, neither are they to be held accountable for any extra costs incurred due to issues resulting from the use and or misuse of the information herein. This book was not written by an engineer so read and apply the information within at your own risk.

ALWAYS VERIFY ANY AND ALL INFORMATION WITHIN THIS BOOK BY WAY OF THE APPROPRIATE CODES, QC DEPARTMENT, MARKED RATINGS, TAGS, STENCILS, FIELD MEASUREMENTS, ETC. ALL ASME, ANSI, API, ETC., CODES ARE PROVIDED WITH THE INFORMATION WHICH PERTAINS TO THEM TO ALLOW FOR FURTHER VERIFICATION OF ALL INFORMATION HEREIN. DO NOT ALLOW THIS BOOK TO BE THE ONLY SOURCE OF INFORMATION CONCERNING THOSE ASPECTS IT ADDRESSES. IT IS MEANT TO CONTRIBUTE TO QUALITY AND SAFETY SO DON'T LET IT CAUSE AN ISSUE WITH EITHER BY WAY OF NOT ATTEMPTING TO VERIFY THE INFORMATION HEREIN BEFORE THE APPLICATION THEREOF. THIS BOOK IS A GOOD REPRESENTATION OF THE MANY CONSIDERATIONS REQUIRED WHEN PERFORMING TASKS WITHIN THE FIELD AND IS PROVIDED AS AN ADDITIONAL REFERENCE TO COMPARE TO OTHER SOURCES OF INFORMATION.

There is no other single job title which encompasses a broader range of duties in the modern construction and maintenance industry of today than that of the 'boilermaker'. Even within the same title, there is a difference between the paper mill side of the business and the refinery and chemical plant side with the latter being more inclined to working equipment such as exchangers, towers, drums, valves, heaters, etc., and their associated piping. In accomplishing such a variety of tasks, one must be a skilled craftsman in a wide range of fields whereby having a knowledge of not only the various types of equipment being worked on, but also aspects of the various trades required to accomplish such (e.g. pipefitting, rigging, welding, hydro's, torque procedures, etc.).

This book is intended to supply a basic reference to the wide spectrum of aspects covered by the title of refinery and chemical plant 'boilermaker' which inevitably will also apply to many more industrial trades and construction sites. I put this information together in one resource after working for years in the industry from my own personal booklet which contained much of the information herein which I have yet to find in any other single reference source. Each section also begins with some tips and information I've acquired over the years pertaining to that particular section heading. Though the information provided is intended for day to day aspects of the craftsman in the field, I've also tried to make the range and scope of the book broad enough to offer a little something for everyone all the way from those performing the tasks to those overseeing and assuring the quality thereof. I hope that the information herein effectively offers something for the various mechanics of the craftsman and execution of the supervisor perspective all the way to the more technical aspects useful to the QC and inspections department, while bringing much of the until now scattered information into the most comprehensive resource on the market for the industrial trades it pertains to.

TABLE OF CONTENTS		
CHAPTER 1	**BLINDS**	1
	Blind Diameter: NPS 1/4 – 24 Class 150 – 2500	2
	Blind Diameter: NPS 26 – 60 Class 75 – 300	3
	Blind Diameter: NPS 26 – 60 Class 400 – 900	4
CHAPTER 2	**PRESSURE RATINGS AND HYDROSTATIC TESTING**	5
	Hydrostatic Test Tree considerations	8
	Safe Working Pressure A106 Grade B Nipples	9
	Safe Working Pressure Formula For Pipe	10
	Working and Test Pressure of A105 Small Bore Gate Valves	12
	Fitting Ratings Correlation to Pipe Schedule Per Class	12
	Typical Test Tree Configuration	13
	Feet Head of Water To PSI	14
	Working and Hydrostatic Test Pressure For Gate Valves	15
	Working and Hydrostatic Test Pressure For Flanges	23
	Blind Pressure Rated Thickness Formula	26
	Basic Allowable Stresses In Tension For Metals	27
	Blind Pressure Rated Thickness: NPS 1/2 – 24 Class 150 – 2500	28
	Blind Pressure Rated Thickness: NPS 26 – 48 Class 150 – 900	29
CHAPTER 3	**GASKETS**	30
	Gasket Color Code Chart For Spiral Wound Gaskets	31
	Gasket OD Centering Ring: NPS 1/4 – 24 Class 150 – 2500	32
	Gasket OD Centering Ring: NPS 26 – 60 Class 75 – 300	33
	Gasket OD Centering Ring: NPS 26 – 60 Class 400 – 900	34
	Gasket ID Sealing Element: NPS 1/4 – 24 Class 150 – 2500	35
	Gasket ID Sealing Element: NPS 26 – 60 Class 75 – 300	36
	Gasket ID Sealing Element: NPS 26 – 60 Class 400 – 900	37
	Gasket ID Inner Ring: NPS 1/2 – 24 Class 150 – 2500	38
	Gasket ID Inner Ring: NPS 26 – 60 Class 150 – 300	39
	Gasket ID Inner Ring: NPS 26 – 60 Class 400 – 900	40
CHAPTER 4	**STUD BOLTS**	41
	Threads Per Inch	42
	Wrench Size Per Stud Diameter	42
	Stud Dimensions: NPS 1/2 – 24 Class 150	43
	Stud Dimensions: NPS 1/2 – 24 Class 300	44
	Stud Dimensions: NPS 1/2 – 24 Class 400	45
	Stud Dimensions: NPS 1/2 – 24 Class 600	46
	Stud Dimensions: NPS 1/2 – 24 Class 900	47
	Stud Dimensions: NPS 1/2 – 24 Class 1500	48
	Stud Dimensions: NPS 1/2 – 24 Class 2500	49
	Stud Dimensions: Orifice Flange NPS 1–24 Class 300 – 900	50
	Stud Dimensions: Orifice Flange NPS 1–24 Class 1500 – 2500	51
	Stud Dimensions: NPS 26 – 60 Class 75	52
	Stud Dimensions: NPS 26 – 60 Class 150	53
	Stud Dimensions: NPS 26 – 60 Class 300	54
	Stud Dimensions: NPS 26 – 60 Class 400	55
	Stud Dimensions: NPS 26 – 60 Class 600	56
	Stud Dimensions: NPS 26 – 48 Class 900	57

CHAPTER 5	**FLANGES**	58
	Dimensions: NPS 1/2 – 24 Class 150 – 300	59
	Dimensions: NPS 1/2 – 24 Class 400 – 600	60
	Dimensions: NPS 1/2 – 24 Class 900 – 1500	61
	Dimensions: NPS 1/2 – 24 Class 2500	62
	Weights: NPS 1/2 – 24 Class 150	63
	Weights: NPS 1/2 – 24 Class 300	64
	Weights: NPS 1/2 – 24 Class 400	65
	Weights: NPS 1/2 – 24 Class 600	66
	Weights: NPS 1/2 – 24 Class 900	67
	Weights: NPS 1/2 – 24 Class 1500	68
	Weights: NPS 1/2 – 24 Class 2500	69
	Dimensions: NPS 26 – 60 Class 75 Series B	70
	Dimensions: NPS 26 – 60 Class 150 Series A	71
	Dimensions: NPS 26 – 60 Class 150 Series B	72
	Dimensions: NPS 26 – 60 Class 300 Series A	73
	Dimensions: NPS 26 – 60 Class 300 Series B	74
	Dimensions: NPS 26 – 60 Class 400 Series A	75
	Dimensions: NPS 26 – 60 Class 400 Series B	76
	Dimensions: NPS 26 – 60 Class 600 Series A	77
	Dimensions: NPS 26 – 60 Class 600 Series B	78
	Dimensions: NPS 26 – 48 Class 900 Series A and B	79
	Weights: NPS 26 – 60 Class 75 – 150 Series A and B	80
	Weights: NPS 26 – 60 Class 300 – 400 Series A and B	81
	Weights: NPS 26 – 60 Class 600 – 900 Series A and B	82
CHAPTER 6	**VALVES**	83
	Common Valve Body/Bonnet Materials	84
	Valve Trim Number Reference	85
	Valve Identification Plate	86
	Weights: NPS 2 – 24 Class 150 – 300	87
	Weights: NPS 2 – 24 Class 600 – 900	88
	Weights: NPS 2 – 24 Class 1500 – 2500	89
	Weights: NPS 26 – 60 Class 150 – 300	90
	Weights: NPS 30 – 42 Class 600	91
CHAPTER 7	**PIPE**	92
	Pipe Dimensions: Wall, ID and OD	93
	Pipe Internal Area	93
	Pipe Weight Per Line Foot	100
CHAPTER 8	**PLATE AND TUBING**	103
	Weight of Carbon Steel Plate	103
	Tubing Wall Thickness Gauge to Inches Conversion	103
	Stainless Steel Tubing Wall Thickness, ID and Weight	104
CHAPTER 9	**TORQUING**	105
	Bolt Sequence Charts	107
	Load in Pounds on Alloy Studs Per Torque Load	114
CHAPTER 10	**UNIT CONVERSIONS AND FORMULAS**	115
	Conversion Constants	116
	Fraction to Decimal to Millimeter Conversion	118
	Decimal of a Foot	120
	Geometric Area and Volume Formulas	121
	Cubic Feet to Gallons to Liters and Gallons Per Minute	123

CHAPTER 11	TRIGONOMETRY	124
	Finding Angles When Lengths are Known	124
	Finding Length When Angle and Other Length are Known	125
	Trig Charts	126
CHAPTER 12	FITTING AND WELDING	128
	SMAW Electrode Identification and Amperage Range	130
	Common GTAW and SMAW Filler Metals	131
	Example of Filler Metals as Used in Welding Procedures	135
	Preheat Requirements and Recommendations	136
	Post Weld Heat Treatment Requirements	137
	Bevel Takeoffs Per Wall Thickness	139
	Victor Cutting Torch Tip Chart and Tap and Drill Sizes	141
	Various Manufacturers Cutting Torch Tip Chart	142
	Estimating Pounds of Welding Filler Metal	143
	Pounds of Carbon Filler Metal for Butt Welds	145
	Pounds of Carbon Filler Metal for Socket and Fillet Welds	146
	Maximum Exposure Times For Low Hydrogen Electrodes	146
	Degrees of Flange Bolt Holes	147
CHAPTER 13	MATERIAL GRADES	148
	ASME B16.5 List of Material Specifications	149
	ASTM Specification Index	151
	ASTM Material Reference Per ASME B31.3	154
	ASTM Bolting Materials Per ASME B31.3	167
	Example of Material Grade Variations Per Temperature	170
CHAPTER 14	RIGGING	171
	Stress Distribution Formula	172
	Weight Distribution When Stealing Load	173
	D/d Ratio Chart	174
	D/d Considerations with Eye & Eye Slings	175
	Choker Hitch Reductions	176
	Basket Hitch Reductions	178
	Wire Rope Choker Capacities	179
	Wire Rope Choker Two Part Bridal Capacities	181
	Wire Rope Choker Three Part Bridal Capacities	182
	Wire Rope Choker Four Part Bridal Capacities	183
	Alloy Master Links Dimensions and Capacities	184
	Alloy Pear Shaped Links Dimensions and Capacities	185
	Eye Bolt Dimensions and Capacities	186
	Screw Pin Shackle Dimensions and Capacities	187
	Wide Body Shackle Dimensions and Capacities	188
	Bolt Type Shackle Dimensions and Capacities	189
	Pad Eyes/Lifting Lugs Design, Dimensions and Capacities	190
	Nylon Flat and Twisted Eye Choker Capacities	191
	Polyester Round Sling Capacities and Color Code	192
	Multiplication Factors For Snatch Block Loads	193
	Calculating Loads on Block and Tackle	194
	Calculating Line Parts for Reeved Blocks	195
	Nominal Strength and Weight of Wire Rope 6×19 - 6×37	196
	Wire Rope Clip Information	197
	Load Capacities-Threaded Hanger Rods and Synthetic Ropes	198

CHAPTER 15	**MAKING CALCULATIONS**	199
	Dollar Plate Calculations	200
	Channel Head Calculations	201
	Bell Head and Bundle Calculations	202
	CG's and the Laws of Leverage	203

NOTES:

CHAPTER 1: BLINDS

TIPS: Blind dimensions are essentially 1/8" less than the outer diameter of the gasket of the same size flange thus allowing for proper clearance of the bolts.

- Though gaskets are not interchangeable through the various piping sizes unless otherwise marked as such as with some small bore gaskets being applicable to more than one class of flange within the same flange bore size (e.g. 2"-3/4/600), blinds can sometimes be cross referenced whereby finding some sizes which are interchangeable as with a smaller bore size higher rated flange having the same outside diameter as a larger bore size lower rated flange (e.g. 1" 2500# = 1-1/2" 150# = 3-1/4" OD). However, this is only beneficial for isolation purposes as pressure rating thickness will differ among the various size and class blinds.
- When encountering flanges over 24", one might come across two distinctly different bolt patterns, blind dimensions, stud sizes and gasket dimensions for the same series rated piping flange. At these larger diameters, there is series A (MSS SP-44) and series B (API 605). The differences are recorded within the following charts.
- Both MSS SP-44 (Series A) and API 605 (Series B) have the same slip blind dimensions concerning pipe sizes 38"- 60" at 400#, 600# and 900# flange ratings.
- The industry standard for blinding equipment is isolating it at the first flange from the shell of the equipment being worked on and/or entered with blinds being placed within all connected piping flanges. It's also good practice to place vent strips made from flat bar on the shell side of the blind of any nozzle that will hold water whereby allowing it to drain thus allowing for the later inspection of the nozzle after hydro blasting or washing of the shell has taken place.
- Vent strips are also required in blinds which isolate vessels and piping systems which are to be steamed out for decontamination purposes to prevent pressurization of the system if there are no bleeder valves available or if such bleeders are inappropriate.
- Blind locations are often established by the use of Piping and Instrumentation Diagrams or P&ID's which are also useful for establishing flows and piping specs of various piping systems.
- When cutting blinds from plate, you can always use a gasket of the blind size required to mark out the cut line.
- If an orifice plate has to be removed for any reason which is most commonly to allow for the installation of a blind, it is common practice to turn them into the I&E department for inspection and measurements purposes. This is worth asking about if one is removed.

ASME/ANSI B16.5 PADDLE/SLIP BLIND DIAMETER

PIPE SIZE	150#	300#	400#	600#	900#	1500#	2500#
1/4	1-5/8	1-5/8	1-5/8	1-5/8	N/A	N/A	N/A
1/2	1-3/4	2	2	2	2-3/8	2-3/8	2-5/8
3/4	2-1/8	2-1/2	2-1/2	2-1/2	2-5/8	2-5/8	2-7/8
1	2-1/2	2-3/4	2-3/4	2-3/4	3	3	3-1/4
1-1/4	2-7/8	3-1/8	3-1/8	3-1/8	3-3/8	3-3/8	4
1-1/2	3-1/4	3-5/8	3-5/8	3-5/8	3-3/4	3-3/4	4-1/2
2	4	4-1/4	4-1/4	4-1/4	5-1/2	5-1/2	5-5/8
2-1/2	4-3/4	5	5	5	6-3/8	6-3/8	6-1/2
3	5-1/4	5-3/4	5-3/4	5-3/4	6-1/2	6-3/4	7-5/8
3-1/2	6-1/4	6-3/8	6-1/4	6-1/4	7-3/8	7-1/4	N/A
4	6-3/4	7	6-7/8	7-1/2	8	8-1/8	9-1/8
4-1/2	6-7/8	7-5/8	7-1/2	8-1/8	9-1/4	9	N/A
5	7-5/8	8-3/8	8-1/4	9-3/8	9-5/8	9-7/8	10-7/8
6	8-5/8	9-3/4	9-5/8	10-3/8	11-1/4	11	12-3/8
8	10-7/8	12	11-7/8	12-1/2	14	13-3/4	15-1/8
10	13-1/4	14-1/8	14	15-5/8	17	17	18-5/8
12	16	16-1/2	16-3/8	17-7/8	19-1/2	20-3/8	21-1/2
14	17-5/8	19	18-7/8	19-1/4	20-3/8	22-5/8	N/A
16	20-1/8	21-1/8	21	22-1/8	22-1/2	25-1/8	N/A
18	21-1/2	23-3/8	23-1/4	24	25	27-5/8	N/A
20	23-3/4	25-5/8	25-3/8	26-3/4	27-3/8	29-5/8	N/A
24	28-1/8	30-3/8	30-1/8	31	32-7/8	35-3/8	N/A

ASME/ANSI B16.47 LARGE BORE PADDLE/SLIP BLIND DIAMETER					
PIPE SIZE	MSS SP-44 (SERIES A)		API 605 (SERIES B)		
	150#	300#	75#	150#	300#
26	30-3/8	32-3/4	27-3/4	28-7/16	30-1/4
28	32-5/8	35-1/4	29-3/4	30-7/16	32-3/8
30	34-5/8	37-3/8	31-3/4	32-7/16	34-3/4
32	36-7/8	39-1/2	33-3/4	34-9/16	36-7/8
34	38-7/8	41-1/2	35-3/4	36-11/16	39
36	41-1/8	43-7/8	38-3/16	38-3/4	41-1/8
38	43-5/8	41-3/8	40-3/16	41	43-1/8
40	45-5/8	43-3/4	42-3/16	43	45-1/8
42	47-7/8	45-3/4	44-3/16	45	47-1/8
44	50-1/8	47-7/8	46-3/8	47	49-1/8
46	52-1/8	50	48-3/8	49-5/16	51-3/4
48	54-3/8	52	50-3/8	51-5/16	53-3/4
50	56-3/8	54-1/8	52-3/8	53-5/16	55-3/4
52	58-5/8	56-1/8	54-1/2	55-5/16	57-3/4
54	60-7/8	58-5/8	56-1/2	57-1/2	60-1/8
56	63-1/8	60-5/8	58-3/4	59-1/2	62-5/8
58	65-3/8	62-5/8	60-3/4	62-1/16	65-1/16
60	67-3/8	64-5/8	62-3/4	64-1/16	67-1/16

ASME/ANSI B16.47 LARGE BORE PADDLE/SLIP BLIND DIAMETER						
PIPE SIZE	MSS SP-44 (SERIES A)			API 605 (SERIES B)		
	400#	600#	900#	400#	600#	900#
26	32-5/8	34	34-5/8	29-1/4	30	32-7/8
28	35	35-7/8	37-1/8	31-3/8	32-1/8	35-3/8
30	37-1/8	38-1/8	39-5/8	33-5/8	34-1/2	37-5/8
32	39-3/8	40-1/8	42-1/8	35-3/4	36-5/8	39-7/8
34	41-3/8	42-1/8	44-5/8	37-3/4	39-1/8	42-1/8
36	43-7/8	44-3/8	47-1/8	40-1/8	41-1/8	44-1/8
BOTH MSS SP-44 (SERIES A) AND API 605 (SERIES B)						
	400#		600#		900#	
38	42-1/8		43-3/8		47-1/8	
40	44-1/4		45-3/8		49-1/8	
42	46-1/4		47-7/8		51-1/8	
44	48-3/8		49-7/8		53-3/4	
46	50-5/8		52-1/8		56-3/8	
48	52-7/8		54-5/8		58-3/8	
50	55-1/8		56-7/8		N/A	
52	57-1/8		58-7/8		N/A	
54	59-5/8		61-1/8		N/A	
56	61-5/8		63-3/8		N/A	
58	63-5/8		65-3/8		N/A	
60	66-1/8		68-1/8		N/A	

Both MSS SP-44 (Series A) and API 605 (Series B) have the same slip blind dimensions concerning pipe sizes 38"- 60" at 400#, 600# and 900# flange ratings.

CHAPTER 2: PRESSURE RATINGS AND HYDROSTATIC TESTING

TIPS: The hydrostatic test of a piping system or vessel should not include any piping component which may hinder water filling, flushing, pressurization or draining. All instruments shall be taken off; all internals for check valves shall be removed preferably and if not possible, the pressurization point should be on the upstream and system should be drained from the downstream side. Preferably, all valves shall be in open position and they must not be used as a test limit. If you are left with no option, then check that the valve seat test pressure (normally done at 1.1 of rated valve pressure) is greater than the system test pressure. Refer to ASME B16.34 to gather such information to then proceed for the inclusion of a valve as a test limit in closed position. Strainers can be included whether with mesh or without mesh, there are no issues there. Remove venturimeters, orifices or other flow measuring devices from the test limit. Also, ensure that all items such as control valves, relief valves, rupture disks, diaphragm instruments, expansion joints, sight glasses on vessels, etc., which could be damaged during pressure test have been removed or isolated and that equipment, such as filters, which have internals that may be damaged during the pressure test are either blocked from test or that their internals have been removed. Steam traps and strainers should be left out of a steam system hydro if the steam service is great enough to disallow a service test in lieu of a hydro which usually begins around the 200# steam range. Closure welds should be considered for non-threaded traps and strainers which are part of a newly fabricated piping system. This will allow for a complete hydro of the rest of the new piping with alternative NDE for the closure welds e.g. PT, X-ray, etc.

- When draining water from the system which has been hydro tested, an internal vacuum can result if the drain line is opened and the high point vent remains closed or gets blocked or plugged in some manner. This isn't a hazardous condition with small hydro tests of piping systems and such which contain lower volumes of water and are structurally stable. However, if considering a tower or large drum filled with high volumes of water and a low point drain is opened allowing enough water to escape which is not replaced by air due to no available opened high point vent, then if the drain is large enough to overcome the vacuum's attempt to stop the water flow (as it often stops the flow with small hydro tests) a large enough vacuum could result whereby causing the structural instability of the vessel. This very scenario has led to the collapse of storage tanks and towers. Thus, it's always advisable to make sure the high point vent/bleed is opened completely when draining such systems and is sufficient relative to the drain size and that no trash such as plastic or fire blanket can get sucked on top of it and stop the air flow. This was the cause of one storage tank collapse I read about a while back when the vent was opened while draining but some plastic sheeting stopped the air flow.
- When fabricating a piping system, it's best to do a hydro before the installation of many of the before mentioned piping components. Often a jumper made of a high pressure hose such as from an old hydro pump can be used in the field to connect various systems under one test (if all test at the same pressure) or connect the gap in the test left by the absence of a control valve or other pressure sensitive equipment which was left out if such flanges can't be blind flanged due to needed continuity. Always consider closure welds on new piping systems which will present difficulty in hydro testing due to the lack of high point bleeds, long runs of old pipe with no isolation flange, etc. This allows the testing of all the new piping at the fab shop with only the closure field welds requiring alternative NDE.

- Never use utility water on hydro tests which involve stainless piping, components or equipment such as stainless bundles inside exchangers. Demineralized water such as boiler feed water is considered more appropriate for such hydro tests. If such isn't plausible or readily available, then the available utility water can have its chloride content tested by the lab department to verify if the water is suitable, which sometimes turns out to be. Always ask permission before using the fire water service as a water supply for a hydro. Some plants require notice of its use in general, but also, this service often has a lot of sand in the water supply which the inspection department might not want in their process piping and equipment. Though it may be convenient and does supply a high volume, it's always best to ask first.
- Though it should be considered by the inspection and engineering department beforehand, it doesn't hurt to consider the structural integrity of the available permanent supports of a piping system which is to be filled with water for hydro. Some engineered piping systems weren't constructed for the extra weight of a fluid medium such as water especially when dealing with the larger diameter piping as often they are gas service and water becomes very heavy at the larger bore volumes. I've had to place several temporary supports on large bore flare lines to avoid doing a pneumatic test due to its inherent dangers in favor of a hydrostatic test which the available permanent supports weren't engineered to support.
- When testing systems which have great enough changes in elevation for the feet head pressure of water to effect the gauge pressure at lower elevations, the gauge must be placed at the top of the system under test often followed by one at the lower elevation or the feet head pressure must be calculated into the gauge pressure to determine the upper elevations pressure if using only one gauge at the lower elevation. This variation in pressure is best understood as being analogous to the pressure changes of the ocean from the bottom depths to the surface which is the effect of the weight of the water itself increasing the pressure at the greater depths.
- The common rule of thumb for choosing the correct gauge range for a specific test is to choose a gauge which is 1-1/2 to 4 times the test pressure. Thus, a 200 psi test could use a calibrated test gauge from 300-800 psi. Some plants allow the use of two non-calibrated gauges on the same test tree in lieu of a calibrated one if such can't be found.
- Most hydrostatic testing is done at a test pressure of 1.5 times the design pressure (at the temperature range at which the test will be performed) which is usually below 100°F) of the vessel or piping component under test. The same is true for most valve shell tests performed at the factory, while the valve seat is more often tested at 1.1 times the maximum working pressure with both being rounded up to the next nearest 25psi increment. I have provided a list of valve working pressures and valve seat and shell test pressures in this section in the case that a permanent existing closed valve must be incorporated as the boundary limit of a hydro due to such things as the alternative being to test a long run of old pipe on the other side of the existing valve to be closed due to the lack of a flange in which to insert a pressure rated blind isolation. If it is found that the seat test pressure of the valve is greater than the test pressure being performed, then the QC and inspections department might consider using the closed valve as a boundary. This may often be the case with equipment tests, but if considering a piping system being tested per the flange ratings, then any bolt in or weld in valve with those same flange ratings will generally have a shell test pressure (@ 1.5) equal to the piping test pressure, but the seat test pressure of the valve will be less due to the 1.1 pressure factor at which it is tested. Thus, it's not a good practice to test against flanged or weld in valves in the closed position to the full 1.5 pressure factor generated by the flange rating of that valve and accompanying piping system. The shell is tested at these pressures, but the seat is not. Small bore weld in valves may often be found to have a seat test pressure suitable for the piping test pressure. It's a case by case scenario.

- Gaskets should also be considered when doing a hydro test. There are many different styles of paper type Garlock, Gylon, etc., gaskets with various pressure ratings, depending upon the material used to construct them, which are seldom used for final makeup of flanges but are often used for isolation purposes. My research shows an average of 800 psi - 1200 psi maximum pressure depending on the material type. To my knowledge, most of these styles are only provided precut with torque information for the 150 & 300 class range which would put them at an operating pressure around the 740 psi range with a 300 class A105 flange with a hydro pressure of 1125 psi. I say this because it is common practice to cut gaskets from sheets of such material for various sized and rated flanges whereby the material may not be suitable (pressure rated) for a potentially required hydrostatic test which will involve those flanges. One should always verify the pressure rating of the gasket material being used especially if hydro pressures will reach the 1000 psi range. When in doubt, it's much safer just to use a spiral wound final makeup Flex gasket per the piping spec of the system being worked on which should be rated for the flange's maximum pressure rating. Injuries have occurred due to paper gaskets being over pressured during hydro testing and blowing out, releasing the internal pressure upon craftsmen.

HYDROSTATIC TEST TREE CONSIDERATIONS:

The hydrostatic testing tree used to perform hydro tests is often overlooked in terms of its allowable working pressures. It isn't well defined in the industry at just what pressure these trees are good for as more often they are constructed from the fitting from the free issue trailer which is generally threaded fittings of 160 schedule nipples, 800 class gate valves and 3000 pound fittings. If it is foreseen that there will be some high pressure tests during the turnaround whether on certain equipment or piping with higher pressure class flanges, then some welded trees may sometimes be constructed. The thing about the safe working pressure of a hydro tree is that it is constructed of various components such as fittings, nipples and valves which all have different safe working pressures at various temperatures and being as pressure will find the weakest link then we really are mostly concerned with the particular component which has the least safe working pressure for a specific configuration. Even a welded test tree will still have threaded components as with the test gauge (which is designed for its pressure range with its threaded connection in mind) and fittings on the pump hose. Also, keep in mind that though these test tree components have their own individual hydro test pressures which are generally time and a half that of the safe working pressure at that temperature, the repeated use of the test tree means that we should go by the safe working pressure rather than the maximum hydro pressure of the various fittings and components whereby we don't continually overpressure the system to its max. Thus, the fittings, nipples and valves used in the test tree to test other fittings, nipples, valves and equipment which will find themselves in service soon will generally have to be operating within their safe working pressure range which must be great enough to bring the components under test up to their hydro test pressure range which is generally about 1.5 times the design pressure and often rounded up to the nearest 25psi with piping components such as flanges, valves, etc.

Example: From ASME B16.5 Table F2-1.1 we find that the pressure and temperature ratings for A105 class carbon flanges at 100°F (which is the usual temperature range for a hydro) is 150 class=285; 900 class= 2220 whereby we multiply times 1.5 to receive 150 class=427.5; 900 class= 3330. Round these values up to the nearest 25psi and you receive 150 class= 450psig; 900 class=3350psig as seen from the hydro test charts on the following pages.

You might consider that one could construct a hydro test tree using the piping specs from the piping package or equipment being tested but you'll more often find that this would be a bit of an overkill as most process specs don't allow threaded connections and are generally taking into consideration the much higher operating temperatures which effects the allowable working pressure ratings of all piping components. This is why we are mostly concerned with the 100°F range of most ASME chart specs as most hydro tests will be performed within this temperature range. On the following page I will outline the safe working pressure ratings of the various components of a hydro test tree which covers various ASME and API codes. This should help when considering the proper fittings, nipples and valves needed to construct a test tree which has a safe working pressure rating appropriate for the hydro test pressures of the various equipment and piping components to be tested.

As can be seen on the following charts, various aspects might govern a test trees safe working pressure. For instance, if you were to have a 3/4" threaded tree made of 3000 class fittings, sch. 160 nipples and 800 class gate valves then it is actually the gate valves rating which would govern the safe working pressure of the assembly. However, if the assembly was constructed of sch. 40 nipples while maintaining the same class of valves and fittings, then it would be the nipples rating which would govern the safe working pressure of the assembly. Though it is possible to construct a high pressure threaded tree by the use of 2500 class threaded valves, 6000 class fittings and XXS nipples, its perhaps a good idea to either go to socket weld components or simply back weld the threaded fittings when performing hydro's above a couple thousand pounds. You can never be too safe when working with the higher pressures often required to properly test the higher rated piping systems and equipment found in many refineries.

ASME B31.3 INTERNAL SAFE WORKING PRESSURE OF ASTM A106 GRADE B PLAIN END NIPPLES (psi)				
PIPE SIZE	SCH.40/STD	SCH.80/XS	SCH.160	XXS
1/2	4543	6124	7833	12,250
3/4	3767	5133	7300	10,267
1	3540	4764	6654	9528
1-1/4	2952	4027	5271	8054
1-1/2	2671	3684	5176	7368
2	2269	3212	5069	6425

ASME B31.3 INTERNAL SAFE WORKING PRESSURE OF ASTM A106 GRADE B THREADED NIPPLES (psi)				
PIPE SIZE	SCH.40/STD	SCH.80/XS	SCH.160	XXS
1/2	1821	3404	5112	9529
3/4	1590	2957	5123	8090
1	1424	2648	4538	7412
1-1/4	1275	2351	3595	6378
1-1/2	1206	2219	3712	5904
2	1098	2041	3898	5253

The internal safe working pressures for seamless A106 grade B nipples (which also applies to longer runs of pipe) was calculated using the formula provided in ASME B31.1 Power Piping section 104.1.2 (Straight Pipe Under Internal Pressure) and also in the more familiar code to refineries under the same section heading title ASME B31.3 Process Piping section 304.1.2 (Straight Pipe Under Internal Pressure). Though the formula is essentially the same in both codes, each code will produce a different value due to the fact that their maximum allowable stress values in tension for A106 Gr. A, B and C material differs greatly.

MAXIMUM ALLOWABLE STRESS VALUES IN TENSION FOR A106 SEAMLESS PIPING @ 100°F		
Grade	B31.1 Table A-1	B31.3 Table A-1
A	12,000	16,000
B	15,000	20,000
C	17,500	23,300

Thus, with all other values being equal, the safe working pressures from B31.3 per nominal pipe size will ultimately be higher than those from B31.1. The values given in the tables herein are from B31.3 which is the more applicable code to refinery process piping, even though these calculations do not pertain to actual process piping and are only for hydrostatic test trees for the 100°F rating whereby either code could potentially be used. The formula is as follows.

Solving for minimum thickness: $t_m = \dfrac{PD_o}{2(SE+Py)} + C$

Solving for maximum pressure: $P = \dfrac{2SE(t_m-C)}{D_o-[2y(t_m-C)]}$

Where:

t_m = minimum required wall thickness, including manufacturing tolerance and allowances for corrosion (in.). For A106 seamless pipe, when solving for minimal thickness, 12.5% of the arrived at t_m value must be added back to the thickness to account for the standard manufacturing tolerance when dealing with the listed nominal wall thicknesses. When solving for safe working pressure of listed nominal wall thicknesses, deduct the 12.5% from the nominal wall thickness listed per schedule and pipe diameter.

P = internal design pressure (psi) when solving for minimal thickness and safe working pressure when solving for pressure.

D_o = outside diameter of pipe (in.).

E = joint efficiency factor from B31.3 Table A-1B which will always be = 1 for seamless carbon pipe.

y = coefficient from B31.3 Table 304.1.1 for t < D/6 which will always be = 0.4 @ 100°F for A106 seamless pipe. For t ≥ D/6 the formula shall be: $y = \dfrac{d+2C}{d+D_o+2C}$

d = inside diameter of pipe (in.).
S = maximum allowable stress in material (psi) from B31.3 Table A-1.
C= the sum of the mechanical allowances (thread or groove depth from B1.20.1 Table 2 dimension h) plus corrosion and erosion allowances which is supplied for additional thickness to account for corrosion and the metal removed during the threading of threaded nipples (in.). There are no corrosion allowances in the provided tables being as they are calculated for new piping which will not be in permanent service. The threading depth value is taken from dimension h from ASME B1.20.1 (Pipe Threads, General Purpose) as follows:

ASME B1.20.1 Thread Depth Value From: Table 2	
PIPE SIZE	Height of Thread (h)
1/2	0.05714
3/4	0.05714
1	0.06957
1-1/4	0.06957
1-1/2	0.06957
2	0.06957

Solving for an A106 Gr. B 3/4" sch.160 threaded nipple is as follows:

$$P = \frac{2SE(t_m - C)}{D_o - [2y(t_m - C)]}$$

$$P = 5681.26 = \frac{2 \times 20{,}000 \times 1 \times [0.218 - (0.218 \times 12.5\%) - 0.05714]}{1.05 - [2 \times 0.409 \times \{0.218 - (0.218 \times 12.5\%) - 0.05714\}]}$$

Using this pressure and now double checking by solving for thickness:

$$t_m = \frac{PD_o}{2(SE + Py)} + C$$

$$t_m = .215 = .19075 + (.19075 \times 12.5\%) = \frac{5681.26 \times 1.05}{2 \times (20{,}000 \times 1 + 5681.26 \times 0.409)} + 0.05714$$

WORKING AND TEST PRESSURES OF A105 GATE VALVES BOTH SOCKET WELD AND THREADED THROUGH ALL PIPE SIZES				
CODE	API 602	ASME B16.34		
CLASS	800	1500	2500	4500
PSI OF SHELL TEST @ 1.5	2975	5575	9275	*16,675*
PSI OF SEAT TEST @ 1.1	2175	4100	6800	*12,225*
SAFE WORKING PSI	1975	3705	6170	11,110

800 class pressure rated to 100°F. 1500-4500 class pressure rated to 500°F.
Shell test performed at 1.5 x safe working pressure.
Seat test performed at 1.1 x safe working pressure.

ASME B16.11 CORRELATION OF FITTING CLASSES WITH SCHEDULE NUMBER OR WALL DESIGNATION OF PIPE FOR CALCULATION OF RATINGS			
FITTING CLASS	TYPE OF FITTING	PIPE USED FOR RATING BASIS	
		SCHEDULE	WALL DESIGNATION
2000	THREADED	80	XS
3000	THREADED	160	-
6000	THREADED	-	XXS
3000	SOCKET WELD	80	XS
6000	SOCKET WELD	160	-
9000	SOCKET WELD	-	XXS

This table does not restrict the use of thinner or thicker wall pipe with fittings. Pipe used with these fittings may be thinner or thicker wall. When thinner pipe is used, its strength may govern the rating. When thicker pipe is used, the strength of the fitting may govern the rating of the assembly.

TYPICAL TEST TREE CONFIGURATION

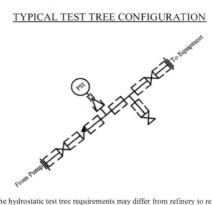

Though the hydrostatic test tree requirements may differ from refinery to refinery, this is a representation of the more common configuration which is a minimal example of the required fittings. I've seen some sites that require two pressure gauges in line. Some require two block valves at the pump end of the tree. Some places require a recently calibrated pressure relief valve threaded into the test tree with a discharge pressure setting at about 10% above the test pressure of the system under test to prevent overpressure. This requires some foresight on the planning department to assure that such relief valves are available and within the appropriate pressure range for every hydro required during the turnaround. The materials list for a 3/4" test tree as shown is as follows:

3/4" Nipple = 7   3/4" Tee = 2   3/4" Gate Valve = 3
3/4" Check Valve = 1 3/4" union = 1 complete   1/2" Coupling = 1
Test Gauge = 1   3/4" x 1/2" Reducer or swage = 1

The pressure ratings and connection type should be determined by the test pressure. Further fittings will generally be required to connect to the system by way of a system bleeder valve, companion flange, etc. When connected to the system through a bleeder valve, always use the test tree block valve at the equipment end of the tree to isolate the tree while zeroing the gauge for the inspections department. Closing the test system's bleeder valve while under full test pressure will effectively be placing the entire test pressure on the seat of the bleeder valve, which might not be rated for such as when the valve shell test is equal to the system test pressure at 1.5 the design pressure, whereby the valves seat test pressure is only 1.1. It's always best not to pressure against any closed system valve if possible.

FEET HEAD OF WATER TO PSI CALCULATION			
Feet Head	PSI	Feet Head	PSI
1	0.43	100	43.31
2	0.87	110	47.64
3	1.30	120	51.97
4	1.73	130	56.30
5	2.17	140	60.63
6	2.60	150	64.96
7	3.03	160	69.29
8	3.46	170	73.63
9	3.90	180	77.96
10	4.33	200	86.62
15	6.50	250	108.27
20	8.66	300	129.93
25	10.83	350	151.58
30	12.99	400	173.24
40	17.32	500	216.55
50	21.65	600	259.85
60	25.99	700	303.16
70	30.32	800	346.47
80	34.65	900	389.78
90	38.98	1000	433.00

One foot of water at 62° F = 0.433 PSI.
To find the PSI for any feet head not listed, multiply the feet head by 0.433.

ASTM Specification	ASME B16.34 & API 600 Working & Hydrostatic Test Pressure For Gate Valves Per Class & Material Group @ 100°F (psi)							
	150#	300#	400#	600#	900#	1500#	2500#	4500#
A105 A216 Gr. WCB A350 Gr. LF2 A515 Gr. 70 A516 Gr. 70 A537 Cl.1 A675 Gr. 70 A672 Gr. B70 A672 Gr. C70 A696 Gr. C	Table 2-1.1A Group 1.1 Materials Standard Class							
	work 285 x1.1 325 x1.5 450	work 740 x1.1 825 x1.5 1125	work 990 x1.1 1100 x1.5 1500	work 1480 x1.1 1650 x1.5 2225	work 2220 x1.1 2450 x1.5 3350	work 3705 x1.1 4100 x1.5 5575	work 6170 x1.1 6800 x1.5 9275	work 11,110 x1.1 12,225 x1.5 16,675
A106 Gr. C A203 Gr. B A203 Gr. E A216 Gr. WCC A350 Gr. LF3 A352 Gr. LCC A352 Gr. LC2 A352 Gr. LC3	Table 2-1.2A Group 1.2 Materials Standard Class							
	work 290 x1.1 325 x1.5 450	work 750 x1.1 825 x1.5 1125	work 1000 x1.1 1100 x1.5 1500	work 1500 x1.1 1650 x1.5 2250	work 2250 x1.1 2475 x1.5 3375	work 3750 x1.1 4125 x1.5 5625	work 6250 x1.1 6875 x1.5 9375	work 11,250 x1.1 12,375 x1.5 16,875
A203 Gr. A A203 Gr. D A352 Gr. LCB A515 Gr. 65 A516 Gr. 65 A675 Gr. 65 A672 Gr. B65 A672 Gr. C65	Table 2-1.3A Group 1.3 Materials Standard Class							
	work 265 x1.1 300 x1.5 400	work 695 x1.1 775 x1.5 1050	work 925 x1.1 1025 x1.5 1400	work 1390 x1.1 1550 x1.5 2100	work 2085 x1.1 2300 x1.5 3150	work 3470 x1.1 3825 x1.5 5225	work 5785 x1.1 6375 x1.5 8700	work 10,415 x1.1 11,475 x1.5 15,625
A106 Gr. B A350 Gr. LF1 A515 Gr. 60 A516 Gr. 60 A672 Gr. B60 A672 Gr. C60 A675 Gr.60 A696 Gr. B	Table 2-1.4A Group 1.4 Materials Standard Class							
	work 235 x1.1 275 x1.5 375	work 620 x1.1 700 x1.5 950	work 825 x1.1 925 x1.5 1250	work 1235 x1.1 1375 x1.5 1875	work 1850 x1.1 2050 x1.5 2775	work 3085 x1.1 3400 x1.5 4650	work 5145 x1.1 5675 x1.5 7725	work 9260 x1.1 10,200 x1.5 13,900

Valve seats are tested at 1.1 and shells are tested at 1.5 of the working pressure per class. Pressures are in PSIG.

ASTM Specification	ASME B16.34 & API 600 Working & Hydrostatic Test Pressure For Gate Valves Per Class & Material Group @ 100°F (psi)							
	150#	300#	400#	600#	900#	1500#	2500#	4500#
A182 Gr. F1 A204 Gr. A A204 Gr. B A217 Gr. WC1 A352 Gr. LC1 A691 Gr. CM70	Table 2-1.5A Group 1.5 Materials Standard Class							
	work 265 x1.1 300 x1.5 400	work 695 x1.1 775 x1.5 1050	work 925 x1.1 1025 x1.5 1400	work 1390 x1.1 1550 x1.5 2100	work 2085 x1.1 2300 x1.5 3150	work 3470 x1.1 3825 x1.5 5225	work 5785 x1.1 6375 x1.5 8700	work 10,415 x1.1 11,475 x1.5 15,625
A335 Gr. P1 A369 Gr. FP1 A387 Gr. 12 Cl.1 A387 Gr. 2 Cl.1 A387 Gr. 2 Cl.2 A691 Gr. 1/2 CR	Table 2-1.6A Group 1.6 Materials Standard Class							
	work 225 x1.1 250 x1.5 350	work 590 x1.1 650 x1.5 900	work 790 x1.1 875 x1.5 1200	work 1185 x1.1 1325 x1.5 1800	work 1775 x1.1 1975 x1.5 2675	work 2955 x1.1 3275 x1.5 4450	work 4930 x1.1 5425 x1.5 7400	work 8870 x1.1 9775 x1.5 13,325
A182 Gr. F2 A204 Gr. C A217 Gr. WC4 A217 Gr. WC5 A691 Gr. CM75	Table 2-1.7A Group 1.7 Materials Standard Class							
	work 290 x1.1 325 x1.5 450	work 750 x1.1 825 x1.5 1125	work 1000 x1.1 1100 x1.5 1500	work 1500 x1.1 1650 x1.5 2250	work 2250 x1.1 2475 x1.5 3375	work 3750 x1.1 4125 x1.5 5625	work 6250 x1.1 6875 x1.5 9375	work 11,250 x1.1 12,375 x1.5 16,875
A335 Gr. P11 A335 Gr. P12 A335 Gr. P22 A369 Gr. P11 A369 Gr. P12 A369 Gr. P22 A387 Gr. P11 Cl.1 A387 Gr. P12 Cl.2 A387 Gr. P22 Cl.1 A691 Gr. 1 CR A691 Gr. 1-1/4CR A691 Gr. 2-1/4CR	Table 2-1.8A Group 1.8 Materials Standard Class							
	work 235 x1.1 275 x1.5 375	work 620 x1.1 700 x1.5 950	work 825 x1.1 925 x1.5 1250	work 1235 x1.1 1375 x1.5 1875	work 1860 x1.1 2050 x1.5 2800	work 3085 x1.1 3400 x1.5 4650	work 5145 x1.1 5675 x1.5 7725	work 9260 x1.1 10,200 x1.5 13,900

Valve seats are tested at 1.1 and shells are tested at 1.5 of the working pressure per class. Pressures are in PSIG.

ASTM Specification	ASME B16.34 & API 600 Working & Hydrostatic Test Pressure For Gate Valves Per Class & Material Group @ 100°F (psi)							
	150#	300#	400#	600#	900#	1500#	2500#	4500#
	Table 2-1.9A Group 1.9 Materials Standard Class							
A182 Gr. F12 Cl.2 A182 Gr. F11 Cl.2 A217 Gr. WC6 A387 Gr. 11 Cl.2 A739 Gr. B11	work 290 x1.1 325 x1.5 450	work 750 x1.1 825 x1.5 1125	work 1000 x1.1 1100 x1.5 1500	work 1500 x1.1 1650 x1.5 2250	work 2250 x1.1 2475 x1.5 3375	work 3750 x1.1 4125 x1.5 5625	work 6250 x1.1 6875 x1.5 9375	work 11,250 x1.1 12,375 x1.5 16,875
	Table 2-1.10A Group 1.10 Materials Standard Class							
A182 Gr. F22 Cl.3 A217 Gr. WC9 A387 Gr. 22 Cl.2 A739 Gr. B22	work 290 x1.1 325 x1.5 450	work 750 x1.1 825 x1.5 1125	work 1000 x1.1 1100 x1.5 1500	work 1500 x1.1 1650 x1.5 2250	work 2250 x1.1 2475 x1.5 3375	work 3750 x1.1 4125 x1.5 5625	work 6250 x1.1 6875 x1.5 9375	work 11,250 x1.1 12,375 x1.5 16,875
	Table 2-1.11A Group 1.11 Materials Standard Class							
A182 Gr. F21 A302 Gr. A A302 Gr. B A302 Gr. C A302 Gr. D A387 Gr. 21 Cl.2 A537 Cl. 2	work 290 x1.1 325 x1.5 450	work 750 x1.1 825 x1.5 1125	work 1000 x1.1 1100 x1.5 1500	work 1500 x1.1 1650 x1.5 2250	work 2250 x1.1 2475 x1.5 3375	work 3750 x1.1 4125 x1.5 5625	work 6250 x1.1 6875 x1.5 9375	work 11,250 x1.1 12,375 x1.5 16,875
	Table 2-1.12A Group 1.12 Materials Standard Class							
A335 Gr. P5 A335 Gr. P5b A369 Gr. FP5 A387 Gr. Cl.1 A387 Gr. 5 Cl.2 A691 Gr. 5CR	work 235 x1.1 275 x1.5 375	work 615 x1.1 700 x1.5 925	work 825 x1.1 925 x1.5 1250	work 1235 x1.1 1375 x1.5 1875	work 1850 x1.1 2050 x1.5 2775	work 3085 x1.1 3400 x1.5 4650	work 5145 x1.1 5675 x1.5 7725	work 9255 x1.1 10,200 x1.5 13,900

Valve seats are tested at 1.1 and shells are tested at 1.5 of the working pressure per class. Pressures are in PSIG.

ASTM Specification	ASME B16.34 & API 600 Working & Hydrostatic Test Pressure For Gate Valves Per Class & Material Group @ 100°F (psi)							
	150#	300#	400#	600#	900#	1500#	2500#	4500#
	Table 2-1.13A Group 1.13 Materials Standard Class							
A182 Gr. F5 A182 Gr. F5a A217 Gr. C5	work 290 x1.1 325 x1.5 450	work 750 x1.1 825 x1.5 1125	work 1000 x1.1 1100 x1.5 1500	work 1500 x1.1 1650 x1.5 2250	work 2250 x1.1 2475 x1.5 3375	work 3750 x1.1 4125 x1.5 5625	work 6250 x1.1 6875 x1.5 9375	work 11,250 x1.1 12,375 x1.5 16,875
	Table 2-1.14A Group 1.14 Materials Standard Class							
A182 Gr. F9 A217 Gr. C12	work 290 x1.1 325 x1.5 450	work 750 x1.1 825 x1.5 1125	work 1000 x1.1 1100 x1.5 1500	work 1500 x1.1 1650 x1.5 2250	work 2250 x1.1 2475 x1.5 3375	work 3750 x1.1 4125 x1.5 5625	work 6250 x1.1 6875 x1.5 9375	work 11,250 x1.1 12,375 x1.5 16,875
A182 Gr. F304 A182 Gr. F304H A240 Gr. 304 A240 Gr. 304H A312 Gr. TP304 A312 Gr. TP304H A351 Gr. CF3 A351 Gr. CF8 A358 Gr. 304 A376 Gr. TP304 A376 Gr. TP304H A430 Gr. FP304 A430 Gr. FP304H A479 Gr. 304 A479 Gr. 304H	Table 2-2.1A Group 2.1 Materials Standard Class							
	work 275 x1.1 325 x1.5 425	work 720 x1.1 800 x1.5 1100	work 960 x1.1 1075 x1.5 1450	work 1440 x1.1 1600 x1.5 2175	work 2160 x1.1 2400 x1.5 3250	work 3600 x1.1 3975 x1.5 5400	work 6000 x1.1 6600 x1.5 9000	work 10,800 x1.1 11900 x1.5 16,200

Valve seats are tested at 1.1 and shells are tested at 1.5 of the working pressure per class. Pressures are in PSIG.

ASTM Specification	ASME B16.34 & API 600 Working & Hydrostatic Test Pressure For Gate Valves Per Class & Material Group @ 100°F (psi)							
	150#	300#	400#	600#	900#	1500#	2500#	4500#
A182 Gr. F316 A182 Gr. F316H A240 Gr. 316 A240 Gr. 316H A240 Gr. 317 A312 Gr. TP316 A312 Gr. TP316H A312 Gr. TP317 A351 Gr. CF3A A351 Gr. CF3H A351 Gr. CF8A A351 Gr. CF8H A358 Gr. 316 A376 Gr. TP316 A376 Gr. TP316H A430 Gr. FP316 A430 Gr. FP316H A479 Gr. 316 A479 Gr. 316H A351 Gr. CG8H	Table 2-2.2A Group 2.2 Materials Standard Class							
	work 275 x1.1 325 x1.5 425	work 720 x1.1 800 x1.5 1100	work 960 x1.1 1075 x1.5 1450	work 1440 x1.1 1600 x1.5 2175	work 2160 x1.1 2400 x1.5 3250	work 3600 x1.1 3975 x1.5 5400	work 6000 x1.1 6600 x1.5 9000	work 10,800 x1.1 11900 x1.5 16,200
A182 Gr. 304L A182 Gr. 316L A240 Gr. 304L A240 Gr. 316L A312 Gr. TP304L A312 Gr. TP316L A479 Gr. 304L A479 Gr. 316L	Table 2-2.3A Group 2.3 Materials Standard Class							
	work 230 x1.1 275 x1.5 350	work 600 x1.1 675 x1.5 900	work 800 x1.1 900 x1.5 1200	work 1200 x1.1 1325 x1.5 1800	work 1800 x1.1 2000 x1.5 2700	work 3000 x1.1 3300 x1.5 4500	work 5000 x1.1 5500 x1.5 7500	work 9000 x1.1 9900 x1.5 13,500
A182 Gr. F321 A182 Gr. F321H A240 Gr. 321 A240 Gr. 321H A312 Gr. TP321 A312 Gr. TP321H A358 Gr. 321 A376 Gr TP321 A376 Gr. TP321H A430 Gr. FP321 A430 Gr. FP321H A479 Gr. 321 A479 Gr. 321H	Table 2-2.4A Group 2.4 Materials Standard Class							
	work 275 x1.1 325 x1.5 425	work 720 x1.1 800 x1.5 1100	work 960 x1.1 1075 x1.5 1450	work 1440 x1.1 1600 x1.5 2175	work 2160 x1.1 2400 x1.5 3250	work 3600 x1.1 3975 x1.5 5400	work 6000 x1.1 6600 x1.5 9000	work 10,800 x1.1 11,900 x1.5 16,200

Valve seats are tested at 1.1 and shells are tested at 1.5 of the working pressure per class. Pressures are in PSIG.

ASTM Specification	ASME B16.34 & API 600 Working & Hydrostatic Test Pressure For Gate Valves Per Class & Material Group @ 100°F (psi)							
	150#	300#	400#	600#	900#	1500#	2500#	4500#
A182 Gr. F347 A182 Gr. F347H A182 Gr. F348 A182 Gr. F348H A240 Gr. 347 A240 Gr. 347H A240 Gr. 348 A240 Gr. 348H A312 Gr. TP347 A312 Gr. TP347H A312 Gr. TP348 A312 Gr. TP348H A351 Gr. CF8C A358 Gr. 347 A376 Gr TP347 A376 Gr. TP347H A376 Gr. TP348 A430 Gr. FP347 A430 Gr. FP347H A479 Gr. 347 A479 Gr. 347H A479 Gr. 348 A479 Gr. 348H	Table 2-2.5A Group 2.5 Materials Standard Class							
	work 275 x1.1 325 x1.5 425	work 720 x1.1 800 x1.5 1100	work 960 x1.1 1075 x1.5 1450	work 1440 x1.1 1600 x1.5 2175	work 2160 x1.1 2400 x1.5 3250	work 3600 x1.1 3975 x1.5 5400	work 6000 x1.1 6600 x1.5 9000	work 10,800 x1.1 11900 x1.5 16,200
A240 Gr. 309S A312 Gr. TP309H A351 Gr. CH8 A240 Gr. 309H A351 Gr. CH20 A358 Gr. 309H	Table 2-2.6A Group 2.6 Materials Standard Class							
	work 260 x1.1 300 x1.5 400	work 670 x1.1 750 x1.5 1025	work 895 x1.1 1000 x1.5 1350	work 1345 x1.1 1500 x1.5 2025	work 2015 x1.1 2225 x1.5 3025	work 3360 x1.1 3700 x1.5 5050	work 5600 x1.1 6175 x1.5 8400	work 10,080 x1.1 11,100 x1.5 15,125
A182 Gr. F310H A240 Gr. 310S A240 Gr. 310H A312 Gr. TP310H A351 Gr. CK20 A479 Gr. 310H A358 Gr. 310H A479 Gr. 310S	Table 2-2.7A Group 2.7 Materials Standard Class							
	work 260 x1.1 300 x1.5 400	work 670 x1.1 750 x1.5 1025	work 895 x1.1 1000 x1.5 1350	work 1345 x1.1 1500 x1.5 2025	work 2015 x1.1 2225 x1.5 3025	work 3360 x1.1 3700 x1.5 5050	work 5600 x1.1 6175 x1.5 8400	work 10,080 x1.1 11,100 x1.5 15,125

Valve seats are tested at 1.1 and shells are tested at 1.5 of the working pressure per class. Pressures are in PSIG.

ASTM Specification	ASME B16.34 & API 600 Working & Hydrostatic Test Pressure For Gate Valves Per Class & Material Group @ 100°F (psi)							
	150#	300#	400#	600#	900#	1500#	2500#	4500#
A182 Gr. F44 A182 Gr. F51 A479 Gr. S31254	Table 2-2.8A Group 2.8 Materials Standard Class							
A312 Gr. S31254 A358 Gr. S31254 A182 Gr. F53 A240 Gr. S31803 A479 Gr. S31803 A789 Gr. S31803 A790 Gr. S31803 A240 Gr. S31254 A240 Gr. S32750 A479 Gr. S32750 A789 Gr. S32750 A790 Gr. S32750 A351 Gr. CK3MCuN	work 290 x1.1 325 x1.5 450	work 750 x1.1 825 x1.5 1125	work 1000 x1.1 1100 x1.5 1500	work 1500 x1.1 1650 x1.5 2250	work 2250 x1.1 2475 x1.5 3375	work 3750 x1.1 4125 x1.5 5625	work 6250 x1.1 6875 x1.5 9375	work 11250 x1.1 12375 x1.5 16875

Valve seats are tested at 1.1 and shells are tested at 1.5 of the working pressure per class. Pressures are in PSIG.

API 602 Working and Hydrostatic Test Pressure For Class 800 Gate Valves Per Material Group @ 100° (psi)					
Material Group Number	ASTM SPECIFICATION	Working Pressure	x1.1 Seat Test Pressure	x1.5 Shell Test Pressure
1.1	A105 A350-LF2 A216-WCB	1975	2175	2975
1.2	A350-LF3 A352-LC2 A352-LC3	2000	2200	3000
1.3	A352-LCB	1855	2050	2800
1.9	A182-F11 A217-WC6	2000	2200	3000
1.10	A182-F22 A217-WC9	2000	2200	3000
1.13	A182-F5 A182-F5a A217-C5	2000	2200	3000
1.14	A182-F9 A217-C12	2000	2200	3000
2.1	A182-F304 A351-CF3 A351-CF8	1920	2125	2900
2.2	A182-F316 A351-CF3M A351-CF8M	1920	2125	2900
2.3	A182-F304L A182-F316L	1600	1775	2400
2.5	A182-F347H A351-CF8C	1920	2125	2900

Pressures are in PSIG.

ASTM Forgings Specification	ASME B16.5 & B16.47 Working & Hydrostatic Test Pressure For FLANGES Per Class & Material Group @ 100°F (psi)						
	150#	300#	400#	600#	900#	1500#	2500#
A105 A350 Gr. LF2 A350 Gr. LF3 A350 Gr. LF6 Cl.1	Table F2-1.1 Group 1.1 Materials						
	work 285 hydro 450	work 740 hydro 1125	work 985 hydro 1500	work 1480 hydro 2225	work 2220 hydro 3350	work 3705 hydro 5575	work 6170 hydro 9275
A350 Gr. LF6 Cl.2	Table F2-1.2 Group 1.2 Materials						
	work 290 hydro 450	work 750 hydro 1125	work 1000 hydro 1500	work 1500 hydro 2250	work 2250 hydro 3375	work 3750 hydro 5625	work 6250 hydro 9375
A350 Gr. LF1 Cl.1	Table F2-1.4 Group 1.4 Materials						
	work 235 hydro 375	work 615 hydro 925	work 825 hydro 1250	work 1235 hydro 1875	work 1850 hydro 2775	work 3085 hydro 4650	work 5145 hydro 7725
A182 Gr. F1	Table F2-1.5 Group 1.5 Materials						
	work 265 hydro 400	work 695 hydro 1050	work 930 hydro 1400	work 1395 hydro 2100	work 2090 hydro 3150	work 3480 hydro 5225	work 5805 hydro 8725
A182 Gr. F2	Table F2-1.7 Group 1.7 Materials						
	work 290 hydro 450	work 750 hydro 1125	work 1000 hydro 1500	work 1500 hydro 2250	work 2250 hydro 3375	work 3750 hydro 5625	work 6250 hydro 9375
A182 Gr. F11 Cl.2	Table F2-1.9 Group 1.9 Materials						
	work 290 hydro 450	work 750 hydro 1125	work 1000 hydro 1500	work 1500 hydro 2250	work 2250 hydro 3375	work 3750 hydro 5625	work 6250 hydro 9375

ASTM Forgings Specification	ASME B16.5 & B16.47 Working & Hydrostatic Test Pressure For FLANGES Per Class & Material Group @ 100°F (psi)						
	150#	300#	400#	600#	900#	1500#	2500#
	Table F2-1.10 Group 1.10 Materials						
A182 Gr. F22 Cl.3	work 290 hydro 450	work 750 hydro 1125	work 1000 hydro 1500	work 1500 hydro 2250	work 2250 hydro 3375	work 3750 hydro 5625	work 6250 hydro 9375
	Table F2-1.13 Group 1.13 Materials						
A182 Gr. F5a	work 290 hydro 450	work 750 hydro 1125	work 1000 hydro 1500	work 1500 hydro 2250	work 2250 hydro 3375	work 3750 hydro 5625	work 6250 hydro 9375
	Table F2-1.14 Group 1.14 Materials						
A182 Gr. F9	work 290 hydro 450	work 750 hydro 1125	work 1000 hydro 1500	work 1500 hydro 2250	work 2250 hydro 3375	work 3750 hydro 5625	work 6250 hydro 9375
	Table F2-1.15 Group 1.15 Materials						
A182. Gr. F91	work 290 hydro 450	work 750 hydro 1125	work 1000 hydro 1500	work 1500 hydro 2250	work 2250 hydro 3375	work 3750 hydro 5625	work 6250 hydro 9375
	Table F2-1.17 Group 1.17 Materials						
A182 Gr. F12 Cl.2 A182 Gr. F5	work 290 hydro 450	work 750 hydro 1125	work 1000 hydro 1500	work 1500 hydro 2250	work 2250 hydro 3375	work 3750 hydro 5625	work 6250 hydro 9375
	Table F2-2.1 Group 2.1 Materials						
A182 Gr. F304 A182 Gr. F304H	work 275 hydro 325	work 720 hydro 1100	work 960 hydro 1450	work 1440 hydro 2175	work 2160 hydro 3250	work 3600 hydro 5400	work 6000 hydro 9000

ASTM Forgings Specification	ASME B16.5 & B16.47 Working & Hydrostatic Test Pressure For FLANGES Per Class & Material Group @ 100°F (psi)						
	150#	300#	400#	600#	900#	1500#	2500#
	Table F2-2.2 Group 2.2 Materials						
A182 Gr. F316 A182 Gr. F316H A182 Gr. F317	work 275 hydro 325	work 720 hydro 1100	work 960 hydro 1450	work 1440 hydro 2175	work 2160 hydro 3250	work 3600 hydro 5400	work 6000 hydro 9000
	Table F2-2.3 Group 2.3 Materials						
A182 Gr. F316L A182 Gr. F304L A182 Gr. F317L	work 230 hydro 350	work 600 hydro 900	work 800 hydro 1200	work 1200 hydro 1800	work 1800 hydro 2700	work 3000 hydro 4500	work 5000 hydro 7500
	Table F2-2.4 Group 2.4 Materials						
A182 Gr. F321 A182 Gr. F321H	work 275 hydro 325	work 720 hydro 1100	work 960 hydro 1450	work 1440 hydro 2175	work 2160 hydro 3250	work 3600 hydro 5400	work 6000 hydro 9000
	Table F2-2.5 Group 2.5 Materials						
A182 Gr. F347 A182 Gr. F347H A182 Gr. F348 A182 Gr. F348H	work 275 hydro 325	work 720 hydro 1100	work 960 hydro 1450	work 1440 hydro 2175	work 2160 hydro 3250	work 3600 hydro 5400	work 6000 hydro 9000
	Table F2-2.7 Group 2.7 Materials						
A182 Gr. F310	work 275 hydro 325	work 720 hydro 1100	work 960 hydro 1450	work 1440 hydro 2175	work 2160 hydro 3250	work 3600 hydro 5400	work 6000 hydro 9000
	Table F2-2.8 Group 2.8 Materials						
A182 Gr. F44 A182 Gr. F51 A182 Gr. F53 A182 Gr. F55	work 290 hydro 450	work 750 hydro 1125	work 1000 hydro 1500	work 1500 hydro 2250	work 2250 hydro 3375	work 3750 hydro 5625	work 6250 hydro 9375

PADDLE/SLIP BLIND PRESSURE RATED THICKNESS FORMULA

ASME B31.5 section 304.5.3 provides a formula for determining the thickness of a slip blind per design or hydro pressure. This calculated thickness will almost always be slightly different than the thickness you get from B16.48.

$$t_m = d_g \sqrt{\frac{3P}{16SE}} + c$$

t_m = minimal blind thickness (in.)
d_g = inside diameter (in.) of gasket for raised or flat face flanges, or the gasket pitch diameter for ring joint and fully retained gasket flanges (raised face info provided in gasket section under inner ring ID)
E = quality factor from Table A-1A or A-1B (seamless plate = 1)
P = design gauge pressure (psig)
S = stress value for material from B31.3 Table A-1 (supplied on following page)
c = sum of allowances defined in B31.3 section 304.1.1

In this formula d_g is found in ASME B16.20 and is the gasket ID for a given size of flange which can also be found under the gasket inner ring ID charts in the gasket section of this book. P is the design pressure which you can take from B16.5 standards for in service blinding and pressures per material grade or it can be any verified hydro pressure required as with a vessel hydro which might be at a lesser value than what the flanges are rated for thus allowing for a thinner blind than would be required for a piping hydro. S is the allowable stress value for your chosen material from Table A-1 in B31.3 (provided on following page) and is usually per the 100°F rating for hydro testing, and E is 1 unless the material is welded or cast in which case you get a quality factor from B31.3 Table A1-A or A1-B. The c is for a corrosion allowance which can be whatever you want, but is usually zero for blanks being used for lockout safety reasons. If the blank is being used for a section of piping being kept out of service with full contact with process fluids on one or both sides, a corrosion factor makes sense but if it's for a blind being cut from new plate which will be used for a hydro, then a corrosion allowance is unnecessary. If you have a defined thickness already then you can also solve for max pressure per that thickness. This formula does not apply to bolted plate blind flanges fastened to the end of a flange due to the bolting moments of the blind flange.

Determine the required thickness t_m of an ASTM A36 seamless material blank in an A105 10" 300 class flange testing at 1125 psig. Where: P = 1125 psig; S = 17,800 psi @ 100° F (from B31.3 Table A-1); c = 0; E = 1 (typical for seamless plate); d_g = 10.56"

Then: $t_m = 10.56 \sqrt{\frac{3 \times 1125}{16 \times 17{,}800}} = 1.15$ in. Blind Thickness

ASME B31.3 TABLE A-1: BASIC ALLOWABLE STRESSES IN TENSION FOR METALS

CARBON STEEL PLATES AND SHEETS

SPEC. NO.	GRADE	S VALUE	SPEC. NO.	GRADE	S VALUE
A285	A	15,000	A283	A	13,800
A285	B	16,700	A570	30	15,000
A516	55	18,300	A283	B	15,300
A285	C	18,300	A570	33	15,900
A516	60	20,000	A570	36	16,300
A515	60	20,000	A283	C	16,900
A516	65	21,700	A570	40	16,900
A515	65	21,700	A36	-	17,800
A516	70	23,300	A283	D	18,400
A515	70	23,300	A570	45	18,400
A537†	Cl.1	23,300	A570	50	19,900
A299	-	25,000	-	-	-

STAINLESS STEEL PLATES AND SHEETS

SPEC. NO.	GRADE	S VALUE	SPEC. NO.	GRADE	S VALUE
A240	304L	16,700	A240	316	20,000
A240	316L	16,700	A167	309	20,000
A167	308	20,000	A240	347	20,000
A240	304	20,000	A167	347	20,000

This table is supplied to provide the "S" value for the blind thickness equation on the previous pages. Table A-1 contains much more information but for the purpose of blinding information only the provided materials and values were considered necessary. The S values provided are for minimal temperature per material to 100°F which is suitable for blinding values whereby the higher temperature values from the table aren't required as they address design and operating temperatures.

† ($\leq$ 2-1/2 in. thick)

ASME/ANSI B16.5 PADDLE/SLIP BLIND PRESSURE RATED THICKNESS PER B16.48

PIPE SIZE	150#	300#	600#	900#	1500#	2500#
1/2	1/8	1/4	1/4	1/4	1/4	3/8
3/4	1/8	1/4	1/4	1/4	3/8	3/8
1	1/8	1/4	1/4	1/4	3/8	3/8
1-1/4	1/4	1/4	3/8	3/8	3/8	1/2
1-1/2	1/4	1/4	3/8	3/8	1/2	5/8
2	1/4	3/8	3/8	1/2	1/2	5/8
2-1/2	1/4	3/8	1/2	1/2	5/8	3/4
3	1/4	3/8	1/2	5/8	3/4	7/8
3-1/2	3/8	1/2	5/8	-	-	-
4	3/8	1/2	5/8	3/4	7/8	1-1/8
5	3/8	5/8	3/4	7/8	1-1/8	1-3/8
6	1/2	5/8	7/8	1	1-3/8	1-5/8
8	1/2	7/8	1/1/8	1-3/8	1-5/8	2-1/8
10	5/8	1	1-3/8	1-5/8	2	2-5/8
12	3/4	1-1/8	1-5/8	1-7/8	2-3/8	3-1/8
14	3/4	1-1/4	1-3/4	2-1/8	2-5/8	-
16	7/8	1-1/2	2	2-3/8	3	-
18	1	1-5/8	2-1/8	2-5/8	3-3/8	-
20	1/1/8	1-3/4	2-1/2	2-7/8	3-3/4	-
22	1-1/4	1-7/8	2-3/4	-	-	-
24	1-1/4	2	2-7/8	3-1/2	4-3/8	-

ASME/ANSI B16.47 SERIES A PADDLE/SLIP BLIND PRESSURE RATED THICKNESS

PIPE SIZE	150#	300#	600#	900#
26	1-1/2	2	3-1/8	3-3/4
28	1-5/8	2-1/8	3-3/8	4-1/8
30	1-3/4	2-3/8	3-5/8	4-3/8
32	1-3/4	2-1/2	3-3/4	4-3/4
34	1-7/8	2-5/8	4-1/8	5
36	2	2-3/4	4-1/4	5-1/4
38	2-1/8	3	4-1/2	5-1/2
40	2-1/4	3-1/8	4-3/4	5-7/8
42	2-3/8	3-1/4	5	6-1/8
44	2-1/2	3-3/8	5-1/4	6-3/8
46	2-1/2	3-5/8	5-1/2	6-3/4
48	2-5/8	3-3/4	5-3/4	7

Sizes 26-48 are for MSS SP-44 (Series A) and do not represent those required thicknesses of API 605 (Series B). Sizes and thicknesses meet the following specifications: ASME 16.48, API 590, ASME 16.5

The thicknesses were calculated using the equation for blanks in ANSI B31.3 as follows: $t_m = d_g \sqrt{\dfrac{3P}{16SE}} + c$

where: C = 0.02; d_g = I.D. of ring gaskets (inches); t_m = Blank Thickness (inches); SE = 24,400 psi

CHAPTER 3: GASKETS

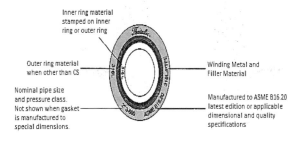

TIPS: Gasket materials and construction will vary per piping specs and should be referenced to such when doing final makeup of flanges.

Verification of the proper gasket in a previously bolted flange should be done by assuring that there is no more than 1/8" clearance of the gaskets outer ring anywhere within the bolt circle of the flange.

ASME B16.20 GASKET COLOR CODE CHART FOR SPIRAL WOUND GASKET METALLIC WINDING AND NON-METALLIC FILLERS	
METALLIC WINDING	**RING COLOR**
304 Stainless Steel	YELLOW
316L Stainless Steel	GREEN
317L Stainless Steel	MAROON
321 Stainless Steel	TURQUOISE
347 Stainless Steel	BLUE
MONEL®	ORANGE
Nickel 200	RED
Titanium	PURPLE
Alloy 20	BLACK
INCONEL® 600/625	GOLD
HASTELLOY® B2	BROWN
HASTELLOY® C276	BEIGE
INCOLOY® 800/825	WHITE
Carbon Steel	SILVER
NON-METALLIC FILLER	**STRIPE COLOR**
Flexicarb	GREY
PTFE	WHITE
Ceramic	LT. GREEN
Flexite Super®	PINK
Thermiculite ® 835	LT. BLUE

ASME/ANSI B16.5 GASKET OUTSIDE DIAMETER OF CENTERING RING PER ASME B16.20

PIPE SIZE	150#	300#	400#	600#	900#	1500#	2500#
1/4	1-3/4	1-3/4	1-3/4	1-3/4	N/A	N/A	N/A
1/2	1-7/8	2-1/8	2-1/8	2-1/8	2-1/2	2-1/2	2-3/4
3/4	2-1/4	2-5/8	2-5/8	2-5/8	2-3/4	2-3/4	3
1	2-5/8	2-7/8	2-7/8	2-7/8	3-1/8	3-1/8	3-3/8
1-1/4	3	3-1/4	3-1/4	3-1/4	3-1/2	3-1/2	4-1/8
1-1/2	3-3/8	3-3/4	3-3/4	3-3/4	3-7/8	3-7/8	4-5/8
2	4-1/8	4-3/8	4-3/8	4-3/8	5-5/8	5-5/8	5-3/4
2-1/2	4-7/8	5-1/8	5-1/8	5-1/8	6-1/2	6-1/2	6-5/8
3	5-3/8	5-7/8	5-7/8	5-7/8	6-5/8	6-7/8	7-3/4
3-1/2	6-3/8	6-1/2	6-3/8	6-3/8	7-1/2	7-3/8	N/A
4	6-7/8	7-1/8	7	7-5/8	8-1/8	8-1/4	9-1/4
4-1/2	7	7-3/4	7-5/8	8-1/4	9-3/8	9-1/8	N/A
5	7-3/4	8-1/2	8-3/8	9-1/2	9-3/4	10	11
6	8-3/4	9-7/8	9-3/4	10-1/2	11-3/8	11-1/8	12-1/2
8	11	12-1/8	12	12-5/8	14-1/8	13-7/8	15-1/4
10	13-3/8	14-1/4	14-1/8	15-3/4	17-1/8	17-1/8	18-3/4
12	16-1/8	16-5/8	16-1/2	18	19-5/8	20-1/2	21-5/8
14	17-3/4	19-1/8	19	19-3/8	20-1/2	22-3/4	N/A
16	20-1/4	21-1/4	21-1/8	22-1/4	22-5/8	25-1/4	N/A
18	21-5/8	23-1/2	23-3/8	24-1/8	25-1/8	27-3/4	N/A
20	23-7/8	25-3/4	25-1/2	26-7/8	27-1/2	29-3/4	N/A
24	28-1/4	30-1/2	30-1/4	31-1/8	33	35-1/2	N/A

PIPE SIZE	MSS SP-44 (SERIES A)		API 605 (SERIES B)		
	150#	300#	75#	150#	300#
26	30-1/2	32-7/8	27-7/8	28-9/16	30-3/8
28	32-3/4	35-3/8	29-7/8	30-9/16	32-1/2
30	34-3/4	37-1/2	31-7/8	32-9/16	34-7/8
32	37	39-5/8	33-7/8	34-11/16	37
34	39	41-5/8	35-7/8	36-13/16	39-1/8
36	41-1/4	44	38-5/16	38-7/8	41-1/4
38	43-3/4	41-1/2	40-5/16	41-1/8	43-1/4
40	45-3/4	43-7/8	42-5/16	43-1/8	45-1/4
42	48	45-7/8	44-5/16	45-1/8	47-1/4
44	50-1/4	48	46-1/2	47-1/8	49-1/4
46	52-1/4	50-1/8	48-1/2	49-7/16	51-7/8
48	54-1/2	52-1/8	50-1/2	51-7/16	53-7/8
50	56-1/2	54-1/4	52-1/2	53-7/16	55-7/8
52	58-3/4	56-1/4	54-5/8	55-7/16	57-7/8
54	61	58-3/4	56-5/8	57-5/8	60-1/4
56	63-1/4	60-3/4	58-7/8	59-5/8	62-3/4
58	65-1/2	62-3/4	60-7/8	62-3/16	65-3/16
60	67-1/2	64-3/4	62-7/8	64-3/16	67-3/16

ASME/ANSI B16.47 LARGE BORE GASKET OUTSIDE DIAMETER OF CENTERING RING PER ASME B16.20

ASME/ANSI B16.47 LARGE BORE GASKET OUTSIDE DIAMETER OF CENTERING RING PER ASME B16.20

PIPE SIZE	MSS SP-44 (SERIES A)			API 605 (SERIES B)		
	400#	600#	900#	400#	600#	900#
26	32-3/4	34-1/8	34-3/4	29-3/8	30-1/8	33
28	35-1/8	36	37-1/4	31-1/2	32-1/4	35-1/2
30	37-1/4	38-1/4	39-3/4	33-3/4	34-5/8	37-3/4
32	39-1/2	40-1/4	42-1/4	35-7/8	36-3/4	40
34	41-1/2	42-1/4	44-3/4	37-7/8	39-1/4	42-1/4
36	44	44-1/2	47-1/4	40-1/4	41-1/4	44-1/4
BOTH MSS SP-44 (SERIES A) AND API 605 (SERIES B)						
	400#		600#		900#	
38	42-1/4		43-1/2		47-1/4	
40	44-3/8		45-1/2		49-1/4	
42	46-3/8		48		51-1/4	
44	48-1/2		50		53-7/8	
46	50-3/4		52-1/4		56-1/2	
48	53		54-3/4		58-1/2	
50	55-1/4		57		N/A	
52	57-1/4		59		N/A	
54	59-3/4		61-1/4		N/A	
56	61-3/4		63-1/2		N/A	
58	63-3/4		65-1/2		N/A	
60	66-1/4		68-1/4		N/A	

Both MSS SP-44 (Series A) and API 605 (Series B) have the same gasket OD concerning pipe sizes 38"- 60" at 400#, 600# and 900# flange ratings.

ASME/ANSI B16.5 GASKET INSIDE DIAMETER OF SEALING ELEMENT PER ASME B16.20

PIPE SIZE	150#	300#	400#	600#	900#	1500#	2500#
1/4	1/2	1/2	1/2	1/2	-	-	-
1/2	3/4	3/4	3/4	3/4	3/4	3/4	3/4
3/4	1	1	1	1	1	1	1
1	1-1/4	1-1/4	1-1/4	1-1/4	1-1/4	1-1/4	1-1/4
1-1/4	1-7/8	1-7/8	1-7/8	1-7/8	1-9/16	1-9/16	1-9/16
1-1/2	2-1/8	2-1/8	2-1/8	2-1/8	1-7/8	1-7/8	1-7/8
2	2-3/4	2-3/4	2-3/4	2-3/4	2-5/16	2-5/16	2-5/16
2-1/2	3-1/4	3-1/4	3-1/4	3-1/4	2-3/4	2-3/4	2-3/4
3	4	4	4	4	3-3/4	3-5/8	3-5/8
3-1/2	4-1/2	4-1/2	4-1/8	4-1/8	4-1/8	4-1/8	-
4	5	5	4-3/4	4-3/4	4-3/4	4-5/8	4-5/8
4-1/2	5-1/2	5-1/2	5-5/16	5-5/16	5-5/16	5-5/16	-
5	6-1/8	6-1/8	5-13/16	5-13/16	5-13/16	5-5/8	5-5/8
6	7-3/16	7-3/16	6-7/8	6-7/8	6-7/8	6-3/4	6-3/4
8	9-3/16	9-3/16	8-7/8	8-7/8	8-3/8	8-1/2	8-1/2
10	11-5/16	11-5/16	10-13/16	10-13/16	10-7/8	10-1/2	10-5/8
12	13-3/8	13-3/8	12-7/8	12-7/8	12-3/4	12-3/4	12-1/2
14	14-5/8	14-5/8	14-1/4	14-1/4	14	14-1/4	-
16	16-5/8	16-5/8	16-1/4	16-1/4	16-1/4	16	-
18	18-11/16	18-11/16	18-1/2	18-1/2	18-1/4	18-1/4	-
20	20-11/16	20-11/16	20-1/2	20-1/2	20-1/2	20-1/4	-
24	24-3/4	24-3/4	24-3/4	24-3/4	24-3/4	24-1/4	-

ASME/ANSI B16.47 LARGE BORE GASKET INSIDE DIAMETER OF SEALING ELEMENT PER ASME B16.20

PIPE SIZE	MSS SP-44 (SERIES A)		API 605 (SERIES B)		
	150#	300#	75#	150#	300#
26	26-1/2	27	26-1/4	26-1/2	26-1/2
28	28-1/2	29	28-1/4	28-1/2	28-1/2
30	30-1/2	31-1/4	30-1/4	30-1/2	30-1/2
32	32-1/2	33-1/2	32-1/4	32-1/2	32-1/2
34	34-1/2	35-1/2	34-1/4	34-1/2	34-1/2
36	36-1/2	37-5/8	36-1/4	36-1/2	36-1/2
38	38-1/2	38-1/2	-	38-3/8	39-3/4
40	40-1/2	40-1/4	-	40-1/4	41-3/4
42	42-1/2	42-1/4	42-1/4	42-1/2	43-3/4
44	44-1/2	44-1/2	-	44-1/4	45-3/4
46	46-1/2	46-3/8	-	46-1/2	47-7/8
48	48-1/2	48-5/8	48-3/8	48-1/2	49-3/4
50	50-1/2	51	-	50-1/2	51-7/8
52	52-1/2	53	-	52-1/2	53-7/8
54	54-1/2	55-1/4	54-3/8	54-1/2	55-1/4
56	56-1/2	57-1/4	-	56-7/8	58-1/4
58	58-1/2	59-1/2	-	59-1/16	60-7/16
60	60-1/2	61-1/2	60-1/2	61-5/16	62-9/16

ASME/ANSI B16.47 LARGE BORE GASKET INSIDE DIAMETER OF SEALING ELEMENT PER ASME B16.20

PIPE SIZE	MSS SP-44 (SERIES A)			API 605 (SERIES B)		
	400#	600#	900#	400#	600#	900#
26	27	27	27	26-1/4	26-1/8	27-1/4
28	29	29	29	28-1/8	27-3/4	29-1/4
30	31-1/4	31-1/4	31-1/4	30-1/8	30-5/8	30-3/4
32	33-1/2	33-1/2	33-1/2	32	32-3/4	34
34	35-1/2	35-1/2	35-1/2	34-1/8	35	36-1/4
36	37-5/8	37-5/8	37-3/4	36-1/8	37	37-1/4

	BOTH MSS SP-44 (SERIES A) AND API 605 (SERIES B)		
	400#	600#	900#
38	38-1/4	39	40-3/4
40	40-3/8	41-1/4	43-1/4
42	42-3/8	43-1/2	45-1/4
44	44-1/2	45-3/4	47-1/2
46	47	47-3/4	50
48	49	50	52
50	51	52	-
52	53	54	-
54	55-1/4	56-1/4	-
56	57-1/4	58-1/4	-
58	59-1/4	60-1/2	-
60	61-3/4	62-3/4	-

Both MSS SP-44 (Series A) and API 605 (Series B) have the same gasket ID concerning pipe sizes 38"- 60" at 400#, 600# and 900# flange ratings.

ASME/ANSI B16.5 GASKET INSIDE DIAMETER OF INNER RING PER ASME B16.20							
PIPE SIZE	150#	300#	400#	600#	900#	1500#	2500#
1/2	0.56	0.56	0.56	0.56	0.56	0.56	0.56
3/4	0.81	0.81	0.81	0.81	0.81	0.81	0.81
1	1.06	1.06	1.06	1.06	1.06	1.06	1.06
1-1/4	1.50	1.50	1.50	1.50	1.31	1.31	1.31
1-1/2	1.75	1.75	1.75	1.75	1.63	1.63	1.63
2	2.19	2.19	2.19	2.19	2.06	2.06	2.06
2-1/2	2.62	2.62	2.62	2.62	2.50	2.50	2.50
3	3.19	3.19	3.19	3.19	3.10	3.10	3.10
4	4.19	4.19	4.04	4.04	4.04	3.85	3.85
5	5.19	5.19	5.05	5.05	5.05	4.90	4.90
6	6.19	6.19	6.10	6.10	6.10	5.80	5.80
8	8.50	8.50	8.10	8.10	7.75	7.75	7.75
10	10.56	10.56	10.05	10.05	9.69	9.69	9.69
12	12.50	12.50	12.10	12.10	11.50	11.50	11.50
14	13.75	13.75	13.50	13.50	12.63	12.63	-
16	15.75	15.75	15.35	15.35	14.75	14.50	-
18	17.69	17.69	17.25	17.25	16.75	16.75	-
20	19.69	19.69	19.25	19.25	19.00	18.75	-
24	23.75	23.75	23.25	23.25	23.25	22.75	-

PIPE SIZE	MSS SP-44 (SERIES A)		API 605 (SERIES B)	
	150#	300#	150#	300#
26	25-3/4	25-3/4	25-3/4	25-3/4
28	27-3/4	27-3/4	27-3/4	27-3/4
30	29-3/4	29-3/4	29-3/4	29-3/4
32	31-3/4	31-3/4	31-3/4	31-3/4
34	33-3/4	33-3/4	33-3/4	33-3/4
36	35-3/4	35-3/4	35-3/4	35-3/4
38	37-3/4	37-1/2	37-3/4	38-1/4
40	39-3/4	39-1/2	39-3/4	40-1/4
42	41-3/4	41-1/2	41-3/4	42-3/4
44	43-3/4	43-1/2	43-3/4	44-1/4
46	45-3/4	45-5/8	45-3/4	46-3/8
48	47-3/4	47-5/8	47-3/4	48-1/2
50	49-3/4	49	49-3/4	49-7/8
52	51-3/4	52	51-3/4	51-7/8
54	53-1/2	53-1/4	53-3/4	53-3/4
56	55-1/2	55-1/4	56	56-1/4
58	57-1/2	57	58-3/16	58-7/16
60	59-1/2	60	60-7/16	61-5/16

ASME/ANSI B16.47 LARGE BORE GASKET INSIDE DIAMETER OF INNER RING PER ASME B16.20

ASME/ANSI B16.47 LARGE BORE GASKET INSIDE DIAMETER OF INNER RING PER ASME B16.20						
PIPE SIZE	MSS SP-44 (SERIES A)			API 605 (SERIES B)		
	400#	600#	900#	400#	600#	900#
26	26	25-1/2	26	25-3/4	25-3/8	26-1/4
28	28	27-1/2	28	27-5/8	27	28-1/4
30	29-3/4	29-3/4	30-1/4	29-5/8	29-5/8	30-3/4
32	32	32	32	31-1/2	31-1/4	33
34	34	34	34	33-1/2	33-1/2	35-1/4
36	36-1/8	36-1/8	36-1/4	35-3/8	35-1/2	36-1/4
BOTH MSS SP-44 (SERIES A) AND API 605 (SERIES B)						
	400#			600#		900#
38	37-1/2			37-1/2		39-3/4
40	39-3/8			39-3/4		41-3/4
42	41-3/8			42		43-3/4
44	43-1/2			43-3/4		45-1/2
46	46			45-3/4		48
48	47-1/2			48		50
50	49-1/2			50		-
52	51-1/2			52		-
54	53-1/4			54-1/4		-
56	55-1/4			56-1/4		-
58	57-1/4			58		-
60	59-3/4			60-1/4		-

Both MSS SP-44 (Series A) and API 605 (Series B) have the same gasket ID concerning pipe sizes 38"- 60" at 400#, 600# and 900# flange ratings.

CHAPTER 4: STUD BOLTS

TIPS: Stud bolt length can be calculated by means of the following formula: Length =Gasket Thickness + 2(Nut Thickness + Flange Thickness + Raised Face Thickness + Excess Thread Required)

Nut Thickness = diameter of stud
Flange Thickness = listed in flange dimension tables per rating and pipe size in this book
Raised Face Thickness = found with appropriate flange dimension table in this book
Excess Thread = varies per site inspection department but one rule of thumb is 1/3 times bolt diameter
Gasket Thickness = factored at 1/8"

When cutting stud bolts down to the size required, never cut the stamped end off of the end to be used. This will allow for future proper identification of the stud once it is installed into the flange. It's also good practice and shows good craftsmanship to do a final bolt up with all of the stamped ends of the studs facing the same way for ease of inspections. This is sometimes a requirement of the inspections department. The direction faced should be in the easiest direction to view.

Its common practice to anti-seize only one side of a stud bolt and place that side in the position whereby that nut will be the one required to come off to allow stud removal in the future if dealing with an obstruction on one side. Applying anti seize opposite of the stamped end of the stud while leaving that nut off and then stabbing studs from the same side of the flange every time will generally accomplish a uniform bolt up with the stamps on the same side and the anti-seize on the obstructed side.

COARSE THREAD (UNC) THREADS PER INCH (TPI) PER STUD DIAMETER

STUD DIA.	TPI	STUD DIA.	TPI
1/4	20	1-1/2	6
5/16	18	1-5/8	5
3/8	16	1-3/4	5
7/16	14	1-7/8	4-1/2
1/2	13	2	4-1/2
9/16	12	2-1/4	4-1/2
5/8	11	2-1/2	4
3/4	10	2-3/4	4
7/8	9	3	4
1	8	3-1/4	4
1-1/8	7	3-1/2	4
1-1/4	7	3-3/4	4
1-3/8	6	4	4

Process Piping usually goes to unified inch 8 thread series (8 UN) for all stud bolts larger than 1 in. diameter in accordance with ANSI/ASME B1.1 whereby always having 8 TPI despite the stud diameter.

WRENCH SIZE PER STUD DIAMETER

STUD DIAMETER	WRENCH SIZE	STUD DIAMETER	WRENCH SIZE
1/2	7/8	1-3/4	2-3/4
5/8	1-1/16	1-7/8	2-15/16
3/4	1-1/4	2	3-1/8
7/8	1-7/16	2-1/4	3-1/2
1	1-5/8	2-1/2	3-7/8
1-1/8	1-13/16	2-3/4	4-1/4
1-1/4	2	3	4-5/8
1-3/8	2-3/16	3-1/2	5-3/8
1-1/2	2-3/8	3-3/4	5-3/4
1-5/8	2-9/16	4	6-1/8

The rule of thumb in figuring wrench size from bolt diameter is:
1-1/2×bolt diameter + 1/8". Example: 1-1/2×1/2"=3/4+1/8=7/8"

ASME/ANSI B16.5 STUD BOLT DIMENSIONS
CLASS 150 FLANGES

PIPE SIZE	QTY	SIZE	BLIND THCK	RING No.	MACHINE BOLTS LENGTH RF	STUD BOLTS RAISED FACE LENGTH	STUD BOLTS RING JOINT LENGTH
1/2	4	1/2	1/8	N/A	2	2-1/4	N/A
3/4	4	1/2	1/8	N/A	2	2-1/2	N/A
1	4	1/2	1/8	R-15	2-1/4	2-1/2	3
1-1/4	4	1/2	1/4	R-17	2-1/4	2-3/4	3-1/4
1-1/2	4	1/2	1/4	R-19	2-1/2	2-3/4	3-1/4
2	4	5/8	1/4	R-22	2-3/4	3-1/4	3-3/4
2-1/2	4	5/8	1/4	R-25	3	3-1/2	4
3	4	5/8	1/4	R-29	3	3-1/2	4
3-1/2	8	5/8	3/8	R-33	3	3-1/2	4
4	8	5/8	3/8	R-36	3	3-1/2	4
5	8	3/4	3/8	R-40	3-1/4	3-3/4	4-1/4
6	8	3/4	1/2	R-43	3-1/4	4	4-1/2
8	8	3/4	1/2	R-48	3-1/2	4-1/4	4-3/4
10	12	7/8	5/8	R-52	4	4-1/2	5
12	12	7/8	3/4	R-56	4	4-3/4	5-1/4
14	12	1	3/4	R-59	4-1/2	5-1/4	5-3/4
16	16	1	7/8	R-64	4-1/2	5-1/4	5-3/4
18	16	1-1/8	1	R-68	5	5-3/4	6-1/4
20	20	1-1/8	1/1/8	R-72	5-1/2	6-1/4	6-3/4
22	20	1-1/4	1-1/4	R-80	5-3/4	6-1/2	7
24	20	1-1/4	1-1/4	R-76	6	6-3/4	7-1/4

USE PRESSURE RATED BLIND THICKNESS VALUES PROVIDED TO FACTOR BLINDING LENGTHS. 1/8" MUST ALSO BE ADDED FOR THE EXTRA BLIND GASKET. ALL STUD DIMENSIONS WERE TAKEN DIRECTLY FROM ASME B16.5 PER THEIR APPLICATION OF THE FORMULA CONTAINED IN ANNEX D AND ARE AS MEASURED FROM THREAD TO THREAD AND DO NOT INCLUDE HEIGHT OF POINTS. MACHINE BOLT LENGTHS ARE AS MEASURED FROM BOTTOM OF BOLT HEAD TO POINT AND DO NOT INCLUDE HEAD THICKNESS.

ASME/ANSI B16.5 STUD BOLT DIMENSIONS
CLASS 300 FLANGES

PIPE SIZE	QTY	SIZE	BLIND THCK	RING No.	MACHINE BOLTS LENGTH RF	STUD BOLTS RAISED FACE LENGTH	STUD BOLTS RING JOINT LENGTH
1/2	4	1/2	1/4	R-11	2-1/4	2-1/2	3
3/4	4	5/8	1/4	R-13	2-1/2	3	3-1/2
1	4	5/8	1/4	R-16	2-1/2	3	3-1/2
1-1/4	4	5/8	1/4	R-18	2-3/4	3-1/4	3-3/4
1-1/2	4	3/4	1/4	R-20	3	3-1/2	4
2	8	5/8	3/8	R-23	3	3-1/2	4
2-1/2	8	3/4	3/8	R-26	3-1/4	4	4-1/2
3	8	3/4	3/8	R-31	3-1/2	4-1/4	4-3/4
3-1/2	8	3/4	1/2	R-34	3-3/4	4-1/4	5
4	8	3/4	1/2	R-37	3-3/4	4-1/2	5
5	8	3/4	5/8	R-41	4-1/4	4-3/4	5-1/4
6	12	3/4	5/8	R-45	4-1/4	4-3/4	5-1/2
8	12	7/8	7/8	R-49	4-3/4	5-1/2	6
10	16	1	1	R-53	5-1/2	6-1/4	6-3/4
12	16	1-1/8	1-1/8	R-57	5-3/4	6-3/4	7-1/4
14	20	1-1/8	1-1/4	R-61	6-1/4	7	7-1/2
16	20	1-1/4	1-1/2	R-65	6-1/2	7-1/2	8
18	24	1-1/4	1-5/8	R-69	6-3/4	7-3/4	8-1/4
20	24	1-1/4	1-3/4	R-73	7-1/4	8	8-3/4
22	24	1-1/2	1-7/8	R-81	8	9	10
24	24	1-1/2	2	R-77	8	9	10

USE PRESSURE RATED BLIND THICKNESS VALUES PROVIDED TO FACTOR BLINDING LENGTHS. 1/8" MUST ALSO BE ADDED FOR THE EXTRA BLIND GASKET. ALL STUD DIMENSIONS WERE TAKEN DIRECTLY FROM ASME B16.5 PER THEIR APPLICATION OF THE FORMULA CONTAINED IN ANNEX D AND ARE AS MEASURED FROM THREAD TO THREAD AND DO NOT INCLUDE HEIGHT OF POINTS. MACHINE BOLT LENGTHS ARE AS MEASURED FROM BOTTOM OF BOLT HEAD TO POINT AND DO NOT INCLUDE HEAD THICKNESS.

ASME/ANSI B16.5 STUD BOLT DIMENSIONS
CLASS 400 FLANGES

PIPE SIZE	QTY	SIZE	RAISED FACE LENGTH	BLIND THCK	RING No.	RING JOINT LENGTH
1/2	4	1/2	3	-	R-11	3
3/4	4	5/8	3-1/2	-	R-13	3-1/2
1	4	5/8	3-1/2	-	R-16	3-1/2
1-1/4	4	5/8	3-3/4	-	R-18	3-3/4
1-1/2	4	3/4	4-1/4	-	R-20	4-1/4
2	8	5/8	4-1/4	-	R-23	4-1/4
2-1/2	8	3/4	4-3/4	-	R-26	4-3/4
3	8	3/4	5	-	R-31	5
3-1/2	8	7/8	5-1/2	-	R-34	5-1/2
4	8	7/8	5-1/2	-	R-37	5-1/2
5	8	7/8	5-3/4	-	R-41	5-3/4
6	12	7/8	6	-	R-45	6
8	12	1	6-3/4	-	R-49	6-3/4
10	16	1-1/8	7-1/2	-	R-53	7-1/2
12	16	1-1/4	8	-	R-57	8
14	20	1-1/4	8-1/4	-	R-61	8-1/4
16	20	1-3/8	8-3/4	-	R-65	8-3/4
18	24	1-3/8	9	-	R-69	9
20	24	1-1/2	9-1/2	-	R-73	9-3/4
22	24	1-5/8	10	-	R-81	10-1/2
24	24	1-3/4	10-1/2	-	R-77	11

USE PRESSURE RATED BLIND THICKNESS VALUES TO FACTOR BLINDING LENGTHS. 1/8" MUST ALSO BE ADDED FOR THE EXTRA BLIND GASKET. ALL STUD DIMENSIONS WERE TAKEN DIRECTLY FROM ASME B16.5 PER THEIR APPLICATION OF THE FORMULA CONTAINED IN ANNEX D AND ARE AS MEASURED FROM THREAD TO THREAD AND DO NOT INCLUDE HEIGHT OF POINTS. BLIND THICKNESSES FOR 400# SERIES ARE NOT LISTED IN ASME B16.48 BUT CAN BE CALCULATED USING THE FORMULA PROVIDED THEREIN WHICH CAN BE FOUND IN THE BLINDING SECTION OF THIS BOOK.

ASME/ANSI B16.5 STUD BOLT DIMENSIONS CLASS 600 FLANGES						
PIPE SIZE	QTY	SIZE	RAISED FACE LENGTH	BLIND THCK	RING No.	RING JOINT LENGTH
1/2	4	1/2	3	1/4	R-11	3
3/4	4	5/8	3-1/2	1/4	R-13	3-1/2
1	4	5/8	3-1/2	1/4	R-16	3-1/2
1-1/4	4	5/8	3-3/4	3/8	R-18	3-3/4
1-1/2	4	3/4	4-1/4	3/8	R-20	4-1/4
2	8	5/8	4-1/4	3/8	R-23	4-1/4
2-1/2	8	3/4	4-3/4	1/2	R-26	4-3/4
3	8	3/4	5	1/2	R-31	5
3-1/2	8	7/8	5-1/2	5/8	R-34	5-1/2
4	8	7/8	5-3/4	5/8	R-37	5-3/4
5	8	1	6-1/2	3/4	R-41	6-1/2
6	12	1	6-3/4	7/8	R-45	6-3/4
8	12	1-1/8	7-1/2	1/1/8	R-49	7-3/4
10	16	1-1/4	8-1/2	1-3/8	R-53	8-1/2
12	20	1-1/4	8-3/4	1-5/8	R-57	8-3/4
14	20	1-3/8	9-1/4	1-3/4	R-61	9-1/4
16	20	1-1/2	10	2	R-65	10
18	20	1-5/8	10-3/4	2-1/8	R-69	10-3/4
20	24	1-5/8	11-1/4	2-1/2	R-73	11-1/2
22	24	1-3/4	12	2-3/4	R-81	12-1/2
24	24	1-7/8	13	2-7/8	R-77	13-1/4

USE PRESSURE RATED BLIND THICKNESS VALUES TO FACTOR BLINDING LENGTHS. 1/8" MUST ALSO BE ADDED FOR THE EXTRA BLIND GASKET. ALL STUD DIMENSIONS WERE TAKEN DIRECTLY FROM ASME B16.5 PER THEIR APPLICATION OF THE FORMULA CONTAINED IN ANNEX D AND ARE AS MEASURED FROM THREAD TO THREAD AND DO NOT INCLUDE HEIGHT OF POINTS.

ASME/ANSI B16.5 STUD BOLT DIMENSIONS CLASS 900 FLANGES

PIPE SIZE	QTY	SIZE	RAISED FACE LENGTH	BLIND THCK	RING No.	RING JOINT LENGTH
1/2	4	3/4	4-1/4	1/4	R-12	4-1/4
3/4	4	3/4	4-1/2	1/4	R-14	4-1/2
1	4	7/8	5	1/4	R-16	5
1-1/4	4	7/8	5	3/8	R-18	5
1-1/2	4	1	5-1/2	3/8	R-20	5-1/2
2	8	7/8	5-3/4	1/2	R-24	5-3/4
2-1/2	8	1	6-1/4	1/2	R-27	6-1/4
3	8	7/8	5-3/4	5/8	R-31	5-3/4
4	8	1-1/8	6-3/4	3/4	R-37	6-3/4
5	8	1-1/4	7-1/2	7/8	R-41	7-1/2
6	12	1-1/8	7-1/2	1	R-45	7-3/4
8	12	1-3/8	8-3/4	1-3/8	R-49	8-3/4
10	16	1-3/8	9-1/4	1-5/8	R-53	9-1/4
12	20	1-3/8	10	1-7/8	R-57	10
14	20	1-1/2	10-3/4	2-1/8	R-62	11
16	20	1-5/8	11-1/4	2-3/8	R-66	11-1/2
18	20	1-7/8	12-3/4	2-5/8	R-70	13-1/4
20	20	2	13-3/4	2-7/8	R-74	14-1/4
24	20	2-1/2	17-1/4	3-1/2	R-78	18

USE PRESSURE RATED BLIND THICKNESS VALUES TO FACTOR BLINDING LENGTHS. 1/8" MUST ALSO BE ADDED FOR THE EXTRA BLIND GASKET. ALL STUD DIMENSIONS WERE TAKEN DIRECTLY FROM ASME B16.5 PER THEIR APPLICATION OF THE FORMULA CONTAINED IN ANNEX D AND ARE AS MEASURED FROM THREAD TO THREAD AND DO NOT INCLUDE HEIGHT OF POINTS.

ASME/ANSI B16.5 STUD BOLT DIMENSIONS
CLASS 1500 FLANGES

PIPE SIZE	QTY	SIZE	RAISED FACE LENGTH	BLIND THCK	RING No.	RING JOINT LENGTH
1/2	4	3/4	4-1/4	1/4	R-12	4-1/4
3/4	4	3/4	4-1/2	3/8	R-14	4-1/2
1	4	7/8	5	3/8	R-16	5
1-1/4	4	7/8	5	3/8	R-18	5
1-1/2	4	1	5-1/2	1/2	R-20	5-1/2
2	8	7/8	5-3/4	1/2	R-24	5-3/4
2-1/2	8	1	6-1/4	5/8	R-27	6-1/4
3	8	1-1/8	7	3/4	R-35	7
4	8	1-1/4	7-3/4	7/8	R-39	7-3/4
5	8	1-1/2	9-3/4	1-1/8	R-44	9-3/4
6	12	1-3/8	10-1/4	1-3/8	R-46	10-1/2
8	12	1-5/8	11-1/2	1-5/8	R-50	12-3/4
10	12	1-7/8	13-1/4	2	R-54	13-1/2
12	16	2	14-3/4	2-3/8	R-58	15-1/4
14	16	2-1/4	16	2-5/8	R-63	16-3/4
16	16	2-1/2	17-1/2	3	R-67	18-1/2
18	16	2-3/4	19-1/2	3-3/8	R-71	20-3/4
20	16	3	21-1/4	3-3/4	R-75	22-1/4
24	16	3-1/2	24-1/4	4-3/8	R-79	25-1/2

USE PRESSURE RATED BLIND THICKNESS VALUES TO FACTOR BLINDING LENGTHS. 1/8" MUST ALSO BE ADDED FOR THE EXTRA BLIND GASKET. ALL STUD DIMENSIONS WERE TAKEN DIRECTLY FROM ASME B16.5 PER THEIR APPLICATION OF THE FORMULA CONTAINED IN ANNEX D AND ARE AS MEASURED FROM THREAD TO THREAD AND DO NOT INCLUDE HEIGHT OF POINTS.

ASME/ANSI B16.5 STUD BOLT DIMENSIONS
CLASS 2500 FLANGES

PIPE SIZE	QTY	SIZE	RAISED FACE LENGTH	BLIND THCK	RING No.	RING JOINT LENGTH
1/2	4	3/4	4-3/4	3/8	R-13	4-3/4
3/4	4	3/4	5	3/8	R-16	5
1	4	7/8	5-1/2	3/8	R-18	5-1/2
1-1/4	4	1	6	1/2	R-21	6
1-1/2	4	1-1/8	6-3/4	5/8	R-23	6-3/4
2	8	1	7	5/8	R-26	7
2-1/2	8	1-1/8	7-3/4	3/4	R-28	8
3	8	1-1/4	8-3/4	7/8	R-32	9
4	8	1-1/2	10	1-1/8	R-38	10-1/4
5	8	1-3/4	11-3/4	1-3/8	R-42	12-1/4
6	8	2	13-1/2	1-5/8	R-47	14
8	12	2	15	2-1/8	R-51	15-1/2
10	12	2-1/2	19-1/4	2-5/8	R-55	20
12	12	2-3/4	21-1/4	3-1/8	R-60	22

USE PRESSURE RATED BLIND THICKNESS VALUES TO FACTOR BLINDING LENGTHS. 1/8" MUST ALSO BE ADDED FOR THE EXTRA BLIND GASKET. ALL STUD DIMENSIONS WERE TAKEN DIRECTLY FROM ASME B16.5 PER THEIR APPLICATION OF THE FORMULA CONTAINED IN ANNEX D AND ARE AS MEASURED FROM THREAD TO THREAD AND DO NOT INCLUDE HEIGHT OF POINTS.

ASME/ANSI B16.36 ORIFICE FLANGE STUD DIMENSIONS

PIPE SIZE	300 CLASS				400 CLASS			
	QTY	DIA.	LENGTH RF	LENGTH RTJ	QTY	DIA.	LENGTH RF	LENGTH RTJ
1	4	5/8	5.00		4	5/8	5.00	5.50
1-1/2	4	3/4	5.25		4	3/4	5.25	5.50
2	8	5/8	5.00		8	5/8	5.00	5.50
2-1/2	8	3/4	5.25		8	3/4	5.25	5.75
3	8	3/4	5.25		8	3/4	5.25	5.75
4	8	3/4	5.25		8	7/8	5.50	6.00
6	12	3/4	5.25		12	7/8	6.25	6.50
8	12	7/8	5.75		12	1	6.75	7.25
10	16	1	6.50		16	1-1/8	7.50	8.00
12	16	1-1/8	7.00		16	1-1/4	8.00	8.50
14	20	1-1/8	7.25		20	1-1/4	8.25	9.00
16	20	1-1/4	7.75		20	1-3/8	8.75	9.25
18	24	1-1/4	8.00		24	1-3/8	9.25	9.50
20	24	1-1/4	8.50		24	1-1/2	9.75	10.25
24	24	1-1/2	9.50		24	1-3/4	11.00	11.50

Stud dimensions for 300 class RTJ not specified in ASME B16.36.

ASME/ANSI B16.36 ORIFICE FLANGE STUD DIMENSIONS

PIPE SIZE	600 CLASS				900 CLASS			
	QTY	DIA.	LENGTH RF	LENGTH RTJ	QTY	DIA.	LENGTH RF	LENGTH RTJ
1	4	5/8	5.00	5.50	4	7/8	6.00	6.25
1-1/2	4	3/4	5.25	5.50	4	1	6.25	6.50
2	8	5/8	5.00	5.50	8	7/8	6.00	6.50
2-1/2	8	3/4	5.25	5.75	8	1	6.50	7.00
3	8	3/4	5.25	5.75	8	7/8	6.00	6.50
4	8	7/8	6.00	6.50	8	1-1/8	7.00	7.50
6	12	1	7.00	7.50	12	1-1/8	7.75	8.25
8	12	1-1/8	7.75	8.25	12	1-3/8	9.00	9.50
10	16	1-1/4	8.75	9.25	16	1-3/8	9.50	10.00
12	20	1-1/4	9.00	9.50	20	1-3/8	10.25	10.75
14	20	1-3/8	9.50	10.00	20	1-1/2	11.00	11.50
16	20	1-1/2	10.25	10.75	20	1-5/8	11.50	12.00
18	20	1-5/8	11.00	11.50	20	1-7/8	13.00	13.75
20	24	1-5/8	11.75	12.50	20	2	14.00	14.75
24	24	1-7/8	13.25	13.75	20	2-1/2	17.50	18.50

ASME/ANSI B16.36 ORIFICE FLANGE STUD DIMENSIONS

PIPE SIZE	1500 CLASS				2500 CLASS			
	QTY	DIA.	LENGTH		QTY	DIA.	LENGTH	
			RF	RTJ			RF	RTJ
1	4	7/8	6.00	6.25	4	7/8	6.00	6.25
1-1/2	4	1	6.25	6.50	4	1-1/8	7.00	7.50
2	8	7/8	6.00	6.50	8	1	7.25	7.75
2-1/2	8	1	6.50	7.00	8	1-1/8	8.00	8.50
3	8	1-1/8	7.25	7.25	8	1-1/4	9.00	9.50
4	8	1-1/4	8.00	8.50	8	1-1/2	10.25	10.75
6	12	1-3/8	10.50	11.00	8	2	13.75	14.50
8	12	1-5/8	11.75	12.25	12	2	15.25	16.00
10	12	1-7/8	13.50	14.00	12	2-1/2	19.25	20.25
12	12	2	15.00	15.75	12	2-3/4	21.25	22.50
14	16	2-1/4	16.25	17.50				
16	16	2-1/2	17.75	19.00				
18	16	2-3/4	19.75	21.00				
20	16	3	21.50	22.50				
24	16	3-1/2	24.50	26.00				

ASME/ANSI B16.47 LARGE BORE STUD BOLT DIMENSIONS CLASS 75 FLANGES			
PIPE SIZE	API 605 (SERIES B)		
	Qty	SIZE	LENGTH
26	36	5/8	4.50
28	40	5/8	4.50
30	44	5/8	4.50
32	48	5/8	4.75
34	52	5/8	4.75
36	40	3/4	5.25
38	40	3/4	5.50
40	44	3/4	5.50
42	48	3/4	5.50
44	36	7/8	6.00
46	40	7/8	6.25
48	44	7/8	6.50
50	44	7/8	6.50
52	48	7/8	6.75
54	48	7/8	6.75
56	40	1	7.25
58	44	1	7.25
60	44	1	7.75

PIPE SIZE	ASME/ANSI B16.47 LARGE BORE STUD BOLT DIMENSIONS CLASS 150 FLANGES						
	MSS SP-44 (SERIES A)			API 605 (SERIES B)		
	Qty	SIZE	LENGTH	Qty	SIZE	LENGTH
26	24	1-1/4	8.75	36	3/4	5.50
28	28	1-1/4	9.00	40	3/4	5.75
30	28	1-1/4	9.25	44	3/4	6.00
32	28	1-1/2	10.50	48	3/4	6.25
34	32	1-1/2	10.50	40	7/8	6.75
36	32	1-1/2	11.00	44	7/8	6.75
38	32	1-1/2	11.00	40	1	7.50
40	36	1-1/2	11.00	44	1	7.75
42	36	1-1/2	11.50	48	1	7.75
44	40	1-1/2	12.00	52	1	8.00
46	40	1-1/2	12.00	40	1-1/8	8.50
48	44	1-1/2	12.50	44	1-1/8	8.75
50	44	1-3/4	13.25	48	1-1/8	9.00
52	44	1-3/4	13.75	52	1-1/8	9.25
54	44	1-3/4	14.00	56	1-1/8	9.50
56	48	1-3/4	14.25	60	1-1/8	9.75
58	48	1-3/4	14.75	48	1-1/4	10.00
60	52	1-3/4	15.00	52	1-1/4	10.25

PIPE SIZE	ASME/ANSI B16.47 LARGE BORE STUD BOLT DIMENSIONS CLASS 300 FLANGES					
	MSS SP-44 (SERIES A)			API 605 (SERIES B)		
	Qty	SIZE	LENGTH	Qty	SIZE	LENGTH
26	28	1-5/8	10.75	32	1-1/4	10.50
28	28	1-5/8	11.25	36	1-1/4	10.50
30	28	1-3/4	12.00	36	1-3/8	11.25
32	28	1-7/8	12.50	32	1-1/2	12.00
34	28	1-7/8	13.00	36	1-1/2	12.00
36	32	2	13.50	32	1-5/8	12.50
38	32	1-1/2	12.50	36	1-5/8	13.00
40	32	1-5/8	13.25	40	1-5/8	13.50
42	32	1-5/8	13.75	36	1-3/4	14.00
44	32	1-3/4	14.25	40	1-3/4	14.50
46	28	1-7/8	15.00	36	1-7/8	15.00
48	32	1-7/8	15.25	40	1-7/8	15.25
50	32	2	16.00	44	1-7/8	15.75
52	32	2	16.50	48	1-7/8	16.00
54	28	2-1/4	17.50	48	1-7/8	16.00
56	28	2-1/4	17.75	36	2-1/4	17.75
58	32	2-1/4	18.00	40	2-1/4	18.00
60	32	2-1/4	18.50	40	2-1/4	18.00

ASME/ANSI B16.47 LARGE BORE STUD BOLT DIMENSIONS CLASS 400 FLANGES						
PIPE SIZE	MSS SP-44 (SERIES A)			API 605 (SERIES B)		
	Qty	SIZE	LENGTH	Qty	SIZE	LENGTH
26	28	1-3/4	12.50	28	1-3/8	11.25
28	28	1-7/8	13.25	24	1-1/2	12.00
30	28	2	14.00	28	1-1/2	12.50
32	28	2	14.25	28	1-5/8	13.25
34	28	2	14.75	32	1-5/8	13.50
36	32	2	15.00	28	1-3/4	14.50
BOTH MSS SP-44 (SERIES A) AND API 605 (SERIES B)						
PIPE SIZE	Qty	SIZE	LENGTH			
38	32	1-3/4	14.75			
40	32	1-7/8	15.50			
42	32	1-7/8	15.75			
44	32	2	16.50			
46	36	2	17.00			
48	28	2-1/4	18.00			
50	32	2-1/4	18.50			
52	32	2-1/4	18.75			
54	28	2-1/2	20.00			
56	32	2-1/2	20.25			
58	32	2-1/2	20.50			
60	32	2-5/8	21.75			

400# FLANGES OF BOTH MSS SP-44 (SERIES A) AND API 605 (SERIES B) HAVE THE SAME STUD QTY, SIZE AND LENGTH FROM PIPE SIZES 38"-60"

ASME/ANSI B16.47 LARGE BORE STUD BOLT DIMENSIONS CLASS 600 FLANGES						
PIPE SIZE	MSS SP-44 (SERIES A)			API 605 (SERIES B)		
	Qty	SIZE	LENGTH	Qty	SIZE	LENGTH
26	28	1-7/8	14.50	28	1-5/8	13.50
28	28	2	15.00	28	1-3/4	14.25
30	28	2	15.50	28	1-7/8	15.25
32	28	2-1/4	16.50	28	2	16.00
34	28	2-1/4	16.75	24	2-1/4	17.25
36	28	2-1/2	17.75	28	2-1/4	17.75

BOTH MSS SP-44 (SERIES A) AND API 605 (SERIES B)				
PIPE SIZE	Qty	SIZE	LENGTH	
38	28	2-1/4	18.25	
40	32	2-1/4	18.75	
42	28	2-1/2	19.75	600# FLANGES OF BOTH MSS SP-44 (SERIES A) AND API 605 (SERIES B) HAVE THE SAME STUD QTY, SIZE AND LENGTH FROM PIPE SIZES 38"-60"
44	32	2-1/2	20.25	
46	32	2-1/2	20.75	
48	32	2-3/4	22.25	
50	28	3	23.25	
52	32	3	23.75	
54	32	3	24.25	
56	32	3-1/4	25.50	
58	32	3-1/4	26.00	
60	28	3-1/2	27.25	

ASME/ANSI B16.47 LARGE BORE STUD BOLT DIMENSIONS CLASS 900 FLANGES						
PIPE SIZE	MSS SP-44 (SERIES A)			API 605 (SERIES B)		
	Qty	SIZE	LENGTH	Qty	SIZE	LENGTH
26	20	2-3/4	18.75	20	2-1/2	17.75
28	20	3	19.75	20	2-3/4	19.50
30	20	3	20.50	20	3	20.50
32	20	3-1/4	22.00	20	3	21.00
34	20	3-1/2	23.00	20	3-1/4	22.50
36	20	3-1/2	23.75	24	3	22.25

BOTH MSS SP-44 (SERIES A) AND API 605 (SERIES B)			
PIPE SIZE	Qty	SIZE	LENGTH
38	20	3-1/2	24.50
40	24	3-1/2	25.00
42	24	3-1/2	25.75
44	24	3-3/4	27.00
46	24	4	28.50
48	24	4	29.00

900# FLANGES OF BOTH MSS SP-44 (SERIES A) AND API 605 (SERIES B) HAVE THE SAME STUD QTY, SIZE AND LENGTH FROM PIPE SIZES 38"-48"

CHAPTER 5: FLANGES

TIPS: The facing of a flange determines the type of gasket to be used with it. For example, two flat faced flanges often require a full faced gasket and two raised faced flanges generally require a spiral wound gasket. Ring Joint facings require the appropriate ring gasket which typically may be oval or octagonal with both being interchangable on the modern octagonal type grooved flanges. There are other facings and groovings for flanges but those mentioned are the most common in refineries.

- Always try to prevent misallignment (high/low) when making up a flange for service. Also check to assure that the gap is equal all the way around the flange when fully tightened to prevent 'bird mouth' of the gap.
- Cast flanges should never be tightened with an impact and should only be hand wrenched tight to the proper torque due to the tendency for impacting the flange to cause a broken or craked hub. These flanges are often found around cooling tower water services in typical refineries and require special attention when wedging open also.
- It's often a good practice to see if the inspection departments wants to do a visual on flanges once they are opened.
- Minor flange pitting and corrosion on the sealing surface can sometimes be repaired by doing weld build up with a Tig set up (which is always prefered over stick rod for such applications) after which the machinist may reface the flange or it may be acceptable to smooth out the area with a tiger disc which should be determined by the inspections department.
- Generally when more than one flange class uses the same gasket within a nominal pipe size such as 2" 3/4/600 class, whereby the flanges will also bolt together as with using a different class blind flange to seal a pipe flange, the higher rated flanges will still generally be thicker thus allowing for their higher pressure rating despite the other dimensions being equal.

ASME/ANSI B16.5 FLANGE DIMENSIONS

PIPE SIZE	150 LB. FLANGES				300 LB. FLANGES			
	Flange O.D.	Thickness	Bolt Circle Dia.	#/Dia. Holes	Flange O.D.	Thickness	Bolt Circle Dia.	#/Dia. Holes
1/2	3.50	0.38	2.38	4-0.62	3.75	0.50	2.62	4-0.63
3/4	3.88	0.44	2.75	4-0.62	4.62	0.56	3.25	4-0.75
1	4.25	0.50	3.12	4-0.62	4.88	0.62	3.50	4-0.75
1-1/4	4.62	0.56	3.50	4-0.62	5.25	0.69	3.88	4-0.75
1-1/2	5.00	0.62	3.88	4-0.62	6.12	0.75	4.50	4-0.88
2	6.00	0.69	4.75	4-0.75	6.50	0.81	5.00	8-0.75
2-1/2	7.00	0.81	5.50	4-0.75	7.50	0.94	5.88	8-0.88
3	7.50	0.88	6.00	4-0.75	8.25	1.06	6.62	8-0.88
3-1/2	8.50	0.88	7.00	8-0.75	9.00	1.12	7.25	8-0.88
4	9.00	0.88	7.50	8-0.75	10.00	1.19	7.88	8-0.88
5	10.00	0.88	8.50	8-0.88	11.00	1.31	9.25	8-0.88
6	11.00	0.94	9.50	8-0.88	12.50	1.38	10.62	12-0.88
8	13.50	1.06	11.75	8-0.88	15.00	1.56	13.00	12-1.00
10	16.00	1.12	14.25	12-1.00	17.50	1.81	15.25	16-1.12
12	19.00	1.19	17.00	12-1.00	20.50	1.94	17.75	16-1.25
14	21.00	1.31	18.75	12-1.12	23.00	2.06	20.25	20-1.25
16	23.50	1.38	21.25	16-1.12	25.50	2.19	22.50	20-1.38
18	25.00	1.50	22.75	16-1.25	28.00	2.31	24.75	24-1.38
20	27.50	1.62	25.00	20-1.25	30.50	2.44	27.00	24-1.38
22	29.50	1.75	27.25	20-1.38	33.00	2.57	29.25	24-1.63
24	32.00	1.81	29.50	20-1.38	36.00	2.69	32.00	24-1.63

Bolt hole diameters given should be 1/8" larger than actual stud diameter.
Add 1/16" to thickness measurements to account for raised face gasket surface.
Thicknesses are good for weldneck and blind flange at these bore sizes.

ASME/ANSI B16.5 FLANGE DIMENSIONS

PIPE SIZE	400 LB. FLANGES				600 LB. FLANGES			
	Flange O.D.	Thickness	Bolt Circle Dia.	#/Dia. Holes	Flange O.D.	Thickness	Bolt Circle Dia.	#/Dia. Holes
1/2	3.75	0.56	2.62	4-0.63	3.75	0.56	2.62	4-0.63
3/4	4.62	0.62	3.25	4-0.75	4.62	0.62	3.25	4-0.75
1	4.88	0.69	3.50	4-.075	4.88	0.69	3.50	4-0.75
1-1/4	5.25	0.81	3.88	4-0.75	5.25	0.81	3.88	4-0.75
1-1/2	6.12	0.88	4.50	4-0.88	6.12	0.88	4.50	4-0.88
2	6.50	1.00	5.00	8-0.75	6.50	1.00	5.00	8-0.75
2-1/2	7.50	1.12	5.88	8-0.88	7.50	1.12	5.88	8-0.88
3	8.25	1.25	6.62	8-0.88	8.25	1.25	6.62	8-0.88
3-1/2	9.00	1.38	7.25	8-1.00	9.00	1.38	7.25	8-1.00
4	10.00	1.38	7.88	8-1.00	10.75	1.50	8.50	8-1.00
5	11.00	1.50	9.25	8-1.00	13.00	1.75	10.50	8-1.12
6	12.50	1.62	10.62	12-1.00	14.00	1.88	11.50	12-1.12
8	15.00	1.88	13.00	12-1.12	16.50	2.19	13.75	12-1.25
10	17.50	2.12	15.25	16-1.25	20.00	2.50	17.00	16-1.38
12	20.50	2.25	17.75	16-1.38	22.00	2.62	19.25	20-1.38
14	23.00	2.38	20.25	20-1.38	23.75	2.75	20.75	20-1.50
16	25.50	2.50	22.50	20-1.50	27.00	3.00	23.75	20-1.63
18	28.00	2.62	24.75	24-1.50	29.25	3.25	25.75	20-1.75
20	30.50	2.75	27.00	24-1.62	32.00	3.50	28.50	24-1.75
22	33.00	2.88	29.25	24-1.75	34.25	3.75	30.63	24-1.88
24	36.00	3.00	32.00	24-1.88	37.00	4.00	33.00	24-2.00

Bolt hole diameters given should be 1/8" larger than actual stud diameter.
Add 1/4" to thickness measurements to account for raised face gasket surface.
Thicknesses are good for weldneck and blind flange at these bore sizes.

ASME/ANSI B16.5 FLANGE DIMENSIONS							
PIPE SIZE	900 LB. FLANGES				1500 LB. FLANGES			
	Flange O.D.	Thickness	Bolt Circle Dia.	#/Dia. Holes	Flange O.D.	Thickness	Bolt Circle Dia.	#/Dia. Holes
1/2	4.75	0.88	3.25	4-0.88	4.75	0.88	3.25	4-0.88
3/4	5.12	1.00	3.50	4-0.88	5.12	1.00	3.50	4-0.88
1	5.88	1.12	4.00	4-1.00	5.88	1.12	4.00	4-1.00
1-1/4	6.25	1.12	4.38	4-1.00	6.25	1.12	4.38	4-1.00
1-1/2	7.00	1.25	4.88	4-1.12	7.00	1.25	4.88	4-1.12
2	8.50	1.50	6.50	8-1.00	8.50	1.50	6.50	8-1.00
2-1/2	9.62	1.62	7.50	8-1.12	9.62	1.62	7.50	8-1.12
3	9.50	1.50	7.50	8-1.00	10.50	1.88	8.00	8-1.25
4	11.50	1.75	9.25	8-1.25	12.25	2.12	9.50	8-1.38
5	13.75	2.00	11.00	8-1.38	14.75	2.88	11.50	8-1.63
6	15.00	2.19	12.50	12-1.25	15.50	3.25	12.50	12-1.50
8	18.50	2.50	15.50	12-1.50	19.00	3.62	15.50	12-1.75
10	21.50	2.75	18.50	16-1.50	23.00	4.25	19.00	12-2.00
12	24.00	3.12	21.00	20-1.50	26.50	4.88	22.50	16-2.12
14	25.25	3.38	22.00	20-1.63	29.50	5.25	25.00	16-2.38
16	27.75	3.50	24.25	20-1.75	32.50	5.75	27.75	16-2.63
18	31.00	4.00	27.00	20-2.00	36.00	6.38	30.50	16-2.88
20	33.75	4.25	29.50	20-2.13	38.75	7.00	32.75	16-3.12
24	41.00	5.50	35.50	20-2.63	46.00	8.00	39.00	16-3.63

Bolt hole diameters given should be 1/8" larger than actual stud diameter.
Add 1/4" to thickness measurements to account for raised face gasket surface.
Thicknesses are good for weldneck and blind flange at these bore sizes.

ASME/ANSI B16.5 FLANGE DIMENSIONS

2500 LB. FLANGES

PIPE SIZE	Flange O.D.	Thickness	Bolt Circle Dia.	#/Dia. Holes
1/2	5.25	1.19	3.50	4-0.88
3/4	5.50	1.25	3.75	4-0.88
1	6.25	1.38	4.25	4-1.00
1-1/4	7.25	1.50	5.13	4-1.12
1-1/2	8.00	1.75	5.75	4-1.25
2	9.25	2.00	6.75	8-1.12
2-1/2	10.50	2.25	7.75	8-1.25
3	12.00	2.62	9.00	8-1.38
4	14.00	3.00	10.75	8-1.63
5	16.50	3.62	12.75	8-1.88
6	19.00	4.25	14.50	8-2.12
8	21.75	5.00	17.25	12-2.12
10	26.50	6.50	21.25	12-2.63
12	30.00	7.25	24.38	12-2.88

Bolt hole diameters given should be 1/8" larger than actual stud diameter.
Add 1/4" to thickness measurements to account for raised face gasket surface.
Thicknesses are good for weldneck and blind flange at these bore sizes.

ASME/ANSI B16.5 FLANGE WEIGHTS (lbs.)
150 LB. FLANGES

PIPE SIZE	Slip on	Thread	Socket Weld	Lap Joint	Blind Flange	Weld Neck
1/2	1	1	2	1	2	2
3/4	2	2	2	2	2	2
1	2	2	2	2	2	3
1-1/4	3	3	3	3	3	3
1-1/2	3	3	3	3	4	4
2	5	5	5	5	5	6
2-1/2	8	8	8	8	7	10
3	9	9	9	9	9	11.5
3-1/2	11	12	11	11	13	12
4	13	13	13	13	17	16.5
5	15	15	15	15	20	21
6	19	19	19	19	27	26
8	30	30	30	30	47	42
10	43	43	43	43	70	54
12	64	64	64	64	123	88
14	90	90	90	105	140	114
16	106	98	98	140	180	140
18	130	130	130	160	220	165
20	165	165	165	195	285	197
22	185	185	185	245	355	225
24	220	220	220	275	430	268

ASME/ANSI B16.5 FLANGE WEIGHTS (lbs.)
300 LB. FLANGES

PIPE SIZE	Slip on	Thread	Socket Weld	Lap Joint	Blind Flange	Weld Neck
1/2	2	2	3	2	2	2
3/4	3	3	3	3	3	3
1	3	3	3	3	4	4
1-1/4	4.5	4.5	4	4.5	6	5
1-1/2	6.5	6.5	6	6.5	7	7
2	7	7	7	7	8	9
2-1/2	10	10	10	10	12	12
3	13	14	13	14.5	16	18
3-1/2	17	17	17	17	21	20
4	23.5	24	22	24	28	26.5
5	29	31	28	28	37	36
6	39	39	39	39	50	45
8	58	58	58	58	81	69
10	81	81	81	91	124	100
12	115	115	115	140	185	142
14	165	165	165	190	250	206
16	210	220	190	234	315	250
18	253	280	250	305	414	320
20	315	325	315	375	515	400
22	370	370	370	435	640	465
24	490	490	475	550	800	580

ASME/ANSI B16.5 FLANGE WEIGHTS (lbs.)
400 LB. FLANGES

PIPE SIZE	Slip on	Thread	Socket Weld	Lap Joint	Blind Flange	Weld Neck
1/2	2	2	2	2	2	3
3/4	3	3	3	3	3	3.5
1	3.5	3.5	3.5	3.5	4	4
1-1/4	4.5	4.5	4.5	4.5	6	4.5
1-1/2	6.5	6.5	6.5	6.5	8	8
2	8	8	8	8	10	10
2-1/2	12	12	12	11	15	14
3	15	15	15	14	20	18
3-1/2	21	21	21	20	29	26
4	26	26	26	25	33	35
5	31	31	31	29	44	43
6	44	44	44	42	61	57
8	67	67	67	64	100	89
10	91	91	91	110	155	125
12	130	130	130	152	226	175
14	191	191	191	210	310	233
16	253	253	253	280	398	295
18	310	310	310	345	502	360
20	378	378	378	420	621	445
22	405	405	405	455	720	505
24	539	539	539	615	936	640

ASME/ANSI B16.5 FLANGE WEIGHTS (lbs.)
600 LB. FLANGES

PIPE SIZE	Slip on	Thread	Socket Weld	Lap Joint	Blind Flange	Weld Neck
1/2	2	2	2	2	3	3
3/4	3	3	3	3	4	4
1	4	4	4	4	4	4
1-1/4	5	5	5	5	6	6
1-1/2	7	7	7	7	8	8
2	9	9	9	9	10	12
2-1/2	13	13	13	12	15	18
3	16	16	16	15	20	23
3-1/2	21	21	21	20	29	26
4	37	37	37	36	41	42
5	63	63	63	63	68	68
6	80	80	80	78	86	81
8	115	115	115	112	140	120
10	177	177	177	195	231	190
12	215	215	215	240	295	226
14	259	259	259	290	378	347
16	366	366	366	400	527	481
18	476	476	476	469	665	555
20	612	612	612	604	855	690
22	590	590	590	670	1000	720
24	876	876	876	866	1250	977

ASME/ANSI B16.5 FLANGE WEIGHTS (lbs.)
900 LB. FLANGES

PIPE SIZE	Slip on	Thread	Socket Weld	Lap Joint	Blind Flange	Weld Neck
1/2	6	6	6	6	4	7
3/4	6	6	6	6	6	7
1	7.5	7.5	7.5	7.5	9	8.5
1-1/4	10	10	10	10	10	10
1-1/2	14	14	14	14	14	14
2	22	22	22	21	25	24
2-1/2	31	31	31	25	32	31
3	36	36	36	29	35	36
4	53	53	53	51	54	53
5	83	83	83	81	87	86
6	110	110	110	105	115	110
8	172	172	172	190	200	187
10	245	245	245	277	290	268
12	326	326	326	371	415	325
14	400	400	400	415	520	400
16	459	459	459	488	619	495
18	647	647	647	670	880	680
20	792	792	792	810	1107	830
24	1480	1480	1480	1550	2099	1500

ASME/ANSI B16.5 FLANGE WEIGHTS (lbs.)
1500 LB. FLANGES

PIPE SIZE	Slip on	Thread	Socket Weld	Lap Joint	Blind Flange	Weld Neck
1/2	6	6	6	6	4	7
3/4	6	6	6	6	6	7
1	8	8	8	8	9	9
1-1/4	10	10	10	10	10	10
1-1/2	14	14	14	14	14	14
2	25	25	25	25	25	25
2-1/2	36	36	36	35	35	36
3	48	48	48	47	48	48
4	73	73	73	75	73	73
5	132	132	132	140	140	132
6	165	165	165	170	160	165
8	260	260	260	286	302	275
10	436	436	436	485	510	455
12	667	667	667	749	775	690
14	940	940	940	890	975	940
16	1250	1250	1250	1250	1300	1250
18	1625	1625	1625	1475	1750	1625
20	2050	2050	2050	1775	2225	2050
24	2825	2825	2825	2825	3625	3325

ASME/ANSI B16.5 FLANGE WEIGHTS (lbs.)
2500 LB. FLANGES

PIPE SIZE	Slip on	Thread	Socket Weld	Lap Joint	Blind Flange	Weld Neck
1/2	-	7	-	7	7	8
3/4	-	9	-	8	10	9
1	-	12	-	12	12	13
1-1/4	-	18	-	17	18	20
1-1/2	-	25	-	24	25	28
2	-	38	-	37	39	42
2-1/2	-	55	-	53	56	52
3	-	83	-	80	86	94
4	-	127	-	122	133	146
5	-	210	-	204	223	244
6	-	323	-	314	345	378
8	-	485	-	471	533	576
10	-	925	-	897	1025	1068
12	-	1300	-	1262	1464	1525

ASME/ANSI B16.47 LARGE BORE FLANGE DIMENSIONS 75 LB. FLANGES API 605 (SERIES B)

PIPE SIZE	Flange O.D.	Weld Neck Thickness	Blind Flange Thickness	Bolt Circle Dia.	Qty	Dia. Holes
26	30.00	1.25	1.25	28.50	36	0.75
28	32.00	1.25	1.25	30.50	40	0.75
30	34.00	1.25	1.25	32.50	44	0.75
32	36.00	1.32	1.38	34.50	48	0.75
34	38.00	1.32	1.44	36.50	52	0.75
36	40.69	1.38	1.61	39.06	40	0.88
38	42.69	1.44	1.69	41.06	40	0.88
40	44.69	1.44	1.69	43.06	44	0.88
42	46.69	1.50	1.82	45.06	48	0.88
44	49.25	1.63	1.88	47.38	36	1.00
46	51.25	1.69	1.94	49.38	40	1.00
48	53.25	1.75	2.07	51.38	44	1.00
50	55.25	1.82	2.13	53.38	44	1.00
52	57.38	1.82	2.19	55.50	48	1.00
54	59.38	1.88	2.32	57.50	48	1.00
56	62.00	1.94	2.38	59.88	40	1.12
58	64.00	2.00	2.44	61.88	44	1.12
60	66.00	2.13	2.57	63.88	44	1.12

Bolt hole diameters given should be 1/8" larger than actual stud diameter.
Add 1/16" to thickness measurements to account for raised face gasket surface.

ASME/ANSI B16.47 LARGE BORE FLANGE DIMENSIONS 150 LB. FLANGES MSS SP-44 (SERIES A)

PIPE SIZE	Flange O.D.	Weld Neck Thickness	Blind Flange Thickness	Bolt Circle Dia.	Qty	Dia. Holes
26	34.25	2.63	2.63	31.75	24	1.38
28	36.50	2.75	2.75	34.00	28	1.38
30	38.75	2.88	2.88	36.00	28	1.38
32	41.75	3.13	3.13	38.50	28	1.62
34	43.75	3.19	3.19	40.50	32	1.62
36	46.00	3.50	3.50	42.75	32	1.62
38	48.75	3.38	3.38	45.25	32	1.62
40	50.75	3.50	3.50	47.25	36	1.62
42	53.00	3.75	3.75	49.50	36	1.62
44	55.25	3.94	3.94	51.75	40	1.62
46	57.25	4.00	4.00	53.75	40	1.62
48	59.50	4.19	4.19	56.00	44	1.62
50	61.75	4.32	4.32	58.25	44	1.88
52	64.00	4.50	4.50	60.50	44	1.88
54	66.25	4.69	4.69	62.75	44	1.88
56	68.75	4.82	4.82	65.00	48	1.88
58	71.00	5.00	5.00	67.25	48	1.88
60	73.00	5.13	5.13	69.25	52	1.88

Bolt hole diameters given should be 1/8" larger than actual stud diameter.
Add 1/16" to thickness measurements to account for raised face gasket surface.

ASME/ANSI B16.47 LARGE BORE FLANGE DIMENSIONS 150 LB. FLANGES API 605 (SERIES B)

PIPE SIZE	Flange O.D.	Weld Neck Thickness	Blind Flange Thickness	Bolt Circle Dia.	Qty	Dia. Holes
26	30.94	1.57	1.69	29.31	36	0.88
28	32.94	1.69	1.82	31.31	40	0.88
30	34.94	1.69	1.94	33.31	44	0.88
32	37.06	1.75	2.07	35.44	48	0.88
34	39.56	1.88	2.19	37.69	40	1.00
36	41.62	2.00	2.25	39.75	44	1.00
38	44.25	2.07	2.44	42.12	40	1.12
40	46.25	2.13	2.57	44.12	44	1.12
42	48.25	2.25	2.63	46.12	48	1.12
44	50.25	2.32	2.75	48.12	52	1.12
46	52.81	2.38	2.88	50.56	40	1.25
48	54.81	2.50	3.00	52.56	44	1.25
50	56.81	2.63	3.13	54.56	48	1.25
52	58.81	2.69	3.25	56.56	52	1.25
54	61.00	2.75	3.38	58.75	56	1.25
56	63.00	2.82	3.50	60.75	60	1.25
58	65.94	2.88	3.62	63.44	48	1.38
60	67.94	2.94	3.75	65.44	52	1.38

Bolt hole diameters given should be 1/8" larger than actual stud diameter.
Add 1/16" to thickness measurements to account for raised face gasket surface.

ASME/ANSI B16.47 LARGE BORE FLANGE DIMENSIONS 300 LB. FLANGES MSS SP-44 (SERIES A)

PIPE SIZE	Flange O.D.	Weld Neck Thickness	Blind Flange Thickness	Bolt Circle Dia.	Qty	Dia. Holes
26	38.25	3.07	3.25	34.50	28	1.75
28	40.75	3.32	3.50	37.00	28	1.75
30	43.00	3.57	3.69	39.25	28	1.88
32	45.25	3.82	3.88	41.50	28	2.00
34	47.50	3.94	4.07	43.50	28	2.00
36	50.00	4.07	4.32	46.00	32	2.12
38	46.00	4.19	4.19	43.00	32	1.62
40	48.75	4.44	4.44	45.50	32	1.75
42	50.75	4.63	4.63	47.50	32	1.75
44	53.25	4.82	4.82	49.75	32	1.88
46	55.75	5.00	5.00	52.00	28	2.00
48	57.75	5.19	5.19	54.00	32	2.00
50	60.25	5.44	5.44	56.25	32	2.12
52	62.25	5.63	5.63	58.25	32	2.12
54	65.25	5.94	5.94	61.00	28	2.38
56	67.25	6.00	6.00	63.00	28	2.38
58	69.25	6.19	6.19	65.00	32	2.38
60	71.25	6.38	6.38	67.00	32	2.38

Bolt hole diameters given should be 1/8" larger than actual stud diameter.
Add 1/16" to thickness measurements to account for raised face gasket surface.

ASME/ANSI B16.47 LARGE BORE FLANGE DIMENSIONS 300 LB. FLANGES API 605 (SERIES B)

PIPE SIZE	Flange O.D.	Weld Neck Thickness	Blind Flange Thickness	Bolt Circle Dia.	Qty	Dia. Holes
26	34.12	3.44	3.44	31.62	32	1.38
28	36.25	3.44	3.44	33.75	36	1.38
30	39.00	3.63	3.63	36.25	36	1.50
32	41.50	4.00	4.00	38.50	32	1.62
34	43.62	4.00	4.00	40.62	36	1.62
36	46.12	4.00	4.00	42.88	32	1.75
38	48.12	4.31	4.31	44.88	36	1.75
40	50.12	4.50	4.50	46.88	40	1.75
42	52.50	4.63	4.63	49.00	36	1.88
44	54.50	4.94	4.94	51.00	40	1.88
46	57.50	5.00	5.06	53.75	36	2.00
48	59.50	5.00	5.25	55.75	40	2.00
50	61.50	5.38	5.44	57.75	44	2.00
52	63.50	5.56	5.61	59.75	48	2.00
54	65.88	5.32	5.81	62.12	48	2.00
56	69.50	6.00	6.12	65.00	36	2.38
58	71.94	6.00	6.31	67.44	40	2.38
60	73.94	5.88	6.50	69.44	40	2.38

Bolt hole diameters given should be 1/8" larger than actual stud diameter.
Add 1/16" to thickness measurements to account for raised face gasket surface.

ASME/ANSI B16.47 LARGE BORE FLANGE DIMENSIONS 400 LB. FLANGES MSS SP-44 (SERIES A)

PIPE SIZE	Flange O.D.	Weld Neck Thickness	Blind Flange Thickness	Bolt Circle Dia.	Qty	Dia. Holes
26	38.25	3.50	3.88	34.50	28	1.88
28	40.75	3.75	4.12	37.00	28	2.00
30	43.00	4.00	4.38	39.25	28	2.12
32	45.25	4.25	4.56	41.50	28	2.12
34	47.50	4.38	4.81	43.50	28	2.12
36	50.00	4.50	5.06	46.00	32	2.12
38	47.50	4.88	4.88	44.00	32	1.88
40	50.00	5.12	5.12	46.25	32	2.00
42	52.00	5.25	5.25	48.25	32	2.00
44	54.50	5.50	5.50	50.50	32	2.12
46	56.75	5.75	5.75	52.75	36	2.12
48	59.50	6.00	6.00	55.25	28	2.38
50	61.75	6.19	6.25	57.50	32	2.38
52	63.75	6.38	6.44	59.50	32	2.38
54	67.00	6.69	6.75	62.25	28	2.62
56	69.00	6.88	6.94	64.25	32	2.62
58	71.00	7.00	7.12	66.25	32	2.62
60	74.25	7.31	7.44	69.00	32	2.88

Bolt hole diameters given should be 1/8" larger than actual stud diameter.
Add 1/4" to thickness measurements to account for raised face gasket surface.

ASME/ANSI B16.47 LARGE BORE FLANGE DIMENSIONS 400 LB. FLANGES API 605 (SERIES B)

PIPE SIZE	Flange O.D.	Weld Neck Thickness	Blind Flange Thickness	Bolt Circle Dia.	Qty	Dia. Holes
26	33.50	3.50	3.50	30.75	28	1.50
28	36.00	3.75	3.75	33.00	24	1.62
30	38.25	4.00	4.00	35.25	28	1.62
32	40.75	4.25	4.25	37.50	28	1.75
34	42.75	4.38	4.38	39.50	32	1.75
36	45.50	4.69	4.69	42.00	28	1.88
38	47.50	4.88	4.88	44.00	32	1.88
40	50.00	5.12	5.12	46.25	32	2.00
42	52.00	5.25	5.25	48.25	32	2.00
44	54.50	5.50	5.50	50.50	32	2.12
46	56.75	5.75	5.75	52.75	36	2.12
48	59.50	6.00	6.00	55.25	28	2.38
50	61.75	6.19	6.25	57.50	32	2.38
52	63.75	6.38	6.44	59.50	32	2.38
54	67.00	6.69	6.75	62.25	28	2.62
56	69.00	6.88	6.94	64.25	32	2.62
58	71.00	7.00	7.12	66.25	32	2.62
60	74.25	7.31	7.44	69.00	32	2.88

Bolt hole diameters given should be 1/8" larger than actual stud diameter.
Add 1/4" to thickness measurements to account for raised face gasket surface.

ASME/ANSI B16.47 LARGE BORE FLANGE DIMENSIONS 600 LB. FLANGES MSS SP-44 (SERIES A)

PIPE SIZE	Flange O.D.	Weld Neck Thickness	Blind Flange Thickness	Bolt Circle Dia.	Qty	Dia. Holes
26	40.00	4.25	4.94	36.00	28	2.00
28	42.25	4.38	5.19	38.00	28	2.12
30	44.50	4.50	5.50	40.25	28	2.12
32	47.00	4.62	5.81	42.50	28	2.38
34	49.00	4.75	6.06	44.50	28	2.38
36	51.75	4.88	6.38	47.00	28	2.62
38	50.00	6.00	6.12	45.75	28	2.38
40	52.00	6.25	6.38	47.75	32	2.38
42	55.25	6.62	6.75	50.50	28	2.62
44	57.25	6.81	7.00	52.50	32	2.62
46	59.50	7.06	7.31	54.75	32	2.62
48	62.75	7.44	7.69	57.50	32	2.88
50	65.75	7.75	8.00	60.00	28	3.12
52	67.75	8.00	8.25	62.00	32	3.12
54	70.00	8.25	8.56	64.25	32	3.12
56	73.00	8.56	8.88	66.75	32	3.38
58	75.00	8.75	9.12	68.75	32	3.38
60	78.50	9.19	9.56	71.75	28	3.62

Bolt hole diameters given should be 1/8" larger than actual stud diameter.
Add 1/4" to thickness measurements to account for raised face gasket surface.

ASME/ANSI B16.47 LARGE BORE FLANGE DIMENSIONS 600 LB. FLANGES API 605 (SERIES B)

PIPE SIZE	Flange O.D.	Weld Neck Thickness	Blind Flange Thickness	Bolt Circle Dia.	Qty	Dia. Holes
26	35.00	4.38	4.38	31.75	28	1.75
28	37.50	4.56	4.56	34.00	28	1.88
30	40.25	4.94	5.00	36.50	28	2.00
32	42.75	5.12	5.31	38.75	28	2.12
34	45.75	5.56	5.68	41.50	24	2.38
36	47.75	5.75	5.94	43.50	28	2.38
38	50.00	6.00	6.12	45.75	28	2.38
40	52.00	6.25	6.38	47.75	32	2.38
42	55.25	6.62	6.75	50.50	28	2.62
44	57.25	6.81	7.00	52.50	32	2.62
46	59.50	7.06	7.31	54.75	32	2.62
48	62.75	7.44	7.69	57.50	32	2.88
50	65.75	7.75	8.00	60.00	28	3.12
52	67.75	8.00	8.25	62.00	32	3.12
54	70.00	8.25	8.56	64.25	32	3.12
56	73.00	8.56	8.88	66.75	32	3.38
58	75.00	8.75	9.12	68.75	32	3.38
60	78.50	9.19	9.56	71.75	28	3.62

Bolt hole diameters given should be 1/8" larger than actual stud diameter.
Add 1/4" to thickness measurements to account for raised face gasket surface.

ASME/ANSI B16.47 LARGE BORE FLANGE DIMENSIONS 900 LB. FLANGES MSS SP-44 (SERIES A)

PIPE SIZE	Flange O.D.	Weld Neck Thickness	Blind Flange Thickness	Bolt Circle Dia.	Qty	Dia. Holes
26	42.75	5.50	6.31	37.50	20	2.88
28	46.00	5.62	6.75	40.25	20	3.12
30	48.50	5.88	7.18	42.75	20	3.12
32	51.75	6.25	7.62	45.50	20	3.38
34	55.00	6.50	8.06	48.25	20	3.62
36	57.50	6.75	8.44	50.75	20	3.62
38	57.50	7.50	8.50	50.75	20	3.62
40	59.50	7.75	8.81	52.75	24	3.62
42	61.50	8.12	9.12	54.75	24	3.62
44	64.88	8.44	9.56	57.62	24	3.88
46	68.25	8.88	10.06	60.50	24	4.12
48	70.25	9.19	10.38	62.50	24	4.12

ASME/ANSI B16.47 LARGE BORE FLANGE DIMENSIONS 900 LB. FLANGES API 605 (SERIES B)

PIPE SIZE	Flange O.D.	Weld Neck Thickness	Blind Flange Thickness	Bolt Circle Dia.	Qty	Dia. Holes
26	40.25	5.31	6.06	35.50	20	2.62
28	43.50	5.81	6.56	38.25	20	2.88
30	46.50	6.12	6.93	40.75	20	3.12
32	48.75	6.31	7.31	43.00	20	3.12
34	51.75	6.75	7.68	45.50	20	3.38
36	53.00	6.81	7.94	47.25	24	3.12
38	57.50	7.50	8.50	50.75	20	3.62
40	59.50	7.75	8.81	52.75	24	3.62
42	61.50	8.12	9.12	54.75	24	3.62
44	64.88	8.44	9.56	57.62	24	3.88
46	68.25	8.88	10.06	60.50	24	4.12
48	70.25	9.19	10.38	62.50	24	4.12

Bolt hole diameters given should be 1/8" larger than actual stud diameter.
Add 1/4" to thickness measurements to account for raised face gasket surface.

ASME/ANSI B16.47 LARGE BORE FLANGE WEIGHTS 75 LB. FLANGES

PIPE SIZE	API 605 (SERIES B)	
	Weld Neck (lbs.)	Blind Flange (lbs.)
26	80	255
28	85	290
30	90	330
32	105	390
34	110	430
36	145	518
38	160	595
40	170	760
42	185	895
44	230	1065
46	245	1185
48	270	1315
50	290	1505
52	310	1665
54	340	1840
56	400	2110
58	430	2300
60	475	2500

ASME/ANSI B16.47 LARGE BORE FLANGE WEIGHTS 150 LB. FLANGES

PIPE SIZE	MSS SP-44 (SERIES A)		API 605 (SERIES B)	
	Weld Neck (lbs.)	Blind Flange (lbs.)	Weld Neck (lbs.)	Blind Flange (lbs.)
26	300	702	120	373
28	345	833	140	454
30	400	982	150	543
32	505	1237	170	648
34	540	1384	210	783
36	640	1676	240	890
38	720	1819	290	1089
40	775	2040	310	1247
42	890	2381	345	1393
44	990	2717	370	1579
46	1060	2961	435	1824
48	1185	3348	480	2045
50	1270	3716	520	2284
52	1410	4156	550	2547
54	1585	4639	620	2848
56	1760	5132	650	3144
58	1915	5675	780	3560
60	2045	6154	850	3913

ASME/ANSI B16.47 LARGE BORE FLANGE WEIGHTS 300 LB. FLANGES

PIPE SIZE	MSS SP-44 (SERIES A)		API 605 (SERIES B)	
	Weld Neck (lbs.)	Blind Flange (lbs.)	Weld Neck (lbs.)	Blind Flange (lbs.)
26	605	1078	400	907
28	745	1315	450	1023
30	870	1543	550	1249
32	1005	1795	685	1556
34	1145	2068	750	1719
36	1275	2436	840	1921
38	695	2001	915	2257
40	840	2380	990	2549
42	950	2688	1135	2876
44	1055	3079	1235	3304
46	1235	3499	1470	3766
48	1380	3896	1575	4183
50	1530	4442	1710	4629
52	1660	4906	1840	5096
54	2050	5684	1980	5678
56	2155	6098	2595	6642
58	2270	6669	2770	7347
60	2470	7274	2870	7980

ASME/ANSI B16.47 LARGE BORE FLANGE WEIGHTS 400 LB. FLANGES

PIPE SIZE	MSS SP-44 (SERIES A)		API 605 (SERIES B)	
	Weld Neck (lbs.)	Blind Flange (lbs.)	Weld Neck (lbs.)	Blind Flange (lbs.)
26	650	1263	360	874
28	785	1522	450	1081
30	905	1802	530	1302
32	1065	2077	635	1570
34	1200	2415	690	1781
36	1340	2815	855	2160
38	935	2450	935	2450
40	1090	2848	1090	2848
42	1190	3159	1190	3159
44	1375	3635	1375	3635
46	1525	4120	1525	4120
48	1790	4726	1790	4726
50	1950	5303	1950	5303
52	2125	5823	2125	5823
54	2565	6742	2565	6742
56	2710	7352	2710	7352
58	3230	7986	3230	7986
60	3820	9126	3820	9126

ASME/ANSI B16.47 LARGE BORE FLANGE WEIGHTS 600 LB. FLANGES

PIPE SIZE	MSS SP-44 (SERIES A)		API 605 (SERIES B)	
	Weld Neck (lbs.)	Blind Flange (lbs.)	Weld Neck (lbs.)	Blind Flange (lbs.)
26	940	1759	550	1194
28	1060	2061	650	1427
30	1210	2423	810	1802
32	1375	2856	950	2159
34	1540	3237	1205	2645
36	1705	3802	1340	3013
38	1470	3404	1470	3404
40	1630	3838	1630	3838
42	2030	4585	2030	4585
44	2160	5105	2160	5105
46	2410	5758	2410	5758
48	2855	6737	2855	6737
50	3330	7695	3330	7695
52	3560	8426	3560	8426
54	3920	9333	3920	9333
56	4280	10529	4280	10529
58	4640	11414	4640	11414
60	5000	13108	5000	13108

ASME/ANSI B16.47 LARGE BORE FLANGE WEIGHTS 900 LB. FLANGES

PIPE SIZE	MSS SP-44 (SERIES A)		API 605 (SERIES B)	
	Weld Neck (lbs.)	Blind Flange (lbs.)	Weld Neck (lbs.)	Blind Flange (lbs.)
26	1525	2566	1050	2184
28	1810	3178	1520	2762
30	2120	3758	1820	3334
32	2545	4541	2065	3865
34	2970	5425	2450	4576
36	3395	6209	2520	4963
38	3385	6253	3385	6253
40	3620	6940	3620	6940
42	3960	7675	3960	7675
44	4300	8954	4300	8954
46	4640	10426	4640	10426
48	4980	11398	4980	11398

CHAPTER 6: VALVES

TIPS: Valve wieghts can differ greatly by manufacturer and also by the code by which they were built as ASME B16.34 allows for a lesser minimal wall thickness than does API 600 which could translate to a lesser weight. Therefore, I have listed the manufacturer from which these weights were derived. It's best to look up valve weights per manufacturer for verification purposes.

- When removing butterfly valves whose body width is less than the pipe ID to which they are bolted such as the thin wafer type check valves, always make sure that the valve is in the closed position which means that the internal disc is perpendicular to the centerline of the pipe, because if left open the internal disc will be parallel to the centerline of the pipe and will be wider than the body of the valve and will not go through the flanges of the pipe which will cause the valve to be hung up when attempting to remove. This is always an opportunity for some preplanning in terms of removing such valves which are locked open or are pneumatic actuator control butterfly valves which have a normally open default position when the instrument air is disconnected. If it happens to be a normally open butterfly valve which will get hung if in the open position, then arrangements can be made to get the instrumentation and electrician (I&E) group to have some temporary flexible air lines on standby which can be connected in place of the stationary lines once they are removed to keep the valve closed thus allowing for removal. If the valve is locked open, then consult with the operations department to remove the lock and close the valve. Even if given direct permission with the unit operator standing there, it is never a good practice to remove valves with lock, chain and tag isolations on them due to the fact that these valves were or are part of a system isolation and are logged as such. Some may still be pressurized on one side. A reputable refinery never wants to see demo valves lying around with locks and chains on them because they have to account for those locks in the future when the lock boxes are opened and it also shows a breach in the safety proceedure of isolating the unit and equipment. If it is permissible per operations to remove a valve, then they should have no problem removing their lock, chain and tag. If they refuse, then this should cause concern because verbal permits/agreements are no good concerning such things and the responsibilty for any wrong doing which may arise due to such will be your own.
- Valves intended to be bolted on for a hot tap should be full ported to allow clearance of the cutting bit. Such valves should have an independent seat test done at 1.1 times the 100°F operating pressure for the class in which the valve falls before being bolted on to the tee to assure that the valve will hold if tapping into a live piping system, whereby the hot tap machine can be removed without complication. Failure to hold the live

system pressure without leakage could cause major complications for the service which was tapped into, which could result in that service being brought down whereby having the potential to effect one or more units in the plant.

COMMON VALVE BODY/BONNET MATERIALS			
SPEC No./GRADE	MATERIAL	SPEC No./GRADE	MATERIAL
ASTM A351 CN7M	Cast Alloy 20	ASTM A105	Forged Carbon Steel
ASTM A216 WCB	Cast Carbon Steel	ASTM A182 F316L	Forged 316 SS
ASTM A216 WCC	Cast Carbon Steel	ASTM A182 F5	Forged Alloy Steel 5%Cr,0.5%Mo
ASTM A217 C5	Cast Alloy Steel 5%Cr,0.5%Mo	ASTM A182 317	Forged 317 SS
ASTM A217 WC6	Cast Alloy Steel 1.25%Cr,0.5%Mo	ASTM A182 F317L	Forged 317L SS
ASTM A217 WC9	Cast Alloy Steel 2.25%Cr,1%Mo	ASTM A182 F11	Forged Alloy Steel 1.25%Cr,0.5%Mo
ASTM A217 C12	Cast Alloy Steel 9%Cr,1%Mo	ASTM A182 F22	Forged Alloy Steel 2.25%Cr,1%Mo
ASTM A217 C12A	Cast Alloy Steel 9%Cr,1%Mo,V	ASTM A182 F9	Forged Alloy Steel 9%Cr,1%Mo
ASTM A351 CF3	Cast Stainless Steel	ASTM A182 F91	Forged Alloy Steel 9%Cr,1%Mo,V
ASTM A351 CF3M	Cast 316L SS	ASTM A182 F304	Forged 304 SS
ASTM A351 CF8	Cast 304 SS	ASTM A182 F316	Forged 316 SS
ASTM A351 CG3M	Cast 317L SS	ASTM A182 F321	Forged 321 SS
ASTM A351 CF8M	Cast 316 SS	ASTM A126 CLB	Cast Iron
ASTM A351 CF8C	Cast 347 SS	ASTM A352 LCC	Cast Low Temperature Carbon Steel
ASTM A351 CG8M	Cast 317 SS	ASTM A350 LF2	Forged Low Temp. Carbon Steel
ASTM A395	Cast Ductile Iron	ASTM A414 M35	Cast NI Cu (Monel)

API Trim No.	Material	Seat	Disc	Stem and Backseat	Notes
1	F6 (Cr 13)	410	410	410	13% Cr = 410 SS
2	304	304	304	304	
3	F310	310	310	310	
4	Hard 410	Hard 410	Hard 410	410	Seats 750 BHN min.
5	HardFaced (HF)	Stellite	Stellite	410	Full Stellite
5A	HardFaced	Ni-Cr	Ni-Cr	410	Ni-Cr is another alloy used for hardfacing as is stellite
6	410 and Cu-Ni	Cu-Ni	Cu-Ni	410	
7	410 and Hard 410	Hard 410	Hard 410	410	Seats 750 BHN min.
8	410 and HardFaced	Stellite	410	410	Half Stellite
8A	410 and HardFaced	Ni-Cr	410	410	
9	Monel	Monel	Monel	Monel	Monel = Ni-Cu
10	316	316	316	316	
11	Monel and HardFaced	Stellite	Monel	Monel	Monel & Half Stellite
12	316 and HardFaced	Stellite	316	316	316 & Half Stellite
13	Alloy 20	Alloy 20	Alloy 20	Alloy 20	
14	Alloy 20 and HardFaced	Stellite	Alloy 20	Alloy 20	Alloy20 & Half Stellite
15	304 and HardFaced	Stellite	Stellite	304	304 & Full Stellite
16	316 and HardFaced	Stellite	Stellite	316	316 & Full Stellite
17	347 and HardFaced	Stellite	Stellite	347	347 & Full Stellite
18	Alloy 20 and HardFaced	Stellite	Stellite	Alloy 20	Alloy20 & Full Stellite

Monel is a registered trademark of International Nickel Company
HF always refers to Hard Facing using CoCr (Stellite) or NiCr welding alloy.

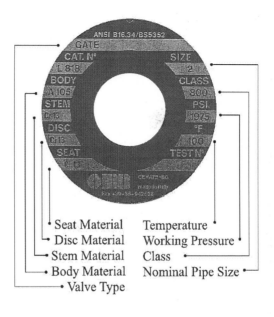

- Seat Material
- Disc Material
- Stem Material
- Body Material
- Valve Type
- Temperature
- Working Pressure
- Class
- Nominal Pipe Size

Above is a typical valve identification plate per MSS SP25 specifications as found in the center of the handle of small bore gate valves and such per ASME B16.34 and API 602. The tag shown represents a 2" 800 class gate valve with a forged carbon steel body, API trim no.1 and a safe working pressure of 1975 psi @ 100°F.

ASME/ANSI B16.5 CAST STEEL API 600 VALVE WEIGHTS (lbs.)
150# CLASS

PIPE SIZE	GATE		GLOBE		SWING CHECK	
	Butt Weld	Flanged	Butt Weld	Flanged	Butt Weld	Flanged
2	42	48	48	55	31	40
2-1/2	50	59	54	58	35	44
3	67	78	82	102	59	78
4	97	117	120	152	98	121
6	180	198	240	280	179	212
8	278	319	405	435	314	360
10	456	515	500	550	513	586
12	646	738	1050	1200	602	823
14	875	954	1700	1850	765	960
16	1120	1200	2300	2500	1120	1300
18	1485	1570	2640	2850	1450	1660
20	1825	1910	2866	3307	1700	2050
24	2870	2960	-	-	2900	3300

All values in this chart were provided by VELAN except for size 20 GLOBE weights which were provided by WALWORTH.

ASME/ANSI B16.5 CAST STEEL API 600 VALVE WEIGHTS (lbs.)
300# CLASS

PIPE SIZE	GATE		GLOBE		SWING CHECK	
	Butt Weld	Flanged	Butt Weld	Flanged	Butt Weld	Flanged
2	46	60	45	60	37	45
2-1/2	55	76	63	72	49	57
3	90	115	88	114	70	96
4	136	166	130	171	110	150
6	245	314	261	337	204	265
8	415	506	447	565	360	455
10	646	762	1000	1150	582	650
12	900	1100	1300	1550	825	945
14	1392	1720	1800	2100	1200	1350
16	1870	2220	2300	2700	1500	1800
18	2405	2960	2640	3200	2000	2400
20	3260	3700	-	-	2600	3000
24	4250	5100	-	-	3000	4050

All values in this chart were provided by VELAN.

ASME/ANSI B16.5 CAST STEEL API 600 VALVE WEIGHTS (lbs.) 600# CLASS						
PIPE SIZE	GATE		GLOBE		SWING CHECK	
	Butt Weld	Flanged	Butt Weld	Flanged	Butt Weld	Flanged
2	60	72	60	72	48	52
2-1/2	89	102	89	100	59	87
3	130	157	130	150	96	130
4	224	275	213	285	167	225
6	394	540	415	515	332	476
8	726	884	1050	1220	525	715
10	1125	1405	1550	1830	1000	1250
12	1490	1812	2293	2293	1500	1750
14	2200	2500	3064	3064	1750	2050
16	3000	3700	-	-	2400	3100
18	4000	4800	-	-	3200	4000
20	5600	6800	-	-	4500	6100
24	8000	9800	-	-	6400	7600

All values in this chart were provided by VELAN except for sizes 12 & 14 GLOBE weights which were provided by WALWORTH.

ASME/ANSI B16.5 CAST STEEL API 600 VALVE WEIGHTS (lbs.) 900# CLASS						
PIPE SIZE	GATE		GLOBE		SWING CHECK	
	Butt Weld	Flanged	Butt Weld	Flanged	Butt Weld	Flanged
2	150	185	-	-	135	165
2-1/2	235	270	-	-	175	210
3	235	270	352	397	175	210
4	270	355	617	705	245	330
6	830	980	1145	1323	485	635
8	1220	1500	2466	2844	700	900
10	2000	2400	3347	3858	1951	2251
12	3170	3670	4206	4850	-	-
14	3900	4460	5560	6393	2833	3263
16	5570	6250	-	-	-	-
18	7280	8535	-	-	-	-
20	8730	10,720	-	-	-	-
24	13,495	16,100	-	-	-	-

Sizes 2-16 GATE & 2-8 SWING CHECK weights provided by VELAN. Sizes 18-24 GATE weights provided by SCV (Southern California Valve). Sizes 3-14 GLOBE & 10-14 SWING CHECK weights provided by WALWORTH.

ASME/ANSI B16.5 CAST STEEL API 600 VALVE WEIGHTS (lbs.) 1500# CLASS

PIPE SIZE	GATE		GLOBE		SWING CHECK	
	Butt Weld	Flanged	Butt Weld	Flanged	Butt Weld	Flanged
2	150	185	231	264	135	165
2-1/2	255	325	328	380	205	275
3	255	325	496	575	205	275
4	430	520	1100	1200	340	430
6	1045	1205	2410	2650	805	965
8	1850	2550	3800	4100	1350	2050
10	2600	3300	5070	5842	-	-
12	7080	8415	6702	7716	-	-
14	7055	9075	-	-	-	-
16	13,230	15,325	-	-	-	-
18	17,065	19,845	-	-	-	-
20	21,080	24,540	-	-	10538	12125
24	30,365	35,875	-	-	-	-

Sizes 2-10 GATE & SWING CHECK weights provided by VELAN. Sizes 12-24 GATE weights provided by SCV (Southern California Valve). Sizes 2-12 GLOBE & 20 SWING CHECK weights provided by WALWORTH.

ASME/ANSI B16.5 CAST STEEL API 600 VALVE WEIGHTS (lbs.) 2500# CLASS

PIPE SIZE	GATE		SWING CHECK	
	Butt Weld	Flanged	Butt Weld	Flanged
2	128	205	-	-
2-1/2	221	331	-	-
3	289	443	-	-
4	1083	1336	-	-
6	2866	3506	-	-
8	4410	5380	-	-
10	8380	10,085	-	-
12	13,230	15,830	-	-

All values in this chart were provided by SCV (Southern Califronia Valve).

ASME/ANSI B16.47 MSS SP-44 (SERIES A) CAST STEEL API 600 VALVE WEIGHTS (lbs.) 150# CLASS				
PIPE SIZE	GATE		SWING CHECK	
	Butt Weld	Flanged	Butt Weld	Flanged
26	3600	3700	3600	4000
28	4400	4500	4300	5000
30	4705	4750	6300	7000
32	5800	6000	-	-
36	6500	6850	8500	9500
40	8400	9000	-	-
42	10,000	11,000	-	-
48	14,000	15,000	-	-
52	18,900	18,800	-	-
54	21,000	23,000	-	-
60	22,600	26,600	-	-

All values in this chart were provided by VELAN except for size 52" which was provided by SCV (Southern California Valve).

ASME/ANSI B16.47 MSS SP-44 (SERIES A) CAST STEEL API 600 VALVE WEIGHTS (lbs.) 300# CLASS				
PIPE SIZE	GATE		SWING CHECK	
	Butt Weld	Flanged	Butt Weld	Flanged
26	5000	5500	4000	5000
28	7000	7500	5000	6000
30	8550	9000	-	-
32	8200	8800	-	-
36	13,500	15,500	-	-
40	13,600	18,650	-	-
42	15,000	20,950	-	-
48	19,850	27,350	-	-

Sizes 26-36 provided by VELAN. Sizes 40-48 provided by SCV.

PIPE SIZE	GATE		SWING CHECK	
	Butt Weld	Flanged	Butt Weld	Flanged
30	12,000	14,000	11883	13668
36	17,000	19,500	-	-
40	18,830	23,260	-	-
42	19,340	24,150	-	-

ASME/ANSI B16.47 MSS SP-44 (SERIES A) CAST STEEL API 600 VALVE WEIGHTS (lbs.) 600# CLASS

Sizes 30-36 GATE weights provided by VELAN. Sizes 40-42 GATE weights provided by SCV. Size 30 SWING CHECK weights provided by WALWORTH.

CHAPTER 7: PIPE

TIPS: A pipes outside diameter, thus also circumference, never changes due to schedule or wall thickness variations. If they did then socket weld and threaded fittings would have to be made per schedule and they are not. A 3/4" 3000 class socket weld fitting will fit any schedule pipe available in 3/4". The ID is what is effected by wall thickness changes.

- The listed nominal pipe size is not the OD of a pipe until 14" pipe and larger. From 12" and smaller the OD is constant, but is not equal to the nominal pipe size. The OD for these sizes can be found on the following pages.
- The time and a half calculation for the takeoff of a 90° fitting is always estimated using the nominal pipe size of the fitting and not the actual OD. A 10" butt weld long radius 90° has a takeoff of 15".
- The takeoff of a butt weld 90° fitting is equal to its radius indicating the pipe centerline arc upon which it is formed. This information is necessary when calculating such things as how to cut a 90° fitting down to various other degrees.
- The bore size of socket weld flanges should always match the pipe bore size to which it is to be welded. This is crucial if using an isolation plug to make the flange weld to an existing pipe as the plug must have proper clearance to allow its later removal as it is always matched to the pipe and wall thickness. If the flange has a smaller bore opening, then the plug could become stuck. The same can happen with the root penetration of a butt weld flange if the root is too heavy.
- The nominal or listed size of tubing is its OD whereby the wall thickness variations determine the ID per the wall thicknesses deduction from the OD. It's often crucial to know the ID of the tubing of exchanger bundles and fin fan banks when selecting certain tooling and plugs.

PIPE SIZE	O.D.	SCHEDULE	WALL (in.)	ID (in.)	AREA (in.^{2})	AREA (Ft.^{2})
1/8	0.405	5, 5S	.035	.335	.0881	.00061
		10, 10S	.049	.307	.0740	.00051
		30	.057	.291	.0665	.00046
		STD, 40, 40S	.068	.269	.0568	.00039
		XS, 80, 80S	.095	.215	.0363	.00025
1/4	0.540	5, 5S	.049	.442	.1534	.00107
		10, 10S	.065	.410	.1320	.00092
		30	.073	.394	.1219	.00085
		STD, 40, 40S	.088	.364	.1041	.00072
		XS, 80, 80S	.119	.302	.0716	.00050
3/8	0.675	5, 5S	.049	.577	.2615	.00182
		10, 10S	.065	.545	.2333	.00162
		30	.073	.529	.2198	.00153
		STD, 40, 40S	.091	.493	.1909	.00133
		XS, 80, 80S	.126	.423	.1405	.00098
1/2	0.840	5, 5S	.065	.710	.3959	.00275
		10, 10S	.083	.674	.3568	.00248
		30	.095	.650	.3318	.00230
		STD, 40, 40S	.109	.622	.3039	.00211
		XS, 80, 80S	.147	.546	.2341	.00163
		120	.170	.500	.1963	.00136
		160	.187	.466	.1706	.00118
		XXS	.294	.252	.0499	.00035
3/4	1.050	5, 5S	.065	.920	.6648	.00462
		10, 10S	.083	.884	.6138	.00426
		30	.095	.860	.5809	.00403
		STD, 40, 40S	.113	.824	.5333	.00370
		XS, 80, 80S	.154	.742	.4324	.00300
		120	.170	.710	.3959	.00275
		160	.219	.612	.2942	.00204
		XXS	.308	.434	.1479	.00103
1	1.315	5, 5S	.065	1.185	1.1029	.00766
		10, 10S	.109	1.097	.9452	.00656
		30	.114	1.087	.9280	.00644
		STD, 40, 40S	.133	1.049	.8643	.00600
		XS, 80, 80S	.179	.957	.7193	.00500
		120	.200	.915	.6576	.00457
		160	.250	.815	.5217	.00362
		XXS	.358	.599	.2818	.00196

PIPE SIZE	O.D.	SCHEDULE	WALL (in.)	ID (in.)	AREA (in.²)	AREA (Ft.²)
1¼	1.660	5, 5S	.065	1.530	1.8385	.01277
		10, 10S	.109	1.442	1.6331	.01134
		30	.117	1.426	1.5971	.01109
		STD, 40, 40S	.140	1.380	1.4957	.01039
		XS, 80, 80S	.191	1.278	1.2828	.00891
		120	.215	1.230	1.1882	.00825
		160	.250	1.160	1.0568	.00734
		XXS	.382	.896	.6305	.00438
1½	1.900	5, 5S	.065	1.770	2.4606	.01709
		10, 10S	.109	1.682	2.2220	.01543
		30	.125	1.650	2.1382	.01485
		STD, 40, 40S	.145	1.610	2.0358	.01414
		XS, 80, 80S	.200	1.500	1.7671	.01227
		120	.225	1.450	1.6513	.01147
		160	.281	1.338	1.4061	.00976
		XXS	.400	1.100	.9503	.00660
2	2.375	5, 5S	.065	2.245	3.9584	.02749
		10, 10S	.109	2.157	3.6542	.02538
		STD, 40, 40S	.154	2.067	3.3556	.02330
		XS, 80, 80S	.218	1.939	2.9529	.02051
		120	.250	1.875	2.7612	.01917
		160	.344	1.687	2.2352	.01552
		XXS	.436	1.503	1.7742	.01232
2½	2.875	5, 5S	.083	2.709	5.7638	.04003
		10, 10S	.120	2.635	5.4532	.03787
		STD, 40, 40S	.203	2.469	4.7878	.03325
		XS, 80, 80S	.276	2.323	4.2383	.02943
		120	.300	2.275	4.0649	.02823
		160	.375	2.125	3.5466	.02463
		XXS	.552	1.771	2.4634	.01711
3	3.500	5, 5S	.083	3.334	8.7301	.06063
		10, 10S	.120	3.260	8.3469	.05796
		STD, 40, 40S	.216	3.068	7.3927	.05134
		XS, 80, 80S	.300	2.900	6.6052	.04587
		120	.350	2.800	6.1575	.04276
		160	.438	2.624	5.4078	.03755
		XXS	.600	2.300	4.1548	.02885
3½	4.000	5, 5S	.083	3.834	11.5450	.08017
		10, 10S	.120	3.760	11.1036	.07711
		STD, 40, 40S	.226	3.548	9.8868	.06866
		XS, 80, 80S	.318	3.364	8.8879	.06172
		XXS	.636	2.728	5.8449	.04059

PIPE SIZE	O.D.	SCHEDULE	WALL (in.)	ID (in.)	AREA (in.²)	AREA (Ft.²)
4	4.500	5, 5S	.083	4.334	14.7526	.10245
		10, 10S	.120	4.260	14.2531	.09898
		STD, 40, 40S	.237	4.026	12.7303	.08840
		60	.281	3.938	12.1798	.08458
		XS, 80, 80S	.337	3.826	11.4969	.07984
		120	.438	3.624	10.3149	.07163
		160	.531	3.438	9.2833	.06447
		XXS	.674	3.152	7.8030	.05419
4 ½	5.000	STD, 40, 40S	.247	4.506	15.9467	.11074
		XS, 80, 80S	.355	4.290	14.4545	.10038
		XXS	.710	3.580	10.0660	.06990
5	5.563	5, 5S	.109	5.345	22.4380	.15582
		10, 10S	.134	5.295	22.0202	.15292
		STD, 40, 40S	.258	5.047	20.0058	.13893
		XS, 80, 80S	.375	4.813	18.1937	.12635
		120	.500	4.563	16.3527	.11356
		160	.625	4.313	14.6099	.10146
		XXS	.750	4.063	12.9653	.09004
6	6.625	5, 5S	.109	6.407	32.2403	.22389
		10, 10S	.134	6.357	31.7391	.22041
		STD, 40, 40S	.280	6.065	28.8902	.20063
		XS, 80, 80S	.432	5.761	26.0667	.18102
		120	.562	5.501	23.7669	.16505
		160	.719	5.187	21.1311	.14674
		XXS	.864	4.897	18.8343	.13079
7	7.625	STD, 40, 40S	.301	7.023	38.7378	.26901
		XS, 80, 80S	.500	6.625	34.4716	.23939
		XXS	.875	5.875	27.1085	.18825
8	8.625	5S	.109	8.407	55.5100	.38549
		10, 10S	.148	8.329	54.4848	.37837
		20	.250	8.125	51.8485	.36006
		30	.277	8.071	51.1616	.35529
		STD, 40, 40S	.322	7.981	50.0270	.34741
		60	.406	7.813	47.9430	.33294
		XS, 80, 80S	.500	7.625	45.6635	.31711
		100	.594	7.437	43.4395	.30166
		120	.719	7.187	40.5681	.28172
		140	.812	7.001	38.4955	.26733
		XXS	.875	6.875	37.1223	.25779
		160	.906	6.813	36.4558	.25317

PIPE SIZE	O.D.	SCHEDULE	WALL (in.)	ID (in.)	AREA (in.^{2})	AREA (Ft.^{2})
9	9.625	STD, 40, 40S	.342	8.941	62.7858	.43601
		XS, 80, 80S	.500	8.625	58.4264	.40574
		XXS	.875	7.875	48.7069	.33824
10	10.75	5, 5S	.134	10.482	86.2934	.59926
		10, 10S	.165	10.420	85.2756	.59219
		20	.250	10.250	82.5158	.57303
		30	.307	10.136	80.6906	.56035
		STD, 40, 40S	.365	10.020	78.8542	.54760
		XS, 60, 80S	.500	9.750	74.6618	.51849
		80	.594	9.562	71.8103	.49868
		100	.719	9.312	68.1044	.47295
		120	.844	9.062	64.4967	.44789
		XXS, 140	1.000	8.750	60.1320	.41758
		160	1.125	8.500	56.7450	.39406
11	11.75	STD, 40, 40S	.375	11.000	95.0331	.65995
		XS, 80, 80S	.500	10.750	90.7625	.63030
		XXS	.875	10.000	78.2398	.54541
12	12.75	5, 5S	.156	12.438	121.5040	.84378
		10, 10S	.180	12.390	120.5680	.83728
		20	.250	12.250	117.8587	.81846
		30	.330	12.090	114.8001	.79722
		STD, 40S	.375	12.000	113.0972	.78540
		40	.406	11.938	111.9316	.77730
		XS, 60, 80S	.500	11.750	108.4339	.75301
		80	.688	11.374	101.6052	.70559
		100	.844	11.062	96.1074	.66741
		XXS, 120	1.000	10.750	90.7625	.63030
		140	1.125	10.500	86.5901	.60132
		160	1.312	10.126	80.5314	.55925
14	14.00	5S	.156	13.688	147.1531	1.02190
		10S	.188	13.624	145.7803	1.01236
		10	.250	13.500	143.1387	.99402
		20	.312	13.376	140.5213	.97584
		STD, 30, 40S	.375	13.250	137.8863	.95754
		40	.438	13.124	135.2764	.93942
		XS, 80S	.500	13.000	132.7322	.92175
		60	.594	12.812	128.9209	.89528
		80	.750	12.500	122.7184	.85221
		100	.938	12.124	115.4467	.80171
		120	1.094	11.812	109.5813	.76098
		140	1.250	11.500	103.8688	.72131
		160	1.406	11.188	98.3093	.68270

PIPE SIZE	O.D.	SCHEDULE	WALL (in.)	ID (in.)	AREA (in.²)	AREA (Ft.²)
16	16.00	5S	.165	15.670	192.8535	1.33926
		10S	.188	15.624	191.7229	1.33141
		10	.250	15.500	188.6917	1.31036
		20	.312	15.376	185.6848	1.28948
		STD, 30, 40S	.375	15.250	182.6540	1.26843
		XS, 40, 80S	.500	15.000	176.7144	1.22718
		60	.656	14.688	169.4396	1.17666
		80	.844	14.312	160.8756	1.11719
		100	1.031	13.938	152.5775	1.05957
		120	1.219	13.562	144.4565	1.00317
		140	1.438	13.124	135.2764	.93942
		160	1.594	12.812	128.9209	.89528
18	18.00	5S	.165	17.670	245.2238	1.702943
		10S	.188	17.624	243.9487	1.69409
		10	.250	17.500	240.5280	1.67033
		20	.312	17.376	237.1314	1.64675
		STD, 40S	.375	17.250	233.7048	1.62295
		30	.438	17.124	230.3032	1.59933
		XS, 80S	.500	17.000	226.9799	1.57625
		40	.562	16.876	223.6807	1.55334
		60	.750	16.500	213.8245	1.48489
		80	.938	16.124	204.1903	1.41799
		100	1.156	15.688	193.2968	1.34234
		120	1.375	15.250	182.6540	1.26843
		140	1.562	14.876	173.8048	1.20698
		160	1.781	14.438	163.7207	1.13695
20	20.00	5S	.188	19.624	302.4577	2.10040
		10S	.218	19.564	300.6110	2.08758
		10	.250	19.500	298.6474	2.07394
		STD, 20, 40S	.375	19.250	291.0389	2.02110
		XS, 30, 80S	.500	19.000	283.5285	1.96895
		40	.594	18.812	277.9454	1.93018
		60	.812	18.376	265.2110	1.84174
		80	1.031	17.938	252.7188	1.75499
		100	1.281	17.438	238.8267	1.65852
		120	1.500	17.000	226.9799	1.57625
		140	1.750	16.500	213.8245	1.48489
		160	1.969	16.062	202.6230	1.40710

PIPE SIZE	O.D.	SCHEDULE	WALL (in.)	ID (in.)	AREA (in.^{2})	AREA (Ft.^{2})
22	22.00	10, 10S	.250	21.500	363.0500	2.52118
		STD, 20, 40S	.375	21.250	354.6561	2.46289
		XS, 30, 80S	.500	21.000	346.3603	2.40528
		40	.688	20.624	334.0683	2.31992
		60	.875	20.250	322.0621	2.23654
		80	1.125	19.750	306.3541	2.12746
		100	1.375	19.250	291.0389	2.02110
		120	1.625	18.750	276.1163	1.91747
		140	1.875	18.250	261.5865	1.81657
		160	2.125	17.750	247.4493	1.71840
24	24.00	5S	.218	33.564	436.1015	3.02848
		10, 10S	.250	23.500	433.7358	3.01205
		STD, 20, 40S	.375	23.250	424.5564	2.94831
		XS, 80S	.500	23.000	415.4753	2.88524
		30	.562	22.876	411.0074	2.85422
		40	.688	22.624	402.0021	2.79168
		60	.969	22.062	382.2780	2.65471
		80	1.219	21.562	365.1469	2.53574
		100	1.531	20.938	344.3181	2.39110
		120	1.812	20.376	326.0824	2.26446
		140	2.062	19.876	310.2755	2.15469
		160	2.344	19.312	292.9166	2.03414
26	26.00	10	.312	25.376	505.7499	3.51215
		STD, 40S	.375	25.250	500.7400	3.47736
		XS, 80S	.500	25.000	490.8734	3.40884
28	28.00	10	.312	27.376	588.6125	4.08759
		STD, 40S	.375	27.250	583.2067	4.05005
		XS, 20, 80S	.500	27.000	572.5548	3.97607
		30	.625	26.750	562.0010	3.90278
30	30.00	10	.312	29.376	677.7583	4.70665
		STD, 40S	.375	29.250	671.9566	4.66637
		XS, 20, 80S	.500	29.000	660.5193	4.58694
		30	.625	28.750	649.1801	4.50820
32	32.00	10	.312	31.376	773.1872	5.36936
		STD	.375	31.250	766.9897	5.32632
		20	.500	31.000	754.7670	5.24144
		30	.625	30.750	742.6424	5.15724
		40	.688	30.624	736.5688	5.11506

PIPE SIZE	O.D.	SCHEDULE	WALL (in.)	ID (in.)	AREA (in.^{2})	AREA (Ft.^{2})
34	34.00	10	.312	33.376	874.8993	6.07569
		STD	.375	33.250	868.3060	6.02990
		20	.500	33.000	855.2979	5.93957
		30	.625	32.750	842.3879	5.84992
		40	.688	32.624	835.9185	5.80499
36	36.00	10	.312	35.376	982.8946	6.82566
		STD, 40S	.375	35.250	975.9055	6.77712
		XS, 20, 80S	.500	35.000	962.1119	6.68133
42	42.00	STD, 40S	.375	41.250	1,336.4029	9.28058
		XS, 80S	.500	41.000	1,320.2532	9.16842
		30	.625	40.750	1,304.2016	6.05696
		40	.750	40.500	1,288.2482	8.94617
48	48.00	STD, 40S	.375	47.250	1,753.4490	12.17673
		XS, 80S	.500	47.000	1,734.9431	12.04822

COMMERCIAL PIPE WEIGHT PER LINE FOOT (lbs.)						
SIZE	SCH5s	SCH5	SCH10s	SCH10	SCH20	SCH30
1/8	-	0.1383	0.1863	0.1863	-	-
1/4	-	0.2570	0.3297	0.3297	-	-
3/8	-	0.3276	0.4235	0.4235	-	-
1/2	0.5383	0.5383	0.6710	0.6710	-	-
3/4	0.6838	0.6838	0.8572	0.8572	-	-
1	0.8678	0.8687	1.404	1.404	-	-
1-1/4	1.107	1.107	1.806	1.806	-	-
1-1/2	1.274	1.274	2.085	2.085	-	-
2	1.604	1.604	2.638	2.638	-	-
2-1/2	2.475	2.475	3.513	3.513	-	-
3	3.029	3.029	4.332	4.332	-	-
3-1/2	3.472	3.472	4.973	4.973	-	-
4	3.915	3.915	5.613	5.613	-	-
5	6.349	6.349	7.770	7.770	-	-
6	7.585	7.585	9.290	9.290	-	-
8	9.914	9.914	13.40	13.40	22.36	24.70
10	15.19	15.19	18.65	18.70	28.04	32.24
12	21.07	22.18	24.16	24.20	33.38	43.77
14	23.07	-	27.73	36.71	45.68	54.57
16	27.90	-	31.75	42.05	52.36	62.58
18	31.43	-	35.73	47.39	59.03	82.06
20	39.78	-	46.05	52.73	78.60	104.1
24	55.37	-	63.41	63.41	94.62	140.8
26	-	-	85.60	85.60	136.17	-
28	-	-	92.26	92.26	146.85	182.73
30	79.43	-	98.93	98.93	157.53	196.08
32	-	-	105.59	105.59	168.21	209.43
34	-	-	112.25	112.25	178.89	222.78
36	-	-	118.92	118.92	-	236.13
42	-	-	-	-	221.61	-

A simple formula to yeild an estimated weight per linear foot of any pipe size is as follows: weight per linear foot = 10.69 x wall thickness x (OD – wall thickness)

COMMERCIAL PIPE WEIGHT PER LINE FOOT (lbs.)						
SIZE	STD	SCH40	SCH60	XS	SCH80	SCH100
1/8	0.2447	0.2447	-	0.3145	0.3145	-
1/4	0.4248	0.4248	-	0.5351	0.5351	-
3/8	0.5676	0.5676	-	0.7338	0.7338	-
1/2	0.8510	0.8510	-	1.088	1.088	-
3/4	1.131	1.131	-	1.474	1.474	-
1	1.679	1.679	-	2.172	2.172	-
1-1/4	2.273	2.273	-	2.997	2.997	-
1-1/2	2.718	2.718	-	3.631	3.631	-
2	3.653	3.653	-	5.022	5.022	-
2-1/2	5.793	5.793	-	7.661	7.661	-
3	7.576	7.576	-	10.25	10.25	-
3-1/2	9.109	9.109	-	12.51	12.51	-
4	10.79	10.79	12.66	14.98	14.98	-
5	14.62	14.62	-	20.78	20.78	-
6	18.97	18.97	-	28.57	28.57	-
8	28.5	28.55	35.64	43.39	43.39	50.87
10	40.48	40.48	54.74	54.74	64.33	76.93
12	49.56	53.53	73.16	65.42	88.51	107.2
14	54.57	63.37	84.91	72.09	106.1	130.7
16	62.58	82.77	107.5	82.77	136.5	164.8
18	70.59	104.8	138.2	93.45	170.8	208.0
20	78.60	122.9	166.4	104.1	208.9	265.1
24	94.62	171.2	238.1	125.5	296.4	367.4
26	102.63	-	-	136.17	-	-
28	110.64	-	-	-	-	-
30	118.65	-	-	157.53	-	-
32	126.66	230.08	-	168.21	-	-
34	134.67	244.77	-	-	-	-
36	142.68	282.35	-	189.57	-	-
42	166.71	330.41	-	221.61	-	-

A simple formula to yeild an estimated weight per linear foot of any pipe size is as follows: weight per linear foot = 10.69 x wall thickness x (OD – wall thickness)

COMMERCIAL PIPE WEIGHT PER LINE FOOT (lbs.)				
SIZE	SCH120	SCH140	SCH160	XXS
1/8	-	-	-	-
1/4	-	-	-	-
3/8	-	-	-	-
1/2	-	-	1.304	1.714
3/4	-	-	1.937	2.441
1	-	-	2.844	3.659
1-1/4	-	-	3.765	5.214
1-1/2	-	-	4.859	6.408
2	-	-	7.444	9.029
2-1/2	-	-	10.01	13.70
3	-	-	14.32	18.58
3-1/2	-	-	-	22.85
4	19.01	-	22.51	27.54
5	27.04	-	32.96	38.55
6	36.39	-	45.30	53.16
8	60.93	67.76	74.69	72.42
10	89.20	104.1	115.7	-
12	125.5	139.7	160.3	-
14	150.7	170.2	189.1	-
16	192.3	223.5	245.1	-
18	244.1	274.2	308.5	-
20	296.4	341.1	397.0	-
24	429.4	483.1	541.9	-

A simple formula to yeild an estimated weight per linear foot of any pipe size is as follows: weight per linear foot = 10.69 x wall thickness x (OD − wall thickness)

CHAPTER 8: PLATE AND TUBING

WEIGHT OF CARBON STEEL PLATE

Thickness	Pounds per sq. foot	Pounds per sq. inch	Thickness	Pounds per sq. foot	Pounds per sq. inch
1/8	5.100	0.0354	1-1/2	61.26	0.4254
3/16	7.650	0.0531	1-3/4	71.47	0.4963
1/4	10.21	0.0765	2	81.68	0.5672
5/16	12.75	0.0885	2-1/4	91.89	0.6381
3/8	15.32	0.1063	2-1/2	102.10	0.7090
7/16	17.85	0.1239	2-3/4	112.31	0.7799
1/2	20.42	0.1418	3	122.52	0.8508
5/8	25.53	0.1773	3-1/2	142.94	0.9926
3/4	30.63	0.2127	4	163.36	1.1344
7/8	35.72	0.2482	4-1/2	183.78	1.2762
1	40.84	0.2836	5	204.20	1.4181
1-1/8	45.95	0.3191	5-1/2	224.62	1.5599
1-1/4	51.05	0.3545	6	245.04	1.7017

TUBING WALL THICKNESS (BWG) GAUGE TO INCHES CONVERSION

GAUGE	INCHES	GAUGE	INCHES	GAUGE	INCHES
00000	0.500	10	0.134	24	0.022
0000	0.454	11	0.120	25	0.020
000	0.425	12	0.109	26	0.018
00	0.380	13	0.095	27	0.016
0	0.340	14	0.083	28	0.014
1	0.300	15	0.072	29	0.013
2	0.284	16	0.065	30	0.012
3	0.259	17	0.058	31	0.010
4	0.238	18	0.049	32	0.009
5	0.220	19	0.042	33	0.008
6	0.203	20	0.035	34	0.007
7	0.180	21	0.032	35	0.005
8	0.165	22	0.028	36	0.004
9	0.148	23	0.025	-	-

304/316 STAINLESS STEEL TUBING
WALL THICKNESS, ID AND WEIGHT

OD	Wall Thickness	ID	Lbs. Per Foot	OD	Wall Thickness	ID	Lbs. Per Foot
0.188	0.350	0.118	0.057		0.049	1.402	0.759
	0.020	0.210	0.050	1.500	0.065	1.370	0.996
	0.028	0.194	0.066		0.083	1.334	1.256
0.250	0.035	0.180	0.080		0.120	1.260	1.769
	0.049	0.152	0.105		0.035	1.680	0.641
	0.065	0.120	0.128	1.750	0.065	1.620	1.170
0.313	0.035	0.243	0.104		0.083	1.584	1.478
	0.049	0.215	0.138	1.875	0.065	1.745	1.257
	0.028	0.319	0.104		0.049	1.902	1.021
0.375	0.035	0.305	0.127	2.000	0.065	1.870	1.343
	0.049	0.277	0.171		0.083	1.834	1.699
	0.065	0.245	0.215		0.120	1.760	2.409
	0.035	0.430	0.174	2.125	0.065	1.995	1.430
0.500	0.049	0.402	0.236		0.065	2.120	1.517
	0.650	0.370	0.302	2.250	0.083	2.084	1.921
	0.035	0.555	0.221		0.120	2.010	2.730
0.625	0.049	0.527	0.301		0.065	2.370	1.690
	0.065	0.495	0.389	2.500	0.083	2.334	2.143
	0.035	0.680	0.267		0.120	2.260	3.050
	0.049	0.652	0.367	2.750	0.065	2.620	1.864
0.750	0.065	0.620	0.476		0.049	2.902	1.540
	0.083	0.584	0.591	3.000	0.065	2.870	2.037
	0.120	0.510	0.807		0.083	2.834	2.586
	0.035	0.805	0.314		0.120	2.760	3.691
0.875	0.049	0.777	0.432	3.250	0.065	3.120	2.210
	0.065	0.745	0.562		0.120	3.010	4.011
	0.120	0.635	0.968	3.500	0.065	3.370	2.385
	0.035	0.930	0.361		0.065	3.870	2.385
	0.049	0.902	0.498	4.000	0.083	3.834	3.472
1.000	0.065	0.870	0.649	4.250	0.120	4.010	5.293
	0.083	0.834	0.813	4.500	0.065	4.370	3.070
	0.095	0.810	0.918		0.065	4.870	3.426
	0.120	0.760	1.128	5.000	0.083	4.834	4.359
1.125	0.065	0.995	0.736		0.120	4.760	6.254
	0.065	1.120	0.823		0.188	4.625	9.662
1.250	0.083	1.084	1.034		0.065	5.870	4.120
	0.120	1.010	1.448	6.000	0.083	5.834	5.245
1.375	0.035	1.305	0.501		0.120	5.760	7.536
				8.000	0.120	7.760	10.099

CHAPTER 9: TORQUING

TIPS: The following pages contain some premade torquing charts per quantity of bolts. Another field method available which can be memorized for times when there is no diagram available or for those bolt quantities not covered herein is to simply make a numbered list which will guide in the sequencing proceedure. All flanges have a total bolt quantity which is always divisible by four. For this reason, it is essential to always make four columns whereby establishing the quartering pattern which will properly sequence the numbering order. Below is an example of how to apply this procedure. It will not produce the exact sequencing shown in the following diagrams but may be sufficient for field applications in some scenarios.

The grey column to the far right represents the total number of bolts in a flange which is the bottom cutoff for any numbering made using this chart. Simply find the total number in the far right column and never count horizontally below that row in which that total number resides. Simply number a flange starting at the 1 in the far left and number vertically rather than moving left to right until the point that the horizontal cutoff row is reached at which point you simply skip a column and start again at the top. This will result in all of the odd numbers being transferred to the flange first at which point the even numbers are then transferred by going back to the column line containing the number 2 and starting over whereby transferring all of the even numbers to the flange as all numbers are to be transferred to the flange in a sequential clockwise ordering.

1	2	3	4
5	6	7	8
9	10	11	12
13	14	15	16
17	18	19	20
21	22	23	24
25	26	27	28
29	30	31	32
33	34	35	36
37	38	39	40
41	42	43	44
45	46	47	48
49	50	51	52
53	54	55	56
57	58	59	60
61	62	63	64
65	66	67	68
69	70	71	72
73	74	75	76
77	78	79	80

Below is a diagram of a 12 bolt flange numbered in this method.

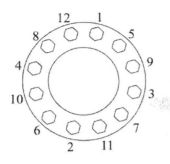

You may notice that this diagram pretty well matches the following diagram for a twelve bolt flange which is included with the other various bolt quantity flanges. However, as the flanges get increasingly larger, the quartering is simply rotated further to ensure a proper crossbolt pattern rather than merely being rotated one bolt at a time as seen when the number five is next to the number one etc. Such a pattern as used in the following diagrams requires more effort but is a preferred sequencing among the larger flanges due to the more accurate crossbolt effect. In some cases the previously mentioned method may be an allowable alternative which can easily be applied directly in the field.

Proper torque of a flange requires crossbolt passes per the torque sequencing to be made at increasing percentages of the final torque value such as a sequenced crossbolt pass of 1/3 of the total final torque value throughout the entire sequence followed by a pass of 2/3 of the final torque value, and then a 100% full torque value pass at the same sequence. A non-crossbolt rotational sequenced progression at 100% is then made as a final pass to ensure proper tensioning throughout and can be repeated as needed until all nuts cease to move. Some final passes are sometimes required per the inspections department after recommisioning of the flange which may take place after the system is back in service. Consult with your QC department concerning the proper proceedure, torque values and accompanying paperwork requried to properly execute and document the torquing of a flange per a specific sites written proceedure per their inspections department.

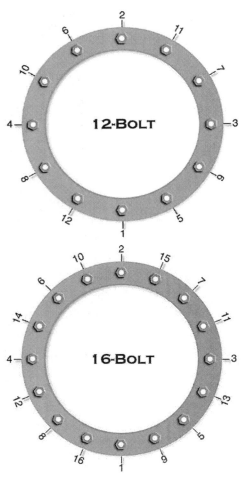

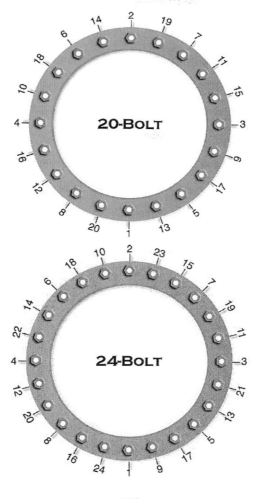

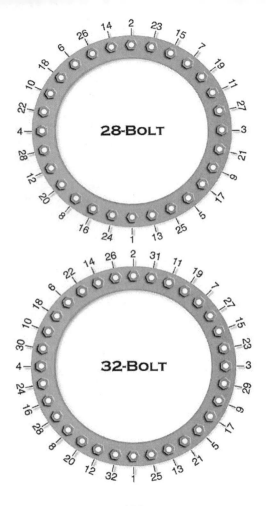

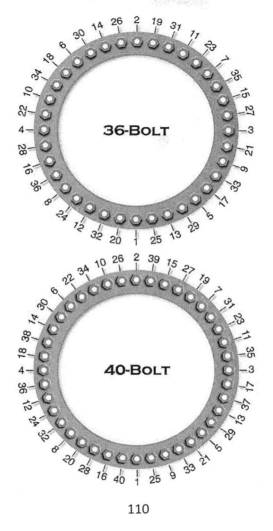

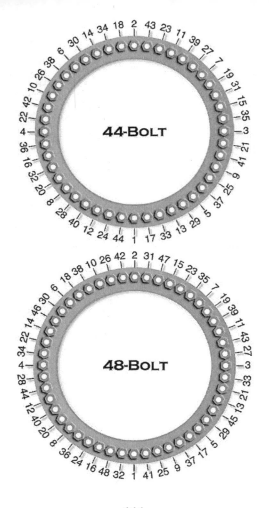

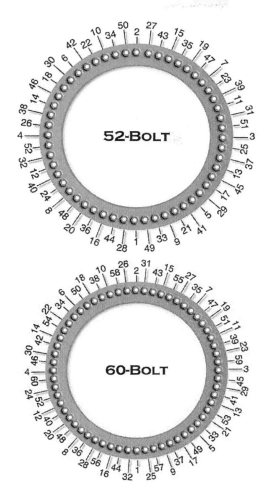

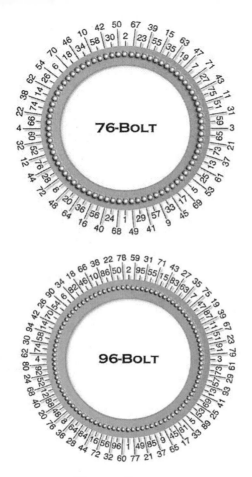

Torque Sequence

LOAD IN POUNDS ON ALLOY STEEL STUD BOLTS WHEN TORQUE LOADS ARE APPLIED

Stud Dia.	TPI	Dia. @ Root of Thread	Area @ Root of Thread	STRESS					
				30,000 psi		45,000 psi		60,000 psi	
				Torque Ft/Lbs.	Load Lbs.	Torque Ft/Lbs.	Load Lbs.	Torque Ft/Lbs.	Load Lbs.
1/4	20	0.185	0.027	4	810	6	1215	8	1620
5/16	18	0.240	0.045	8	1350	12	2025	16	2700
3/8	16	0.294	0.068	12	2040	18	3060	24	4080
7/16	14	0.345	0.093	20	2790	30	4185	40	5580
1/2	13	0.400	0.126	30	3780	45	5670	60	7560
9/16	12	0.454	0.162	45	4860	68	7290	90	9720
5/8	11	0.507	0.202	60	6060	90	9090	120	12,120
3/4	10	0.620	0.302	100	9060	150	13,590	200	18,120
7/8	9	0.731	0.419	160	12,570	240	18,855	320	25,140
1	8	0.838	0.551	245	16,530	368	24,795	490	33,060
1-1/8	8	0.963	0.728	355	21,840	533	32,760	710	43,680
1-1/4	8	1.088	0.929	500	27,870	750	41,805	1000	55,740
1-3/8	8	1.213	1.155	680	34,650	1020	51,975	1360	69,300
1-1/2	8	1.338	1.405	800	42,150	1200	63,225	1600	84,300
1-5/8	8	1.463	1.680	1100	50,400	1650	75,600	2200	100,800
1-3/4	8	1.588	1.980	1500	59,400	2250	89,100	3000	118,800
1-7/8	8	1.713	2.304	2000	69,120	3000	103,680	4000	138,240
2	8	1.838	2.652	2200	79,560	3300	119,340	4400	159,120
2-1//4	8	2.088	3.423	3180	102,690	4770	154,035	6360	205,380
2-1/2	8	2.338	4.292	4400	128,760	6600	193,140	8800	257,520
2-3/4	8	2.588	5.259	5920	157,770	8880	236,655	11,840	315,540
3	8	2.838	6.324	7720	189,720	11,580	284,580	15,440	379,440
3-1/4	8	3.088	7.490	10,000	224,700	15,000	337,050	20,000	449,400
3-1/2	8	3.338	8.750	12,500	262,500	18,750	393,750	25,000	525,000
3-3/4	8	3.589	10.11	15,400	303,300	23,150	454,950	30,900	606,600

CHAPTER 10: UNIT CONVERSIONS AND FORMULAS

TIPS: It takes two dimensions to calculate an area and three dimensions to calculate a volume. Therefore, a volume calculation is generally arrived at by factoring in a third dimension to the associated area calculation of the geometric form in question.

- Always apply the correct unit of measure or make the required conversions of the values of a calculation to the appropriate associated unit of measure. For example, if dealing in square inches, convert all values which are in square feet to square inches before proceeding with the equation. Failure to apply the proper unit of measure or make the proper unit conversions when need be will result in extreme inaccuracies when making calculations of any sort.
- Many calculations you'll come by are nothing more than a constant establishing the relationship of a variable represented by a specific unit of measure with some parameter being questioned as with determining the circumference of a circle by way of multiplying its diameter (variable) by π (constant = 3.14159). If the diameter is measured in inches, then the resulting product will be in inches also. However, if the diameter is measured in millimeters, then the resulting product or circumference will be in millimeters whereby 3.14159 is merely the universal ratio of diameter to circumference and works equally well with either unit of measure. Making further calculations from these arrived at values must assure that the values being factored further within the following equations are also addressing the same unit of measure as inputting a metric value in place of a standard value will produce inaccuracies. There are some tables on the following pages containing the constants by which certain units must be multiplied by to properly convert from one unit of measure to another to allow for accurate calculations.

CONVERSION CONSTANTS		
TO CHANGE:	TO:	MULTIPLY BY
INCHES	FEET	0.0833
INCHES	MILLIMETERS	25.4
FEET	INCHES	12
FEET	YARDS	0.3333
YARDS	FEET	3
SQUARE INCHES	SQUARE FEET	0.00694
SQUARE FEET	SQUARE INCHES	144
SQUARE FEET	SQUARE YARDS	0.11111
SQUARE YARDS	SQUARE FEET	9
CUBIC INCHES	CUBIC FEET	0.00058
CUBIC FEET	CUBIC INCHES	1728
CUBIC FEET	CUBIC YARDS	0.03703
CUBIC YARDS	CUBIC FEET	27
CUBIC INCHES	GALLONS	0.00433
CUBIC FEET	GALLONS	7.48
GALLONS	CUBIC INCHES	231
GALLONS	CUBIC FEET	0.1337
GALLONS	POUNDS OF WATER	8.33
POUNDS OF WATER	GALLONS	0.12004
OUNCES	POUNDS	0.0625
POUNDS	OUNCES	16
psi	kPa	6.895
psi	bar	.06895
kPa	psi	.145
kPa	bar	.01
bar	psi	14.503
bar	kPa	100
INCHES OF WATER	POUNDS PER SQ INCH	0.0361

°F to °C= deduct 32, then multiply by 5, then divide by 9
°C to °F= multiply by 9, then divide by 5, then add 32

CONVERSION CONSTANTS		
TO CHANGE:	TO:	MULTIPLY BY
INCHES OF WATER	INCHES OF MERCURY	0.0735
INCHES OF WATER	OUNCES PER SQ INCH	0.578
INCHES OF WATER	LBS. PER SQ FOOT	5.2
IN. OF MERCURY	INCHES OF WATER	13.6
IN. OF MERCURY	FEET OF WATER	1.1333
IN. OF MERCURY	psi	0.4914
OUNCES PER SQ IN.	INCHES OF MERCURY	0.127
OUNCES PER SQ IN.	INCHES OF WATER	1.733
psi	INCHES OF WATER	27.72
psi	FEET OF WATER	2.310
psi	INCHES OF MERCURY	2.04
psi	ATMOSPHERES	0.0681
FEET OF WATER	psi	0.434
FEET OF WATER	LBS. PER SQ FOOT	62.5
FEET OF WATER	INCHES OF MERCURY	0.8824
ATMOSPHERES	psi	14.696
ATMOSPHERES	INCHES OF MERCURY	29.92
ATMOSPHERES	FEET OF WATER	34
LONG TONS	POUNDS	2240
METRIC TONS	POUNDS	2204.6
SHORT TONS (U.S.)	POUNDS	2000
SHORT TONS (U.S.)	LONG TONS	0.89285
SHORT TONS (U.S.)	METRIC TONS	0.9072
LONG TONS	SHORT TONS (U.S.)	1.12
METRIC TONS	SHORT TONS (U.S.)	1.1023
POUNDS	KILOGRAMS	0.4536
KILOGRAMS	POUNDS	2.2046

FRACTION					DECIMAL	MILLI-METERS
				1/64	0.01563	0.397
			1/32	2/64	0.03125	0.794
				3/64	0.04688	1.191
		1/16	2/32	4/64	0.0625	1.588
				5/64	0.07813	1.984
			3/32	6/64	0.09375	2.381
				7/64	0.10938	2.778
	1/8	2/16	4/32	8/64	0.125	3.175
				9/64	0.14063	3.572
			5/32	10/64	0.15625	3.969
				11/64	0.17188	4.366
		3/16	6/32	12/64	0.1875	4.763
				13/64	0.20313	5.159
			7/32	14/64	0.21875	5.556
				15/64	0.23438	5.953
1/4	2/8	4/16	8/32	16/64	0.250	6.350
				17/64	0.26563	6.747
			9/32	18/64	0.28125	7.144
				19/64	0.29688	7.541
		5/16	10/32	20/64	0.3125	7.938
				21/64	0.32813	8.334
			11/32	22/64	0.34375	8.731
				23/64	0.35938	9.128
	3/8	6/16	12/32	24/64	0.375	9.525
				25/64	0.39063	9.922
			13/32	26/64	0.40625	10.319
				27/64	0.42188	10.716
		7/16	14/32	28/64	0.4375	11.113
				29/64	0.45313	11.509
			15/32	30/64	0.46875	11.906
				31/64	0.48438	12.303
1/2	4/8	8/16	16/32	32/64	0.500	12.700

FRACTION				DECIMAL	MILLI-METERS
				33/64	0.51563	13.097
			17/32	34/64	0.53125	13.494
				35/64	0.54688	13.891
		9/16	18/32	36/64	0.5625	14.288
				37/64	0.57813	14.684
			19/32	38/64	0.59375	15.081
				39/64	0.60938	15.478
	5/8	10/16	20/32	40/64	0.625	15.875
				41/64	0.64063	16.272
			21/32	42/64	0.65625	16.669
				43/64	0.67188	17.066
		11/16	22/32	44/64	0.6875	17.463
				45/64	0.70313	17.859
			23/32	46/64	0.71875	18.256
				47/64	0.73438	18.653
3/4	6/8	12/16	24/32	48/64	0.750	19.050
				49/64	0.76563	19.447
			25/32	50/64	0.78125	19.844
				51/64	0.79688	20.241
		13/16	26/32	52/64	0.8125	20.638
				53/64	0.82813	21.034
			27/32	54/64	0.84375	21.431
				55/64	0.85938	21.828
	7/8	14/16	28/32	56/64	0.875	22.225
				57/64	0.89063	22.622
			29/32	58/64	0.90625	23.019
				59/64	0.92188	23.416
		15/16	30/32	60/64	0.9375	23.813
				61/64	0.95313	24.209
			31/32	62/64	0.96875	24.606
				63/64	0.98438	25.003
1	8/8	16/16	32/32	64/64	1.00000	25.400

DECIMALS OF A FOOT

INCH	0"	1"	2"	3"	4"	5"	6"	7"	8"	9"	10"	11"
0	0	.0833	.1667	.2500	.3333	.4167	.5000	.5833	.6667	.7500	.8333	.9167
1/16	.0052	.0885	.1719	.2552	.3385	.4219	.5052	.5885	.6719	.7552	.8385	.9219
1/8	.0104	.0938	.1771	.2604	.3438	.4271	.5104	.5938	.6771	.7604	.8438	.9271
3/16	.0156	.0990	.1823	.2656	.3490	.4323	.5156	.5990	.6823	.7656	.8490	.9323
1/4	.0208	.1042	.1875	.2708	.3542	.4375	.5208	.6042	.6875	.7708	.8542	.9375
5/16	.0260	.1094	.1927	.2760	.3594	.4427	.5260	.6094	.6927	.7760	.8594	.9427
3/8	.0313	.1146	.1979	.2812	.3646	.4479	.5313	.6146	.6979	.7813	.8646	.9479
7/16	.0365	.1198	.2031	.2865	.3698	.4531	.5365	.6198	.7031	.7865	.8698	.9531
1/2	.0417	.1250	.2083	.2917	.3750	.4583	.5417	.6250	.7083	.7917	.8750	.9583
9/16	.0469	.1302	.2135	.2969	.3802	.4635	.5469	.6302	.7135	.7969	.8802	.9635
5/8	.0521	.1354	.2188	.3021	.3854	.4688	.5521	.6354	.7188	.8021	.8854	.9688
11/16	.0573	.1406	.2240	.3073	.3906	.4740	.5573	.6406	.7240	.8073	.8906	.9740
3/4	.0625	.1458	.2292	.3125	.3958	.4792	.5625	.6458	.7292	.8125	.8958	.9792
13/16	.0677	.1510	.2344	.3177	.4010	.4844	.5677	.6510	.7344	.8177	.9010	.9844
7/8	.0729	.1563	.2396	.3229	.4063	.4896	.5729	.6563	.7396	.8229	.9063	.9896
15/16	.0781	.1615	.2448	.3281	.4115	.4948	.5781	.6615	.7448	.8281	.9115	.9948
1	.0833	.1667	.2500	.3333	.4167	.5000	.5833	.6667	.7500	.8333	.9167	1.000

RECTANGLE	SQUARE

Perimeter= 2l+2w	Perimeter= 4s
Area= lw	Area= s^2

CIRCLE	TRIANGLE

 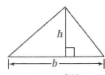

Circumference= $2\pi r$ or πd
Area= πr^2
Arc length= $2\pi r\left(\dfrac{\theta}{360°}\right)$

Area= 1/2bh

TRAPEZOID	PARALLELOGRAM

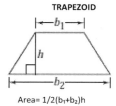 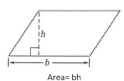

Area= 1/2(b_1+b_2)h

Area= bh

RECTANGULAR PRISM	**PYRAMID**
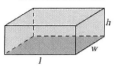	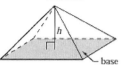
Volume= Bh = lwh	Volume= 1/3Bh = 1/3lwh
SA= 2lw+2lh+2wh	SA= total SA of all sides
CONE	**CYLINDER**
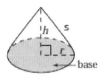	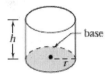
Volume= 1/3Bh = 1/3πr^2h	Volume= Bh = πr^2h
SA closed= $\pi r^2 + \pi rs$	SA closed= $2\pi rh + 2\pi r^2$
SA closed= $\pi r^2 + \pi r\sqrt{r^2 + h^2}$	SA opened= $2\pi rh$
SA opened= πrs	

SPHERE

Volume= 4/3πr^3
SA= $4\pi r^2$

θ= arc angle in degrees
π=3.141592
SA=Surface Area
B=base
note: the volume of a triangular prism can be calculated by multiplying a length dimension with the area calculation of a triangle

CUBIC FEET TO U.S. GALLONS, IMPERIAL GALLONS AND LITERS			
CUBIC FEET	U.S. GALLONS	IMPERIAL GALLONS	LITERS
1	7.5	6.2	28
2	15.0	12.5	57
3	22.4	18.7	85
4	29.9	24.9	113
5	37.4	31.2	142
6	44.9	37.4	170
7	52.4	43.6	198
8	59.8	49.9	227
9	67.3	56.1	255
10	74.8	62.4	283
50	374.0	311.8	1416
100	748.0	623.6	2832
500	3740.3	3117.8	14158
1000	7480.5	6235.5	28317
5000	37402.6	31177.5	141583
10000	74805.2	62355.0	283166
50000	374025.9	311775.0	1415830
100000	748051.9	623550.0	2831660

GALLONS PER MINUTE FROM 1-1/8" HOSE					
psi	gallons	psi	gallons	psi	gallons
10	89	60	222	110	300
20	129	70	240	120	314
30	157	80	257	130	326
40	182	90	272	140	339
50	202	100	287	150	351

CHAPTER 11: TRIGONOMETRY

In my honest opinion, trig is the most benificial math to the construction industry craftsman. It ecompasses needed aspects to many trades and crafts if properly understood as with its usage in pipe fitting, iron working, rigging, general fabrication, etc. Though it can be slightly confusing, it's really not that complicated. It simply estalbishes the relationship of lengths and angles within a right angle triangle, which can be found in the relationship of many systems e.g. piping, rigging, etc. It's simply about the ratio of these parameters to each other required to maintain a right angle triangle. The very essence of establishing a right angle triangle enforces parameters which must be met, which allows for an intrinsic relationship which can be exploited to aquire a tool which has far reaching implications in the construction industry. The following relationships can be calculated with a right angle triangle of known proportions such as the 3, 4, 5 version often used whereby allowing one to become familiar with the math involved.

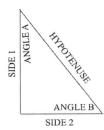

$(SIDE\ 1)^2 + (SIDE\ 2)^2 = (HYPOTENUSE)^2$

ANGLE A + ANGLE B = 90° ALWAYS

SIDE 1= SIDE ADJACENT TO ANGLE A AND OPPOSITE TO ANGLE B
SIDE 2= SIDE ADJACENT TO ANGLE B AND OPPOSITE TO ANGLE A

TO FIND ANGLE A OR B WHEN TWO SIDE LENGTHS ARE KNOWN:

SIDE 1 ÷ HYPOTENUSE = SINE OF ANGLE B AND COSINE OF ANGLE A
SIDE 2 ÷ HYPOTENUSE = SINE OF ANGLE A AND COSINE OF ANGLE B
SIDE 1 ÷ SIDE 2 = TANGENT OF ANGLE B AND COTANGENT OF ANGLE A
SIDE 2 ÷ SIDE 1 = TANGENT OF ANGLE A AND COTANGENT OF ANGLE B
HYPOTENUSE ÷ SIDE 1= SECANT OF ANGLE A AND COSECANT OF ANGLE B
HYPOTENUSE ÷ SIDE 2= SECANT OF ANGLE B AND COSECANT OF ANGLE A

TO FIND LENGTH OF SIDE WHEN ANY ANGLE AND LENGTH ARE KNOWN:

FOR THE LENGTH OF SIDE OPPOSITE:
HYPOTENUSE X SINE OF ANGLE A = SIDE 2
HYPOTENUSE X SINE OF ANGLE B = SIDE 1
HYPOTENUSE ÷ COSECANT OF ANGLE A = SIDE 2
HYPOTENUSE ÷ COSECANT OF ANGLE B = SIDE 1
SIDE 1 X TANGENT OF ANGLE A = SIDE 2
SIDE 2 X TANGENT OF ANGLE B = SIDE 1
SIDE 1 ÷ COTANGENT OF ANGLE A = SIDE 2
SIDE 2 ÷ COTANGENT OF ANGLE B = SIDE 1

FOR THE LENGTH OF SIDE ADJACENT:
HYPOTENUSE X COSINE OF ANGLE A = SIDE 1
HYPOTENUSE X COSINE OF ANGLE B = SIDE 2
HYPOTENUSE ÷ SECANT OF ANGLE A = SIDE 1
HYPOTENUSE ÷ SECANT OF ANGLE B = SIDE 2
SIDE 2 X COTANGENT OF ANGLE A = SIDE 1
SIDE 1 X COTANGENT OF ANGLE B = SIDE 2
SIDE 2 ÷ TANGENT OF ANGLE A = SIDE 1
SIDE 1 ÷ TANGENT OF ANGLE B = SIDE 2

FOR THE LENGTH OF HYPOTENUSE:
SIDE 2 X COSECANT OF ANGLE A = HYPOTENUSE
SIDE 1 X COSECANT OF ANGLE B = HYPOTENUSE
SIDE 2 ÷ SINE OF ANGLE A = HYPOTENUSE
SIDE 1 ÷ SINE OF ANGLE B = HYPOTENUSE
SIDE 2 X SECANT OF ANGLE B = HYPOTENUSE
SIDE 1 X SECANT OF ANGLE A = HYPOTENUSE
SIDE 2 ÷ COSINE OF ANGLE B = HYPOTENUSE
SIDE 1 ÷ COSINE OF ANGLE A = HYPOTENUSE

Angle	Sin	Cos	Tan	Cot	Sec	Csc	
0	.0000	1.000	.0000	∞	1.000	∞	90
1	.0174	.9998	.0175	57.29	1.000	57.30	89
2	.0349	.9994	.0349	28.64	1.001	28.65	88
3	.0523	.9986	.0524	19.08	1.001	19.11	87
4	.0698	.9976	.0699	14.30	1.002	14.34	86
5	.0872	.9962	.0875	11.43	1.004	11.47	85
6	.1045	.9945	.1051	9.514	1.006	9.567	84
7	.1219	.9925	.1228	8.144	1.008	8.206	83
8	.1392	.9903	.1405	7.115	1.010	7.185	82
9	.1564	.9877	.1584	6.314	1.012	6.392	81
10	.1736	.9848	.1763	5.671	1.015	5.759	80
11	.1908	.9816	.1944	5.145	1.019	5.241	79
12	.2079	.9781	.2126	4.705	1.022	4.810	78
13	.2250	.9744	.2309	4.331	1.026	4.445	77
14	.2419	.9703	.2493	4.011	1.031	4.134	76
15	.2588	.9659	.2679	3.732	1.035	3.864	75
16	.2756	.9613	.2867	3.487	1.040	3.628	74
17	.2924	.9563	.3057	3.271	1.046	3.420	73
18	.3090	.9511	.3249	3.078	1.051	3.236	72
19	.3256	.9455	.3443	2.904	1.058	3.072	71
20	.3420	.9397	.3640	2.747	1.064	2.924	70
21	.3584	.9336	.3839	2.605	1.071	2.790	69
22	.3746	.9272	.4040	2.475	1.079	2.669	68
23	.3907	.9205	.4245	2.356	1.086	2.559	67
24	.4067	.9135	.4452	2.246	1.095	2.459	66
	Cos	Sin	Cot	Tan	Csc	Sec	Angle

Angle	Sin	Cos	Tan	Cot	Sec	Csc	
25	.4226	.9063	.4663	2.145	1.103	2.366	65
26	.4384	.8988	.4877	2.050	1.113	2.281	64
27	.4540	.8910	.5095	1.963	1.122	2.203	63
28	.4695	.8829	.5317	1.881	1.133	2.130	62
29	.4848	.8746	.5543	1.804	1.143	2.063	61
30	.5000	.8660	.5774	1.732	1.155	2.000	60
31	.5150	.8572	.6009	1.664	1.167	1.942	59
32	.5299	.8480	.6249	1.600	1.179	1.887	58
33	.5446	.8387	.6494	1.540	1.192	1.836	57
34	.5592	.8290	.6745	1.483	1.206	1.788	56
35	.5736	.8192	.7002	1.428	1.221	1.743	55
36	.5878	.8090	.7265	1.376	1.236	1.701	54
37	.6018	.7986	.7536	1.327	1.252	1.662	53
38	.6157	.7880	.7813	1.280	1.269	1.624	52
39	.6293	.7771	.8098	1.235	1.287	1.589	51
40	.6428	.7660	.8391	1.192	1.305	1.556	50
41	.6561	.7547	.8693	1.150	1.325	1.524	49
42	.6691	.7431	.9004	1.111	1.346	1.494	48
43	.6820	.7314	.9325	1.072	1.367	1.466	47
44	.6947	.7193	.9657	1.036	1.390	1.440	46
45	.7071	.7071	1.000	1.000	1.414	1.414	45
	Cos	Sin	Cot	Tan	Csc	Sec	Angle

The intermediate minute values which further divide each degree into sixty equal parts as seen with the larger trig tables are not supplied due to the extra pages required to properly display such. Though the provided values are perhaps not specific enough for fitting and fabrication in some circumstances, they are sufficient enough to address the math outlined in this book in terms of rigging and such.

CHAPTER 12: FITTING AND WELDING

SMAW = Sheilded Metal Arc Welding (Stick Rod)
GTAW = Gas Tungsten Arc Welding (Tungsten Inert Gas/ TIG)

TIPS: Always PMI all alloys before making any fabrication or welding to verify material grade and filler metal to be used. Mark all drop pieces at the shop with the material grade information to prevent a mishap and to prevent the need of another PMI. Always PMI alloy welds as soon as they are done to free up further NDE requirements which will otherwise be lost time if the wrong filler metal was used and the PMI is performed after final PT's, pre PWHT X-rays, PWHT, post PWHT X-rays, hydro, etc. Verify the filler metal is correct first and then proceed to further procedures and NDE to prevent mishap and lost time. When the wrong filler metal was used on an alloy, always clean the pipe and fitting back to original base metal and perform a pre weld PMI on the weld area of both pieces to verify that all other metals were removed. This may also require another prep PT if either material is old/existing depending upon the QC requirements.

● The common practice is to PT all old fit preperations before welding the new piece on. A closure weld will usually consist of a PT on the prep, root pass and final weld pass with code welds on pressure vessels and such often requiring more PTs or other forms of NDE, sometimes on every pass. Closure welds are done in lieu of hydro whereby an entire drawing may be fabricated and hydro tested at the fab shop leaving only a closure weld to tie the new to old in the field without the need of its hydro after an x-ray is performed.

● Always verify that any piping that must recieve PWHT which has weld in gate valves is assembled with bolted bonnet valves and not welded bonnet valves due to the need of having to remove the valves internal components during PWHT as is also the case for check valve internals, threaded plugs in the end of bleeders, etc., to prevent damage during heat stress. Always properly support any piping that must receive PWHT at the shop in jack stands whereby leaving no unsupported ends which may have enough weight to cause bending/distortion when heated. This is a common problem with small bore piping.

● Always connect your ground lead as close as possible to your work when making welds in the field at refineries to prevent being grounded across a pump seal which could cause problems with the seal when it is back in service, which could be a dangerous situation being as these seals are holding back whatever service the pump is involved with. Many refineries require some form of insulator protection when welding within a certain distance of a pump. This may be nothing more than dropping a bolt up spool out when possible to disallow current flow. It may also require such things as non-metallic gaskets and stud sleeves with non-metallic washers as with a flange insulator kit as used for dissimilar metal flanges which increase corrosion. Extra grounding is sometimes required from the work piece to earth ground along with jumpers across the two work pieces to be welded during initial tacking.

● Always check the job site for lead and asbestos before disturbing any paint or insulation.

● It is common practice to grind the internal root weld penetration smooth in butt weld orifice flanges which will be used for flow measurement rather than just mere flow restriction to assure proper flow characteristics during measurement. Always consult with your inspection and QC department concerning such things as site requirements may differ.

● ASME B31.3 FIG. 328.5.2C MINIMUM WELDING DIMENSIONS FOR SOCKET WELDING COMPONENTS OTHER THAN FLANGES calls for a 1/16" internal gap "before welding" in socket welds at the end of the pipe where it meets the fitting due to thermal expansion. The greatest temperature most fittings will see is during the welding process whereby there is some debate about such gap after the weld as it could close up slightly during the welding process and the code DOES NOT specify the "after welding" gap. From my experience, it is general practice to use approximately a 1/8" gap whereby maintaining a visible gap after welding which is often verified by a visual on open ended flanges or by x-ray examination of a percentage of others. Though it may not be specified within the referenced code, the lack of a gap after welding WILL often cause a complete cut out followed by a refabrication and reweld of that particular fit up whereby maintaining an after weld gap approximately 1/16" to 1/8". Also contained in that particular diagram is specifications for the minimal rise and run length of the legs of the triangle created by a cross section view of a fillet weld of a socket weld fitting, whereby calling for a minimum of 1-1/4 x wall thickness of the pipe being welded to the socket weld fitting but not less than 1/8" allowed. This dimension is as measured up the side of the pipe or across the shouldered face of the fitting and is not the fillet weld "throat" thickness at center.

● The minimum leg length for the fillet weld made inside the ID of a slip-on flange opposite of the hub weld per ASME B31.3 FIG. 328.5.2B is to be the lesser of the thickness of the pipe or 1/4" meaning pipe wall thicknesses less than 1/4" govern the length while wall thicknesses greater than 1/4" are governed by the 1/4" minimum. The minimum leg length for the hub weld is the lesser of 1.4 x pipe wall thickness or the thickness of the hub.

● When seal welding threaded connections you must never leave threads exposed above the weld. Always cut the threads down as needed to accomplish a full engagement of the threads into the fitting while also leaving a minimum area of coverage required to cover the remaining threads with the seal weld.

● Taper boring (transitioning) the ID of a thicker pipe or fitting to match the wall thickness of another pipe or fitting is to have a maximum angle no greater than 30° as measured perpendicular to the centerline of the pipe per ASME B31.3 FIG. 328.4.3. This would be a 1.73:1 ratio of the ID tapper length as measured parallel to the centerline of the pipe to that of the thickness of the metal removed from the ID. A 3:1 ratio as referenced in ASME B16.25 (which is the applicable code to unequal wall thicknesses with one greater than 1-1/2 times the other) is a more common practice and is the recommended ratio per ASME VIII which would translate to 18.43°.

● **4 X Pipe Diameter X Foot of Pipe ÷ Purge Rate (cfh) = Piping Purge Time in Minutes**

The above formula is to estimate the amount of time to purge a line before welding to allow for proper evacuation of the atmospheric air contained within. A good practice is to start at 30 to 45 CFH, after purge is completed turn the flow range down between 8 and 12 CFH.

SMAW ELECTRODE IDENTIFICATION PER AWS A5.1

E XX YY
E XX YY M
E XX YY -1 HZ R

Mandatory Classification Designators:

E - Designates an electrode. This designator may be deleted from the product imprint required for identification of the electrode.

XX - Designates the tensile strength (minimum) in ksi, of the weld metal when produced in accordance with the test assembly preparation procedure of the AWS specification. See Table 2. AWS A5.1

YY - Designates the welding position in which electrodes are usable, the type of covering and the kind of welding current for which the electrodes are suitable. See Table 1. AWS A5.1 or refer to the <u>Common SMAW Welding Electrodes For Carbon Steel</u> on the following page for designations.

M - Designates an electrode (E70 18M) intended to meet most military requirements (greater toughness, lower moisture content — both as-received and after exposure — and mandatory diffusible hydrogen limits for weld metal). See Table 3, 10 and 11 AWS A5.1

Optional Supplemental Designators:

1 - Designates that the electrode (E7016, E7018, or E7024) meets the requirements for improved toughness — and ductility in the case of E7024 — (optional supplemental test requirements shown in Tables 2 and 3). See notes to Tables 2 and 3 AWS A5.1.

HZ - Designates that the electrode meets the requirements of the diffusible hydrogen test (an optional supplemental test of the weld metal from low hydrogen electrodes, as-received or conditioned — with an average value not exceeding "Z" mL of H2 per 100g of deposited metal, where "Z" is 4, 8, or 16). See Table 11 AWS A5.1.

R - Designates that the electrode meets the requirements of the absorbed moisture test (an optional supplemental test for all low hydrogen electrodes except the E701 8M classification, for which the test is required). See Table 10 AWS A5.1.

TYPICAL WELDING ROD AMPERAGE RANGE					
ROD DIA.	EXX10-X EXX11-X	EXX13-X	E7020-X	E7027-X	EXX15-X EXX16-X	EXX18M EXX18-X
3/32	40-80	45-90	-	-	65-110	70-100
1/8	75-125	80-130	100-150	125-185	100-150	115-165
5/32	110-170	105-180	130-190	160-240	140-200	150-220
3/16	140-215	150-230	175-250	210-300	180-255	200-275
7/32	170-250	-	225-310	250-350	240-320	260-340
1/4	210-320	-	275-375	300-420	300-390	315-400
5/16	-	-	-	375-475	-	-

COMMON GTAW WELDING FILLER METALS					
CLASS	SUFFIX	TYPE	CLASS	SUFFIX	TYPE
ER 70 S	2	Carbon steel type	ER 80 S	B6	5Cr-0.5Mo steel
ER 70 S	3		ER 80 S	B8	9Cr-1Mo steel
ER 70 S	4		ER 90 S	B9	9Cr-1Mo-0.2V steel
ER 70 S	6		ER 80 S	Ni1	Ni steel
ER 70 S	7		ER 80 S	Ni2	
ER 70 S	G		ER 80 S	Ni3	
ER 70 S	A1	C-0.5Mo steel	ER 80 S	D2	Mn-Mo steel
ER 80 S	B2	1.25Cr-0.5Mo steel	ER 90 S	D2	
ER 70 S	B2L		ER 100 S	1	Other low alloy steels
ER 90 S	B3	2.25Cr-1Mo steel	ER 110 S	1	
ER 80 S	B3L		ER 120 S	1	

ER: Designates welding electrodes or rods. E: Designates welding electrodes.
S: Designates solid wire. C: Designates composite wire.

COMMON SMAW WELDING ELECTRODES FOR CARBON STEEL					
Classification		Welding Position	Current	Classification	Welding Position	Current
E60	10	F,V,OH,H	DC(+)	E70	14	F,V,OH,H	AC or DC($\pm$)
	11		AC or DC(+)		15		DC(+)
	12		AC or DC(−)		16		AC or DC(+)
	13		AC or DC($\pm$)		18		AC or DC(+)
	18		AC or DC(+)		24	H-Fill,F	AC or DC($\pm$)
	19		AC or DC($\pm$)		28		AC or DC(+)
	20	H-Fill	AC or DC (−)		27	H-Fill F	AC or DC (−)
		F	AC or DC($\pm$)				AC or DC($\pm$)
	22	F,H	AC or DC(−)		48	F,OH,H,V-down	AC or DC(+)
	27	H-Fill F	AC or DC (−)		18M	F,V,OH,H	DC(+)
			AC or DC($\pm$)				

(1) Welding position: F: Flat, H: Horizontal, H-Fill: Horizontal fillet, V-down: Vertical down V: Vertical, OH: Overhead (V and OH are applicable for 5/32" (4.0mm) or smaller electrodes as to E7014, E7015, E7016, E7018, E7018M, and for 3/16" (4.8mm) electrodes as to the other types of electrodes)
(2) Type of current: DC(−) : DC-EN, DC(+) : DC-EP, DC($\pm$) : DC-EP or DC-EN

COMMON SMAW WELDING ELECTRODES FOR LOW-ALLOY STEEL

CLASS		CHEMICAL COMPOSITION							
		C	Mn	Si	P	S	Ni	Cr	Mo	others
ELECTRODES FOR C-Mo STEEL										
E 7010 E 7011 E 7020	A1	0.12	0.60	0.40	0.03	0.03	-	-	0.40-0.65	-
E 7015 E 7016			0.90	0.60						
E 7018			0.90	0.80						
E 7027			1.00	0.40						
ELECTRODES FOR Cr-Mo STEEL										
E 8016 E 8018	B1	0.05-0.12	0.90	0.60 0.80	0.03	0.03	-	0.40-0.65	0.40-0.65	
E 8016 E 8018	B2	0.05-0.12	0.90	0.60 0.80	0.03	0.03	-	1.00-1.50	0.40-0.65	
E 7015 E 7016 E 7018	B2L	0.05	0.90	1.00 0.60 0.80	0.03	0.03	-	1.00-1.50	0.40-0.65	
E 9015 E 9016 E 9018	B3	0.05-0.12	0.90	1.00 0.60 0.80	0.03	0.03	-	2.00-2.50	0.90-1.20	
E 8015 E 8018	B3L	0.05	0.90	1.00 0.80	0.03	0.03	-	2.00-2.50	0.90-1.20	
E 8015	B4L	0.05	0.90	1.00	0.03	0.03	-	1.75-2.25	0.40-0.65	
E 8016	B5	0.07-0.15	0.40-0.70	0.30-0.60	0.03	0.03	-	0.40-0.60	1.00-1.25	V: 0.05
E 8015 E 8016 E 8018	B6	0.05-0.12	1.0	0.90	0.03	0.03	0.40	4.0-6.0	0.45-0.65	
E 8015 E 8016 E 8018	B6L	0.05	1.0	0.90	0.03	0.03	0.40	4.0-6.0	0.45-0.65	
E 8015 E 8016 E 8018	B7	0.05-0.12	1.0	0.90	0.03	0.03	0.40	6.0-8.0	0.45-0.65	
E 8015 E 8016 E 8018	B7L	0.05	1.0	0.90	0.03	0.03	0.40	6.0-8.0	0.45-0.65	

COMMON SMAW WELDING ELECTRODES FOR LOW-ALLOY STEEL Continued

CLASS		CHEMICAL COMPOSITION								
		C	Mn	Si	P	S	Ni	Cr	Mo	others
ELECTRODES FOR Cr-Mo STEEL										
E 8015 E 8016 E 8018	B8L	0.05	1.0	0.90	0.03	0.03	0.40	8.0-10.5	0.85-1.20	-
E 9015 E 9016 E 9018	B9	0.08-0.13	1.20	0.30	0.01	0.01	0.80	8.0-10.5	0.85-1.20	V: 0.15-0.30 Cu: 0.25 Al: 0.04 Nb(Cb): 0.02-0.10 N: 0.02-0.07
ELECTRODES FOR Ni STEEL										
E 8016 E 8018	C1	0.12	1.25	0.60 0.80	0.03	0.03	2.00-2.75	-	-	-
E 7015 E 7016 E 7018	C1L	0.05	1.25	0.50	0.03	0.03	2.00-2.75	-	-	-
E 8016 E 8018	C2	0.12	1.25	0.60 0.80	0.03	0.03	3.00-3.75	-	-	-
E 7015 E 7016 E 7018	C2L	0.05	1.25	0.50	0.03	0.03	3.00-3.75	-	-	-
E 8016 E 8018	C3	0.12	0.40-1.25	0.80	0.03	0.03	0.80-1.10	0.15	0.35	V: 0.05
E 7018	C3L	0.08	0.40-1.40	0.50	0.03	0.03	0.80-1.10	0.15	0.35	V: 0.05
E 8016 E 8018	C4	0.10	1.25	0.60 0.80	0.03	0.03	1.10-2.00	-	-	-
E 9015	C5L	0.05	0.40-1.00	0.50	0.03	0.03	6.00-7.25	-	-	-

SOME COMMON STAINLESS STEEL FILLER METAL APPLICATIONS

BASE METAL	Type 304L Stainless Steel	Type 304H Stainless Steel	Type 316L Stainless Steel	Type 317L Stainless Steel	Type 904L Stainless Steel
Carbon and Low Alloy Steel	ABC	ABC	ABC	ABC	ABC
Type 304L Stainless Steel	D	DE	DF	DG	DC
Type 304H Stainless Steel		E	EF	EG	
Type 316L Stainless Steel			FG	FG	FC
Type 317L Stainless Steel				GC	GC
Type 904L Stainless Steel					C

LEGEND

	SMAW	GTAW
A	E309L-XX	ER309L
B	ENiCrFe-2 or -3 (-2 is Alloy 718 and -3 is Inconel 182)	ERNiCrFe-2 or -3
C	ENiCrMo-3 (Inconel 625)	ERNiCrMo-3
D	E308L-XX	ER308L
E	E308H-XX	ER308H
F	E316L-XX	ER316L
G	E317L-XX	ER317L

EXAMPLE OF SOME COMMON WELDING FILLER METALS AS USED IN SOME WELDING PROCEDURES				
MATERIAL BEING WELDED	P-no./ P-no.	PWHT	FILLER METAL	
			SMAW	GTAW
CARBON	1 - 1	NO	E6010/E7018	ER70S-2
CARBON-1/2 MOLY	3 - 3	NO	E7018-A1	ER80S-D2
1-1/4 CR	4 - 4	YES	E7018-B2L E8018-B2L E8018-B2	ER70S-B2L ER80S-B2L ER80S-B2
1-1/4 CR TO CARBON	4 - 1	YES	E8018-B2L	ER80S-B2L
1-1/4 CR TO CARBON-1/2 MOLY	4 - 3	YES	E8018-B2	ER80S-B2
2-1/4 CR	5A-5A	YES	E9018-B3	ER90S-B3
2-1/4 CR TO 1-1/4 CR	5A-4	YES	E9018-B3	ER90S-B3
5 CR	5B-5B	YES	E502 E8018-B6	ER502 ER80S-B6
9 CR	5B-5B	YES	E505 E8018-B8	ER505 ER80S-B8
9 CR TO CARBON	5B-1	YES	E505	ER505
HASTELLOY C	44-44	NO	ENiCrMo-4	ERNiCrMo-4
HASTELLOY B-2	44-44	NO	ENiMo-10	ERNiMo-10
ALLOY 20	45-45	NO	E320LR	ER320LR
ALLOY 20 TO CARBON	45-1	NO	E320LR	ER320LR
SS TO 1-1/4 CR	8 - 4	YES	ENiCr-3	ERNiCr-3
SS TO 2-1/4 CR	8 -5A	YES	ENiCr-3	ERNiCr-3
INCO 825	45-45	NO	ENiCrMo-3	ERNiCrMo-3
INCO 625	43-43	NO	ENiCrMo-3	ERNiCrMo-3
INCO 625 TO CARBON	43-1	NO	ENiCr-3	ERNiCr-3

PREHEAT REQUIREMENTS AND RECOMMENDATIONS
ASME B31.3 TABLE 330.1.1

Base Metal P-NO S-NO Note 1	Weld Metal A-NO Note 2	BASE METAL GROUP	WALL THICKNESS		SPECIFIED MINIMAL TENSILE STRENGTH BASE METAL		MINIMUM TEMPERATURE			
							REQUIRED		RECO-MENDED	
			in.	mm	ksi	MPa	°F	°C	°F	°C
1	1	Carbon Steel	<1 ≥1 All	<25 ≥25 All	≤71 All >71	≤490 All >490			50 175 175	10 79 79
3	2,11	Alloy Steels, Cr ≤ 1/2%	<1/2 ≥1/2 All	<13 ≥13 All	≤71 All >71	≤490 All >490			50 175 175	10 79 79
4	3	Alloy Steels, 1/2% < Cr ≤ 2%	All	All	All	All	300	149		
5A 5B,5C	4,5	Alloy steels 2-1/4% ≤ Cr ≤ 10%	All	All	All	All	350	177		
6	6	High Alloy Steels Martensitic	All	All	All	All			300[3]	149[3]
7	7	High Alloy Steels Ferritic	All	All	All	All			50	10
8	8,9	High Alloy Steels Austenitic	All	All	All	All			50	10
9A,9B	10	Nickel Alloy Steels	All	All	All	All			200	93
10		Cr – Cu Steel	All	All	All	All	300-400	149-204		
10I		27 Cr Steel	All	All	All	All	300[4]	149[4]		
11A SG1		8 Ni, 9 Ni Steel	All	All	All	All			50	10
11A SG2		5 Ni steel	All	All	All	All	50	10		
21-52			All	All	All	All			50	10

Notes:
1. P-Number or S-Number from BPV Code, Section IX, QW/QB-422.
2. A-Number from Section IX, QW-442.
3. Maximum interpass temperature 316°C (600°F).
4. Maintain interpass temperature between 177°-232°C (350°F-450°).

REQUIREMENTS FOR HEAT TREATMENT (PWHT)
ASME B31.3 TABLE 331.1.1

Base Metal P-NO S-NO Note 1	Weld Metal A-NO Note 2	BASE METAL GROUP	WALL THICKNESS	SPECIFIED MIN. TENSILE STRENGTH BASE METAL	METAL TEMP. RANGE	HOLDING TIME NOMINAL WALL	
			in.	ksi	°F	hr/in	Min. Time, hr
1	1	Carbon Steel	≤3/4 >3/4	All All	None 1100-1200	1	1
3	2,11	Alloy Steels, Cr ≤ 1/2%	≤3/4 >3/4 All	≤71 All >71	None 1100-1325 1100-1325	1 1	1 1
4	3	Alloy Steels, 1/2% < Cr ≤ 2%	≤1/2 >1/2 All	≤71 All >71	None 1300-1375 1300-1375	1 1	2 2
5A 5B,5C	4,5	Alloy steels 2-1/4% ≤ Cr ≤ 10% ≤3%Cr and ≤0.15%C ≤3%Cr and ≤0.15%C >3%Cr and >0.15%C	≤1/2 >1/2 All	All All All	None 1300-1400 1300-1400	1 1	2 2
6	6	High Alloy Steels Martensitic A240 Gr.429	All All	All All	1350-1450 1150-1225	1 1	2 2
7	7	High Alloy Steels Ferritic	All	All	None		
8	8,9	High Alloy Steels Austenitic	All	All	None		
9A,9B	10	Nickel Alloy Steels	≤3/4 >3/4	All All	None 1100-1175	1/2	1
10		Cr – Cu Steel	All	All	1400-1500 [note 5]	1/2	1/2
10H		Duplex Stainless Steel	All	All	[note 7]	1/2	1/2
10I		27 Cr Steel	All	All	1225-1300 [Note 6]	1	1

To understand the greater, less and equal to signs, the expression 1/2% < Cr ≤ 2% is simplying saying Cr greater than 1/2% and less than or equal to 2%. This is relational to how metal composition classifies metals per their P-No.

REQUIREMENTS FOR HEAT TREATMENT (PWHT)
ASME B31.3 TABLE 331.1.1 Continued

Base Metal P-NO S-NO Note 1	Weld Metal A-NO Note 2	BASE METAL GROUP	WALL THICK NESS	SPECIFIED MIN. TENSILE STRENGTH BASE METAL	METAL TEMP. RANGE	HOLDING TIME NOMINAL WALL	
			in.	ksi	°F	hr/in.	Min. Time, hr
11A SG1		8 Ni, 9 Ni Steel	≤2 >2	All All	None 1025-1085 [Note 8]	1	1
11A SG2		5 Ni steel	>2	All	1025-1085 [Note 8]	1	1
62		Zr R60705	All	All	1000-1100 [Note 9]	[Note 9]	1

Notes: (3 and 4 left out intentionally)
1. P-Number or S-Number from BPV Code, Section IX, QW/QB-422
2. A-Number from Section IX, QW-442
5. Cool as rapidly as possible after the hold period.
6. Cooling rate to 1200°F (649°C) shall be less than 100°F (56°C)/hr; thereafter the cooling rate shall be fast enough to prevent embrittlement.
7. Post weld heat treatment is neither required nor prohibited, but any heat treatment applied shall be as required in the material specification.
8. Cooling rate shall be >300°F (167°C)/hr to 600°F (316°C).
9. Heat treat within 14 days after welding. Hold time shall be increased by 1/2 for each 1 in. (25mm) over 25 mm thickness. Cool to 800°F (427°C) at a rate ≥500°F (278°C)/hr, per 1 in. (25mm) nominal thickness, 500°F (278°C)/hr max. Cool in still air from 800°F (427°C).
10. Heat treatment temperatures listed for some P-No. 4 and P-No.5 materials may be higher than the minimum tempering temperatures specified in the ASTM specifications for the base material. For higher-strength normalized and tempered materials, there is consequently a possibility of reducing tensile properties of the base material, particularly if long holding times at the higher temperatures are used.

BEVEL TAKEOFFS PER WALL THICKNESS								
WALL THICK	30° BEV	37.5° BEV	WALL THICK	30° BEV	37.5° BEV	WALL THICK	30° BEV	37.5° BEV
0.049	0.028	0.037	0.148	0.085	0.113	0.276	0.159	0.211
0.065	0.037	0.049	0.154	0.088	0.118	0.277	0.160	0.212
0.068	0.039	0.052	0.156	0.090	0.119	0.280	0.161	0.214
0.083	0.047	0.063	0.165	0.095	0.126	0.281	0.162	0.215
0.088	0.050	0.067	0.179	0.103	0.137	0.294	0.169	0.225
0.091	0.052	0.069	0.180	0.104	0.138	0.300	0.173	0.230
0.095	0.054	0.072	0.188	0.108	0.144	0.307	0.177	0.235
0.109	0.062	0.083	0.191	0.110	0.146	0.308	0.178	0.236
0.113	0.065	0.086	0.200	0.115	0.153	0.312	0.180	0.239
0.119	0.068	0.091	0.203	0.117	0.155	0.318	0.183	0.244
0.120	0.069	0.092	0.216	0.124	0.165	0.322	0.185	0.247
0.126	0.072	0.096	0.218	0.125	0.167	0.330	0.190	0.253
0.133	0.076	0.102	0.219	0.126	0.168	0.337	0.194	0.258
0.134	0.077	0.103	0.226	0.130	0.173	0.344	0.198	0.263
0.140	0.080	0.107	0.237	0.136	0.181	0.358	0.206	0.274
0.145	0.083	0.111	0.250	0.144	0.191	0.365	0.210	0.280
0.147	0.084	0.112	0.258	0.148	0.197	0.375	0.216	0.287

When cutting a bevel from the OD of a pipe with a torch, the cutline must be offset to achieve the proper ID length due to the linear gain caused by the angle. The above values represent such gains whereby the cutline might be offset on the OD thus achieving proper ID (overall) length. Bevel angles are always measured from the line perpendicular to the centerline of the pipe. Thus, for a 37.5 degree bevel, there will be 52.5 degrees as measured from the centerline of pipe. These values are also good for laying out a rear boundary line for bevels to use as a grinding guide to improve hand ground bevels.

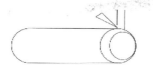

BEVEL TAKEOFFS PER WALL THICKNESS								
WALL THICK	30° BEV	37.5° BEV	WALL THICK	30° BEV	37.5° BEV	WALL THICK	30° BEV	37.5° BEV
0.382	0.220	0.293	0.750	0.433	0.575	1.312	0.757	1.006
0.400	0.230	0.306	0.812	0.468	0.623	1.375	0.793	1.055
0.406	0.234	0.311	0.844	0.487	0.647	1.406	0.811	1.078
0.432	0.249	0.331	0.864	0.498	0.662	1.438	0.830	1.103
0.436	0.251	0.334	0.875	0.505	0.671	1.500	0.866	1.150
0.438	0.252	0.336	0.906	0.523	0.695	1.531	0.883	1.174
0.500	0.288	0.383	0.938	0.541	0.719	1.562	0.901	1.198
0.531	0.306	0.407	0.969	0.559	0.743	1.594	0.920	1.223
0.552	0.318	0.423	1.000	0.577	0.767	1.625	0.938	1.246
0.562	0.324	0.431	1.031	0.595	0.791	1.750	1.010	1.342
0.594	0.342	0.455	1.094	0.631	0.839	1.781	1.028	1.366
0.600	0.346	0.460	1.125	0.649	0.863	1.812	1.046	1.390
0.625	0.360	0.479	1.156	0.667	0.887	1.875	1.082	1.438
0.656	0.378	0.503	1.218	0.703	0.934	1.969	1.136	1.510
0.674	0.389	0.517	1.219	0.704	0.935	2.062	1.190	1.582
0.688	0.397	0.527	1.250	0.721	0.959	2.125	1.226	1.630
0.719	0.415	0.551	1.281	0.739	0.982	2.344	1.353	1.798

When cutting a bevel from the OD of a pipe with a torch, the cutline must be offset to achieve the proper ID length due to the linear gain caused by the angle. The above values represent such gains whereby the cutline might be offset on the OD thus achieving proper ID (overall) length. Bevel angles are always measured from the line perpendicular to the centerline of the pipe. Thus, for a 37.5 degree bevel, there will be 52.5 degrees as measured from the centerline of pipe. These values are also good for laying out a rear boundary line for bevels to use as a grinding guide to improve hand ground bevels.

VICTOR CUTTING TORCH TIP CHART	
METAL THICKNESS	TIP SIZE
UP TO 1/8"	000
1/8" - 1/4"	00
1/4" - 1/2"	0
1/2" - 3/4"	1
3/4" - 1 1/2"	2
1 1/2" - 2 1/2"	3
2 1/2" - 3"	4
3" - 5"	5
5" - 8"	6
8" - 10"	7
10" - 12"	8

TAP AND DRILL SIZES					
DRILL BIT	TAP SIZE	THREADS PER INCH	DRILL BIT	TAP SIZE	THREADS PER INCH
7	1/4	20	49/64	7/8	9
F	5/16	18	53/64	15/16	9
5/16	3/8	16	7/8	1	8
U	7/16	14	63/64	1-1/8	7
27/64	1/2	13	1-7/64	1-1/4	7
31/64	9/16	12	1-13/64	1-3/8	6
17/32	5/8	11	1-11/32	1-1/2	6
19/32	11/16	11	1-29/64	1-5/8	5-1/2
21/32	3/4	10	1-11/16	1-7/8	5
23/32	13/16	10	1-25/32	2	4-1/2

Metal thickness	Victor type seat 2 tapper: 1-101, 3-101, 5-101 GPM-N-P	Airco type seat 3 tapper 144, 164	Harris type seat 2 flat 6290	Oxygen		Acet/Fuel gas		Inches Per Minute
				psig	scfh	psig	scfh	
1/8"	000	00	000	20-25	25	5	5	28-32
1/4"	00	0	00	20-25	35	5	6	25-30
3/8"	0	1	00	25-30	60	5	8	24-28
1/2"	0	1	0	30-35	65	5	10	20-24
3/4"	1	2	1	30-40	85	5	13	17-20
1"	2	2	1	35-50	140	6	16	15-20
1-1/2"	2	3	2	40-50	160	7	18	12-17
2"	3	3	3	40-55	180	9	22	12-15
2-1/2"	3	4	3	45-55	230	10	26	10-13
3"	4	5	4	45-60	280	10	30	9-12
4"	5	5	4	45-60	350	12	36	8-11
5"	5	6	4	50-65	420	12	38	7-9
6"	6	6	5	50-70	450	12	40	6-8
8"	6	6	5	55-75	600	14	44	5-6
10"	7	7	6	68-85	700	14	50	4-5
12"	8	8	6	55-95	900	14	55	3-5

ESTIMATING POUNDS OF WELDING FILLER METAL

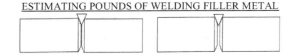

The ability to calculate a close approximation of how many pounds of welding rods are required to do a job could save you a lot of time and money due to the ability to buy in bulk with higher confidence of minimal waste while also decreasing the chance of running out of rods on a given day just because someone forgot to order more or late delivery which creates down time in the fab shop and field whereby causing a loss of production and extension of the job completion. The bevel on a pipe represents the volume of metal that was taken out of the pipe when preping it. Two pipes being fit together creates a valley around the entire circumference of the pipes which must be completely filled with filler metal to achieve proper fusion. Thus, we are effectively replacing the metal we removed by grinding, milling, cutting, etc. to create the bevel with the filler metal of the electrode. If we were to add in an allowance for the gap, root and cap, then we'd have a close approximation of how many pounds of rods it takes to weld various pipe sizes at their associated wall thicknesses as represented by the triangle in the above two diagrams. If we allow for a 1/8" root and cap height, then we merely need to add 1/4" to the wall thickness of a given pipe to receive one of the two needed trig values required to do the calculation. The other value is the 37.5° (tangent = .76733) bevel angle whereby we now can find the side opposite value.

As seen from the geometric relationships of surface area and volume covered in the previous sections, we can find a simple volume measurement of the weld area, which is a triangular prism, by using the surface area formula for a triangle and multiplying it times the circumference of the pipe at the center of the wall or half way between the ID and OD of the pipe which should yeild a more accurate result than just using the ID or OD alone. By doing this we have created a quantitative value of the volume of filler metal within a welded joint. This allows a direct calculation of how many pounds of rods are needed to properly do a complete weld per pipe size by simply factoring in the pounds per volume/cubic inch of the filler metal being used. For carbon steel such as 70S or 7018 filler metal, this value will average around 0.2833 pounds per cubic inch. The density of the various stainless and alloy filler metals is slightly different but is close enough to this value also for the purpose of estimating filler metal.

$$W_{th} + \tfrac{1}{4} = H$$
$$2 \times 0.76733 \times H = B$$
$$\tfrac{1}{2} BHC_c = in^3$$
$$in^3 \times D = pounds\ of\ rods$$

Where:
W_{th} = wall thickness
$\tfrac{1}{4}$ = allowance for gap, root and cap
H = height
0.76733 = tangent of 37.5°
B = base
C_c = circumference of pipe @ center of wall = OD minus single wall thickness x 3.14159 = ID plus single wall thickness x 3.14159
D = density of the filler metal being used

The above formula can be reduced to:

$$0.217385 \times C_c H^2 = pounds\ of\ rods$$

If you'll notice from the two images at the top of the previous page, the left hand image has all of the excess 1/4" above the pipe wall whereby the bottom of the bevels are touching. The right hand image shows the same volume of filler metal being centered in between the two pipes to be welded which leaves a 1/8" excess for the root and cap. In doing so, this establishes about a 3/16" gap factor per the trig involved as seen with 1/8 x 0.76733 x 2= 3/16. Thus, this formula estimates a 1/8" root and cap height fit at a 3/16" gap as is common practice for tig welds.

Simply knowing an estimated quantity and description of total welds should allow a close approximation of how many total pounds of filler metal will be required. The following page contains a chart which estimates these values for many common sizes of pipe. Knowing the average weld deposition rate for a welder allows further estimation of manhours involved per complete welded joint.

- AN AVERAGE WELD DEPOSITION RATE FOR AN SMAW OR GTAW WELDER IS 2 TO 3 POUNDS OF FILLER METAL PER HOUR AND 8-10 LBS./HR. FOR GMAW (MIG).
- A 50LB. BOX OF SMAW (STICK) RODS WILL YEILD APPROXIMATELY 30LBS. OF DEPOSITED FILLER METAL.
- OTHER WASTE RATIO CONSIDERATIONS ALSO APPLY WHEN CALCULATING AN APPROXIMATE QUANTITY OF RODS.

ESTIMATED POUNDS OF CARBON STEEL FILLER METAL TO MAKE A COMPLETE BUTT WELD FROM ROOT TO CAP			
PIPE SIZE	ROD QUANTITY IN POUNDS		
	SCH40	SCH80	SCH160
2	.248 †	.323 ‡	.489
3	.487 †	.661 ‡	.990
4	.690 †	.979 ‡	1.653
6	1.217 †	1.967 ‡	3.786
8	1.855 †	3.121 ‡	7.044
10	2.682 †	4.941	12.428
12	3.627	7.247	19.056
14	4.384	9.049	29.974
16	5.953	12.296	33.455
18	7.851	16.500	45.642
20	9.441	21.223	60.692
24	14.000	33.619	99.487
PIPE SIZE	ROD QUANTITY IN POUNDS		
	STD	XS	
26	6.835	9.795	
28	7.369	10.563	
30	7.903	11.332	
32	8.436	12.100	
34	8.970	12.868	
36	9.503	13.636	
42	11.104	15.942	
48	12.705	18.247	

†INDICATES VALUES THAT APPLY TO STD WALL THICKNESS ALSO.
‡INDICATES VALUES THAT APPLY TO XS WALL THICKNESS ALSO.
FIT UP IS FIGURED WITH A 37.5° STANDARD BEVEL WITH A 3/16" GAP AND A 1/8" TALL ROOT AND CAP PAST FLUSH.

CARBON STEEL TIG WIRE ESTIMATED WEIGHTS			
WIRE DIA.	POUNDS PER 36" ROD	No. of rods per pound	No. of rods per 10 lbs.
3/32"	.070	14.28	142.85
1/8"	.125	8.00	80.00
5/32"	.196	5.10	51.02

ESTIMATED POUNDS OF CARBON STEEL FILLER METAL FOR SOCKET WELD PIPE FITTINGS		
PIPE SIZE	POUNDS PER WELD	WELDS PER POUND
1/2	0.024	40.83
3/4	0.041	24.33
1	0.066	15.10
1-1/4	0.081	12.31
1-1/2	0.117	8.53
2	0.218	4.56

Estimates were made per the minimal leg length of the full fillet weld required as calculated per the sch.160 wall thickness pipe for the nominal pipe size listed.

ESTIMATED POUNDS OF CARBON STEEL FILLER METAL FOR FILLET WELDS		
FILLET WELD SIZE	POUNDS PER LINEAR FOOT	LINEAR FEET PER POUND
1/8	0.026	37.65
1/4	0.106	9.41
3/8	0.239	4.18
1/2	0.424	2.35
5/8	0.663	1.50
3/4	0.956	1.04
7/8	1.301	0.76
1	1.699	0.58

AWS MAXIMUM ATMOSPHERIC EXPOSURE TIMES FOR LOW HYDROGEN COVERED ELECTRODES	
ELETRODE CLASSIFICATION	MAXIMUM TIME IN HOURS
E70XX	4
E80XX	2
E90XX	1
E1XXXX	0.5

Longer times are permissible when appropriate tests show that the moisture content of the electrodes will not exceed specification limits under job-site conditions.

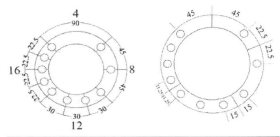

DEGREES BETWEEN FLANGE BOLT HOLES

No. of Holes	Hole to Hole	2 Hole Center to Hole	No. of Holes	Hole to Hole	2 Hole Center to Hole
4	90°	45°	36	10°	5°
8	45°	22.5°	40	9°	4.5°
12	30°	15°	44	8.182°	4.091°
16	22.5°	11.25°	48	7.5°	3.75°
20	18°	9°	52	6.923°	3.462°
24	15°	7.5°	56	6.429°	3.214°
28	12.857°	6.429°	60	6°	3°
32	11.25°	5.625°	64	5.625°	2.813°

The 'Hole to Hole' value is equivalent to the change in degree accomplished by rotating a flange one bolt hole as with the change in degree of a valve stem by way of rotating a bolt in valve one bolt hole. The '2 Hole Center to Hole' value is equivalent to half the 'Hole to Hole' value which is equivalent to the change in degree accomplished by rotating a fitting to be welded to a flange from a two hole fit to a one hole fit or vice versa.

CHAPTER 13: MATERIAL GRADES

TIPS: In this section we'll take a look at the ASTM classification of some common materials along with their material composition and how that plays into the ASME codes on the specifications of these materials. Here you'll find many of the common material markings which you often encounter when trying to identify pipe and its associated fittings such as forged flanges, wrought 90°s and tees, etc., along with casting material information associated with valves. This section also contains the material composition and information on many common stud bolts and nuts.

• The proper material composition and grade is crucial to the quality and safety of a refinery or plant. Different materials have a different tensile strength, yield strength and such at various temperature ranges thus establishing the appropriate material for a specific service per its design temperature and pressure with further considerations being made towards the medium within the service and the effects upon its reactivity with the associated piping, bolting, valves, etc., as with the use of spiral wound Monel gaskets in Alky units due to its high resistance to HF acid. It's not the job of the craftsman to determine the appropriate material composition and grade of the various components of a process system, but it is the job of the craftsman in conjunction with the QC and inspections department to assure that the composition and grade of materials determined by the engineering department is adhered to. Failure to do so can result in catastrophic problems with the safe operation of a process unit. Much effort has been made on behalf of such organizations as ASME, ANSI, ASTM, etc., to standardize many of the aspects which must be considered to address such issues and is the purpose of the various codes such as those referenced within this book, which go further into establishing the various site specific piping specs and such which govern the correct application of the various materials on the market to the various services and conditions within a refinery, chemical plant, power plant, paper mill, etc. Material composition is also important in determining the correct filler metal used during the welding process along with the applicable welding procedure with its considerations towards preheat, PWHT, etc., whereby assuring the continued integrity of the joint to be welded.

ASME B16.5 TABLE 1A: List of Material Specifications

Mat. Group	Nominal Designation	Press. Temp. Table	Applicable ASTM Specifications		
			Forgings	Castings	Plates
1.1	C-Si C-Mn-Si C-Mn-Si-V 3-1/2 Ni	2-1.1	A105 A350 Gr. LF2 A350 Gr. LF6 Cl.1 A350 Gr. LF3	A216 Gr. WCB	A515 Gr. 70 A516 Gr. 70 A537 Cl. 1
1.2	C-Mn-Si C-Mn-Si-V 2-1/2 Ni 3-1/2 Ni	2-1.2	A350 Gr. LF6 Cl.2	A216 Gr. WCC A352 Gr. LCC A352 Gr. LC2 A352 Gr. LC3	A203 Gr. B A203 Gr. E
1.3	C-Si C-Mn-Si 2-1/2 Ni 3-1/2 Ni C-1/2 Mo	2-1.3		A352 Gr. LCB A217 Gr. WC1 A352 Gr. LC1	A515 Gr. 65 A516 Gr. 65 A203 Gr. A A203 Gr. D
1.4	C-Si C-Mn-Si	2-1.4	A350 Gr. LF1 Cl.1		A515 Gr. 60 A516 Gr. 60
1.5	C-1/2 Mo	2-1.5	A182 Gr. F1		A204 Gr. A A204 Gr. B
1.7	1/2 Cr-1/2 Mo Ni-1/2 Cr-1/2 Mo 3/4 Ni-3/4 Cr-1 Mo	2-1.7	A182 Gr. F2	A217 Gr. WC4 A217 Gr. WC5	
1.9	1-1/4 Cr-1/2 Mo 1-1/4 Cr-1/2 Mo-Si	2-1.9	A182 Gr. F11 Cl.2	A217 Gr. WC6	A387 Gr. 11 Cl.2
1.10	2-1/4 Cr-1 Mo	2-1.10	A182 Gr. F22 Cl.3	A217 Gr. WC9	A387 Gr. 22 Cl.2
1.11	C-1/2 Mo	2-1.11			A204 Gr. C
1.13	5 Cr-1/2 Mo	2-1.13	A182 Gr. F5a	A217 Gr. C5	
1.14	9 Cr-1 Mo	2-1.14	A182 Gr. F9	A217 Gr. C12	
1.15	9 Cr-1 Mo-V	2-1.15	A182 Gr. F91	A217 Gr. C12A	A387 Gr. 91 Cl.2
1.17	1 Cr-1/2 Mo 5 Cr-1/2 Mo	2-1.17	A182 Gr. F12 Cl.2 A182 Gr. F5		
2.1	18 Cr-8 Ni	2-2.1	A182 Gr. F304 A182 Gr. F304H	A351 Gr. CF3 A351 Gr. CF8	A240 Gr. 304 A240 Gr. 304H
2.2	16 Cr-12 Ni-2 Mo 18 Cr-13 Ni-3 Mo 19 Cr-10 Ni-3 Mo	2-2.2	A182 Gr. F316 A182 Gr. F316H A182 Gr. F317	A351 Gr. CF3M A351 Gr. CF8M A351 Gr. CG8M	A240 Gr. 316 A240 Gr. 316H A240 Gr. 317

ASME B16.5 TABLE 1A: List of Material Specifications

Mat. Group	Nominal Designation	Press. Temp. Table	Applicable ASTM Specifications		
			Forgings	Castings	Plates
2.3	18 Cr-8 Ni 16 Cr-12 Ni-2 Mo	2-2.3	A182 Gr. F304L A182 Gr. F316L		A240 Gr. 304L A240 Gr. 316L
2.4	18 Cr-10 Ni-Ti	2-2.4	A182 Gr. F321 A182 Gr. F321H		A240 Gr. 321 A240 Gr. 321H
2.5	18 Cr-10 Ni-Cb	2-2.5	A182 Gr. F347 A182 Gr. F347H A182 Gr. F348 A182 Gr. F348H		A240 Gr. 347 A240 Gr. 347H A240 Gr. 348 A240 Gr. 348H
2.6	23 Cr-12 Ni	2-2.6			A240 Gr. 309H
2.7	24 Cr-20 Ni	2-2.7	A182 Gr. F310		A240 Gr. 310H
2.8	20 Cr-18 Ni-6 Mo 22 Cr-5 Ni-3 Mo-N 25 Cr-7 Ni-4 Mo-N 24 Cr-10 Ni-4 Mo-V 25 Cr-5Ni-2Mo-3 Cu 25 Cr-7Ni-3.5Mo-W-Cb 25 Cr-7Ni-3.5Mo-N-Cu-W	2-2.8	A182 Gr. F44 A182 Gr. F51 A182 Gr. F53 A182 Gr. F55	A351 Gr. CK3MCuN A351 Gr. CE8MN A351 Gr. CD4MCu A351Gr.CD3MWCuN	A240 Gr. S31254 A240 Gr. S31803 A240 Gr. S32750 A240 Gr. S32760
2.9	23 Cr-12 Ni 25 Cr-20 Ni	2-2.9			A240 Gr. 309S A240 Gr. 310S
2.10	25 Cr-12 Ni	2-2.10		A351 Gr. CH8 A351 Gr. CH20	
2.11	18 Cr-10 Ni-Cb	2-2.11		A351 Gr. CF8C	
2.12	25 Cr-20 Ni	2-2.12		A351 Gr. CK20	

ASTM SPECIFICATION INDEX

Spec. No.	TITLE
A 36	Structural Steel
A 47	Ferritic Malleable Iron Castings
A 48	Gray Iron Castings
A 53	Pipe, Steel, Black and Hot-Dipped, Zinc Coated, Welded and Seamless
A 105	Forgings, Carbon Steel, for Piping Components
A 106	Seamless Carbon Steel Pipe for High-Temperature Service
A 126	Gray Cast Iron Castings for Valves, Flanges, and Pipe Fittings
A 134	Pipe, Steel, Electric-Fusion (Arc)-Welded (Sizes NPS 16 and Over)
A 135	Electric-Resistance-Welded Steel Pipe
A 139	Electric-Fusion (Arc)-Welded Steel Pipe (NPS 4 and Over)
A 167	Stainless and Heat-Resisting Chromium-Nickel Steel Plate, Sheet and Strip
A 179	Seamless Cold-Drawn Low-Carbon Steel Heat-Exchanger and Condenser Tubes
A 181	Forgings, Carbon Steel For General Purpose Piping
A 182	Forged or Rolled Alloy-Steel Pipe Flanges, Forged Fittings, and Valves and Parts for High-Temperature Service
A 197	Cupola Malleable Iron
A 202	Pressure Vessel Plates, Alloy Steel, Chromium-Manganese-Silicon
A 203	Pressure Vessel Plates, Alloy Steel, Nickel
A 204	Pressure Vessel Plates, Alloy Steel, Molybdenum
A 216	Steel Castings, Carbon, Suitable for Fusion Welding for High-Temperature Service
A 217	Steel Castings, Martensitic Stainless and Alloy, for Pressure-Containing Parts Suitable for High-Temperature Service
A 234	Piping Fittings of Wrought Carbon Steel and Alloy Steel for Moderate and Elevated Temperatures
A 240	Heat-Resisting Chromium and Chromium-Nickel Stainless Steel Plate, Sheet and Strip for Pressure Vessels
A 268	Seamless and Welded Ferritic Stainless Steel Tubing for General Service
A 269	Seamless and Welded Austenitic Stainless Steel Tubing for General Service
A 278	Gray Iron Castings for Pressure-Containing Parts for Temperatures Up to 650°F
A 283	Low and Intermediate Tensile Strength Carbon Steel Plates, Shapes and Bars
A 285	Pressure Vessel Plates, Carbon Steel, Low- and Intermediate-Tensile Strength
A 299	Pressure Vessel Plates, Carbon Steel, Manganese-Silicon
A 302	Pressure Vessel Plates, Alloy Steel, Manganese-Molybdenum and Manganese-Molybdenum-Nickel
A 312	Seamless and Welded Austenitic Stainless Steel Pipe

ASTM SPECIFICATION INDEX

Spec. No.	TITLE
A 333	Seamless and Welded Steel Pipe for Low-Temperature Service
A 334	Seamless and Welded Carbon and Alloy-Steel Tubes for Low-Temperature Service
A 335	Seamless Ferritic Alloy Steel Pipe for High-Temperature Service
A 350	Forgings, Carbon and Low-Alloy Steel Requiring Notch Toughness Testing for Piping Components
A 351	Steel Castings, Austenitic, Austenitic-Ferritic (Duplex) for Pressure-Containing Parts
A 352	Steel Castings, Ferritic and Martensitic, for Pressure-Containing Parts Suitable for Low-Temperature Service
A 353	Pressure Vessel Plates, Alloy Steel, 9 Percent Nickel, Double Normalized and Tempered
A 358	Electric-Fusion-Welded Austenitic Chromium-Nickel Alloy Steel Pipe for High-Temperature Service
A 369	Carbon Steel and Ferritic Alloy Steel Forged and Bored Pipe for High-Temperature Service
A 376	Seamless Austenitic Steel Pipe for High-Temperature Central-Station Service
A 381	Metal-Arc-Welded Steel Pipe for Use with High-Pressure Transmission Systems
A 387	Pressure Vessel Plates, Alloy Steel, Chromium-Molybdenum
A 395	Ferritic Ductile Iron Pressure-Retaining Castings for Use at Elevated Temperatures
A 403	Wrought Austenitic Stainless Steel Piping Fittings
A 409	Welded Large Diameter Austenitic Steel Pipe for Corrosive or High-Temperature Service
A 420	Piping Fittings of Wrought Carbon Steel and Alloy Steel for Low-Temperature Service
A 426	Centrifugally Cast Ferritic Alloy Steel Pipe for High-Temperature Service
A 451	Centrifugally Cast Austenitic Steel Pipe for High-Temperature Service
A 479	Stainless and Heat-Resisting Steel Bars and Shapes for Use in Boilers and Other Pressure Vessels
A 487	Steel Castings Suitable for Pressure Service
A 494	Castings, Nickel and Nickel Alloy
A 515	Pressure Vessel Plates, Carbon Steel, for Intermediate- and Higher-Temperature Service
A 516	Pressure Vessel Plates, Carbon Steel, for Moderate and Lower-Temperature Service
A 524	Seamless Carbon Steel Pipe for Atmospheric and Lower Temperatures
A 537	Pressure Vessel Plates, Heat-Treated, Carbon-Manganese-Silicon Steel

ASTM SPECIFICATION INDEX	
Spec. No.	TITLE
A 553	Pressure Vessel Plates, Alloy Steel, Quenched and Tempered 8 and 9 Percent Nickel
A 570	Hot-Rolled Carbon Steel Sheet and Strip, Structural Quality
A 571	Austenitic Ductile Iron Castings for Pressure-Containing Parts Suitable for Low-Temperature Service
A 587	Electric-Welded Low-Carbon Steel Pipe for the Chemical Industry
A 645	Pressure Vessel Plates, 5 Percent Nickel Alloy Steel, Specially Heat Treated
A 671	Electric-Fusion-Welded Steel Pipe for Atmospheric and Lower Temperatures
A 672	Electric-Fusion-Welded Steel Pipe for High-Pressure Service at Moderate Temperatures
A 691	Carbon and Alloy Steel Pipe, Electric Fusion-Welded for High-Pressure Service at High Temperatures
A 789	Seamless and Welded Ferritic/Austenitic Stainless Steel Tubing for General Service
A 790	Seamless and Welded Ferritic/Austenitic Stainless Steel Pipe
A 815	Wrought Ferritic, Ferritic/Austenitic and Martensitic Stainless Steel Fittings

The ASTM Specification Index can be used in conjunction with the ASTM Material Reference on the following pages to properly identify the ASTM material markings and classifications of the various components it addresses i.e. pipes, tubes, castings such as valve bodies along with forgings and fittings such as flanges, 90° fittings, etc. Referencing the spec. no. from the reference guide to the specification index will give a description of the component under the title column. Often times you will see a spec. no. and grade in the material column of the reference guide concerning another spec. no. and grade as with many pipes and tubes. This is generally understood if the spec. no. in question is a welded seem pipe or tube whereby the accompanying spec. no. and grade in the materials column is referencing the plate spec. from which the pipe or tube was made. Therefore, if you were to look in the 'Plates and Sheets' section of the ASTM Material Reference, you should find that particular spec. no. and grade whereby identifying the plate which was rolled and welded down its seem to form a section of pipe. Seamless pipe is as suggested, whereby it isn't formed in this manner and doesn't have a welded seam.

ASTM MATERIAL REFERENCE PER ASME B31.3			
MATERIAL	SPEC.	GRADE	P/S-No.
CARBON STEEL PIPES AND TUBES			
A 285 Gr. A	A 134	...	1
A 285 Gr. A	A 672	A45	1
Butt weld	API 5L	A25	S-1
Smls & ERW	API 5L	A25	S-1
...	A 179	...	1
Type F	A 53	Gr. A	1
...	A 139	A	S-1
...	A 587	...	1
...	A 53	A	1
...	A 106	A	1
...	A 135	A	1
...	A 369	FPA	1
...	API 5L	A	S-1
A 285 Gr. B	A 134	...	1
A 285 Gr. B	A 672	A50	1
A 285 Gr. C	A 134	...	1
...	A 524	Gr. II	1
...	A 333	1	1
...	A 334	1	1
A 285 Gr. C	A 671	CA55	1
A 285 Gr. C	A 672	A55	1
A 516 Gr. 55	A 672	C55	1
A 516 Gr. 60	A 671	CC60	1
A 515 Gr. 60	A 671	CB60	1
A 515 Gr. 60	A 672	B60	1
A 516 Gr. 60	A672	C60	1
...	A139	B	S-1
...	A 135	B	1
...	A 524	Gr. 1	1
...	A 53	B	1
...	A 106	B	1
...	A 333	6	1
...	A 334	6	1
...	A 369	FPB	1
...	A 381	Y35	S-1
...	API 5L	B	S-1

ASTM MATERIAL REFERENCE PER ASME B31.3			
MATERIAL	SPEC..	GRADE	P/S-No.
CARBON STEEL PIPES AND TUBES continued			
...	A 139	C	S-1
...	A 139	D	S-1
...	API 5L	X42	S-1
...	A 381	Y42	S-1
...	A 381	Y48	S-1
...	API 5L	X46	S-1
...	A 381	Y46	S-1
...	A 381	Y50	S-1
A 516 Gr. 65	A 671	CC65	1
A 515 Gr. 65	A 671	CB65	1
A 515 Gr. 65	A 672	B65	1
A 516 Gr. 65	A 672	C65	1
...	A 139	E	S-1
...	API 5L	X52	S-1
...	A 381	Y52	S-1
A 516 Gr. 70	A 671	CC70	1
A 515 Gr. 70	A 671	CB70	1
A 515 Gr. 70	A 672	B70	1
A 516 Gr. 70	A 672	C70	1
...	A 106	C	1
A 537 Cl. 1 ($\leq$ 2-1/2 in. thick)	A 671	CD70	1
A 537 Cl. 1 ($\leq$ 2-1/2 in. thick)	A 672	D70	1
A 537 Cl. 1 ($\leq$ 2-1/2 in. thick)	A 691	CMSH70	1
	API5L	X56	S-1
...	A 381	Y56	S-1
A 299 (> 1 in. thick)	A 671	CK75	1
A 299 (> 1 in. thick)	A 672	N75	1
A 299 (> 1 in. thick)	A 691	CMS75	1
A 299 ($\leq$ 1 in. thick)	A 671	CK75	1
A 299 ($\leq$ 1 in. thick)	A 672	N75	1
A 299 ($\leq$ 1 in. thick)	A 691	CMS75	1
...	API 5L	X60	S-1
...	API 5L	X65	S-1
...	API 5L	X70	S-1
...	API 5L	X80	S-1
...	A 381	Y60	S-1

ASTM MATERIAL REFERENCE PER ASME B31.3			
MATERIAL	SPEC.	GRADE	P/S-No.
CARBON STEEL STRUCTURAL GRADE PIPES			
A 283 Gr. A	A 134	...	1
A 570 Gr. 30	A 134	...	S-1
A 283 Gr. B	A 134	...	1
A 570 Gr. 33	A 134	...	S-1
A 570 Gr. 36	A 134	...	S-1
A 570 Gr. 40	A 134	...	1
A 36	A 134	...	1
A 283 Gr. D	A 134	...	1
A 570 Gr. 45	A 134	...	S-1
A 570 Gr. 50	A 134	...	1
CARBON STEEL PLATES AND SHEETS			
...	A 285	A	1
...	A 285	B	1
...	A 516	55	1
...	A 285	C	1
...	A 516	60	1
...	A 515	60	1
...	A 516	65	1
...	A 515	65	1
...	A 516	70	1
...	A 515	70	1
($\leq$ 2-1/2 in. thick)	A 537	Cl.1	1
(>1 in. thick)	A 299	...	1
($\leq$ 1 in. thick)	A 299	...	1
...	A 283	A	1
...	A 570	30	S-1
...	A 283	B	1
...	A 570	33	S-1
...	A 570	36	S-1
...	A 283	C	1
...	A 570	40	S-1
...	A 36	...	1
...	A 283	D	1
...	A 570	45	S-1
	A 570	50	S-1

ASTM MATERIAL REFERENCE PER ASME B31.3			
MATERIAL	SPEC.	GRADE	P/S-No.
CARBON STEEL FORGINGS AND FITTINGS			
...	A 350	LF-1	1
...	A 181	Cl. 60	1
...	A 420	WPL-6	1
...	A 234	WPB	1
...	A 350	LF-2	1
...	A 105	...	1
...	A 181	Cl.70	1
...	A 234	WPC	1
CARBON STEEL CASTINGS			
...	A 216	WCA	1
...	A 352	LCB	1
...	A 216	WCB	1
...	A 216	WCC	1
LOW AND INTERMEDIATE ALLOY STEEL PIPES			
1/2 Cr- 1/2 Mo	A 335	P2	3
1/2 Cr- 1/2 Mo A 387 Gr. 2 Cl. 1	A 691	1/2 Cr	3
C- 1/2 Mo	A 335	P1	3
C- 1/2 Mo	A 369	FP1	3
1/2 Cr- 1/2 Mo	A 369	FP2	3
1 Cr- 1/2 Mo A 387 Gr.12 Cl. 1	A 691	1Cr	4
1/2 Cr- 1/2 Mo	A 426	CP2	3
1-1/2 Si- 1/2 Mo	A 335	P15	3
1-1/2 Si- 1/2 Mo	A 426	CP15	3
1 Cr- 1/2 Mo	A 426	CP12	4
5 Cr- 1/2 Mo- 1-1/2 Si	A 426	CP5b	5B
3Cr- Mo	A 426	CP21	5A
3/4 Cr- 3/4 Ni-Cu-Al	A 333	4	4
2 Cr- 1/2 Mo	A 369	FP3b	4
1 Cr- 1/2 Mo	A 335	P12	4
1 Cr- 1/2 Mo	A 369	FP12	4
1-1/4 Cr- 1/2 Mo	A 335	P11	4
1-1/4 Cr- 1/2 Mo	A 369	FP11	4
1-1/4 Cr- 1/2 Mo A387 Gr. 11 Cl.1	A 691	1-1/4 Cr	4
5 Cr- 1/2 Mo A387 Gr. 5 Cl.1	A 691	5Cr	5B
5 Cr- 1/2 Mo	A 335	P5	5B
5 Cr- 1/2 Mo-Si	A 335	P5b	5B
5 Cr- 1/2 Mo-Ti	A 335	P5c	5B
5 Cr- 1/2 Mo	A 369	FP5	5B

ASTM MATERIAL REFERENCE PER ASME B31.3			
MATERIAL	SPEC.	GRADE	P/S-No.
LOW AND INTERMEDIATE ALLOY STEEL PIPES continued			
9 Cr- 1 Mo	A 335	P9	5B
9 Cr- 1 Mo	A 369	FP9	5B
9 Cr- 1 Mo A387 Gr. 9 Cl.1	A 691	9Cr	5B
3 Cr- 1 Mo	A 335	P21	5A
3 Cr- 1 Mo	A 369	FP21	5A
3 Cr- 1 Mo A387 Gr. 21 Cl.1	A 691	3Cr	5A
2-1/4 Cr- 1 Mo A387 Gr. 22 Cl.1	A 691	2-1/4Cr	5A
2-1/4 Cr- 1 Mo	A 369	FP22	5A
2-1/4 Cr- 1 Mo	A 335	P22	5A
2 Ni- 1 Cu	A 333	9	9A
2 Ni- 1 Cu	A 334	9	9A
2-1/4 Ni	A 333	7	9A
2-1/4 Ni	A 334	7	9A
3-1/2 Ni	A 333	3	9B
3-1/2 Ni	A 334	3	9B
C- 1/2 Mo	A 426	CP1	3
C- Mo A204 Gr. A	A 672	L65	3
C-Mo A204 Gr. A	A 691	CM65	3
2-1/4 Ni A203 Gr. B	A 671	CF70	9A
3-1/2 Ni A203 Gr. E	A 671	CF71	9B
C-Mo A204 Gr. B	A 672	L70	3
C-Mo A204 Gr. B	A 691	CM70	3
1-1/4 Cr- 1/2 Mo	A 426	CP11	4
2-1/4 Cr- 1 Mo	A 426	CP22	5A
C- Mo A204 Gr. C	A 672	L75	3
C- Mo A204 Gr. C	A 691	CM75	3
9 Cr- 1 Mo-V ≤ 3 in. thick	A 335	P91	5B
9 Cr- 1 Mo-V ≤ 3 in. thick	A 691	P91	5B
5 Cr- 1/2 Mo	A 426	CP5	5B
9 Cr- 1 Mo	A 426	CP9	5B
9 Ni	A 333	8	11A
9 Ni	A 334	8	11A
LOW AND INTERMEDIATE ALLOY STEEL PLATES			
1/2 Cr- 1/2 Mo	A 387	Gr. 2 Cl.1	3
1 Cr- 1/2 Mo	A 387	Gr. 12 Cl.1	4
9 Cr- 1 Mo	A 387	Gr. 9 Cl.1	5

ASTM MATERIAL REFERENCE PER ASME B31.3

MATERIAL	SPEC.	GRADE	P/S-No.
LOW AND INTERMEDIATE ALLOY STEEL PLATES continued			
1-1/4 Cr- 1/2 Mo	A 387	Gr. 11 Cl.1	4
5 Cr- 1/2 Mo	A 387	Gr. 5 Cl.1	5B
3 Cr- 1 Mo	A 387	Gr. 21 Cl.1	5A
2-1/4 Cr- 1 Mo	A 387	Gr. 22 Cl.1	5A
2-1/4 Ni	A 203	A	9A
3-1/2 Ni	A 203	D	9B
C- 1/2 Mo	A 204	A	3
1 Cr- 1/2 Mo	A 387	Gr. 12 Cl.2	4
2-1/4 Ni	A 203	B	9A
3-1/2 Ni	A 203	E	9B
1/2 Cr- 1/2 Mo	A 387	Gr. 2 Cl.2	3
C-1/2 Mo	A 204	B	3
Cr-n-Si	A 202	A	4
Mn-Mo	A 302	A	3
C- 1/2 Mo	A 204	C	3
1-1/4 Cr- 1/2 Mo	A 387	Gr. 11 Cl.2	4
5 Cr- 1/2 Mo	A 387	Gr. 5 Cl.2	5B
3 Cr- 1/2 Mo	A 387	Gr. 21 Cl.2	5A
2-1/4 Cr- 1 Mo	A 387	Gr. 22 Cl.2	5A
Mn-Mo	A 302	B	3
Mn-Mo-Ni	A 302	C	3
Mn-Mo-Ni	A 302	D	3
Cr-n-Si	A 202	B	4
9 Cr- 1 Mo-V ≤ 3 in. thick	A 387	91 Cl. 2	5B
8 Ni	A 553	Type II	11A
5 Ni	A 645	...	11A
9 Ni	A 553	Type I	11A
9 Ni	A 353	...	11A
LOW AND INTERMEDIATE ALLOY STEEL FORGINGS & FITTINGS			
C- 1/2 Mo	A 234	WP1	3
1 Cr- 1/2 Mo	A 182	F12 Cl.1	4
1 Cr- 1/2 Mo	A 234	WP12 Cl.1	4
1-1/4 Cr- 1/2 Mo	A 182	F11 Cl.1	4
1-1/4 Cr- 1/2 Mo	A 234	WP11b Cl.1	4
2-1/4 Cr- 1 Mo	A 182	F22 Cl.1	...
2-1/4 Cr- 1 Mo	A 234	WP22 Cl.1	5A
5 Cr- 1/2 Mo	A 234	WP5	5B

ASTM MATERIAL REFERENCE PER ASME B31.3			
MATERIAL	SPEC.	GRADE	P/S-No.
LOW AND INTERMEDIATE ALLOY STEEL FORGINGS & FITTINGS continued			
9 Cr- 1 Mo	A 234	WP9	5B
3-1/2 Ni	A 420	WPL3	9B
3-1/2 Ni	A 350	LF3	9B
1/2 Cr- 1/2 Mo	A 182	F2	3
C- 1/2 Mo	A 182	F1	3
1 Cr- 1/2 Mo	A 182	F12 Cl.2	4
1 Cr- 1/2 Mo	A 234	WP12 Cl.2	4
1-1/4 Cr- 1/2 Mo	A 182	F11 Cl.2	4
1-1/4 Cr- 1/2 Mo	A 234	WP11 Cl.2	4
5 Cr- 1/2 Mo	A 182	F5	5B
3 Cr- 1 Mo	A 182	F21	5A
2-1/4 Cr- 1 Mo	A 182	F22 Cl.3	5A
2-1/4 Cr- 1 Mo	A 234	WP22 Cl.3	5A
9 Cr- 1 Mo	A 182	F9	5B
9 Cr- 1 Mo-V ≤ 3 in. thick	A 182	F91	5B
9 Cr- 1 Mo-V ≤ 3 in. thick	A 234	WP91	5B
5 Cr- 1/2 Mo	A 182	F5a	5B
9 Ni	A 420	WPL8	11A
LOW AND INTERMEDIATE ALLOY STEEL CASTINGS			
C- 1/2 Mo	A 352	LC1	3
C- 1/2 Mo	A 217	WC1	3
2-1/2 Ni	A 352	LC2	9A
3-1/2 Ni	A 352	LC3	9B
Ni- Cr- 1/2 Mo	A 217	WC4	4
Ni- Cr- 1 Mo	A 217	WC5	4
1-1/4 Cr- 1/2 Mo	A 217	WC6	4
2-1/4 Cr- 1 Mo	A 217	WC9	5A
5 Cr- 1/2 Mo	A 217	C5	5B
9 Cr- 1 Mo	A 217	C12	5B
STAINLESS STEEL PIPES AND TUBES			
18 Cr- 10 Ni-Ti pipe smls > 3/8 in. thick	A 312	TP321	8
18 Cr- 10 Ni-Ti pipe > 3/8 in. thick	A 376	TP321	8
18 Cr- 8 Ni tube	A 269	TP304L	8
18 Cr- 8 Ni pipe	A 312	TP304L	8
Type 304L A 240	A 358	304L	8
16 Cr- 12 Ni- 2 Mo tube	A 269	TP316L	8
16 Cr- 12 Ni- 2 Mo pipe	A 312	TP316L	8

ASTM MATERIAL REFERENCE PER ASME B31.3			
MATERIAL	SPEC.	GRADE	P/S-No.
STAINLESS STEEL PIPES AND TUBES Continued			
Type 316L A 240	A 358	316L	8
18 Cr- 10 Ni-Ti pipe smls > 3/8 in. thick	A 312	TP321	8
18 Cr- 10 Ni-Ti pipe > 3/8 in. thick	A 376	TP321	8
18 Cr- 10 Ni-i pipe smls > 3/8 in. thick	A 312	TP321H	8
18 Cr- 10 Ni-Ti pipe > 3/8 in. thick	A 376	TP321H	8
23 Cr- 13 Ni	A 451	CPH8	8
25 Cr- 20 Ni	A 451	CPK20	8
11 Cr-Ti tube	A 268	TP409	7
18 Cr-i tube	A 268	TP430Ti	7
15 Cr- 13 Ni- 2 Mo-Cb	A 451	CPF10MC	S-8
16 Cr- 8 Ni- 2 Mo pipe	A 376	16-8-2H	8
12 Cr-Al tube	A 268	TP405	7
13 Cr tube	A 268	TP410	6
16 Cr tube	A 268	TP430	7
18 Cr- 13 Ni- 3 Mo pipe	A 312	TP317L	8
25 Cr- 20 Ni pipe	A 312	TP310	8
Type 310S A 240	A 358	310S	8
25 Cr- 20 Ni pipe	A 409	TP310	8
18Cr-10Ni-Ti pipe smls ≤ 3/8 in. thk & wld	A 312	TP321	8
18 Cr- 10 Ni-Ti pipe	A 358	321	8
18 Cr- 10 Ni-Ti pipe ≤ 3/8 in. thick	A 376	TP321	8
18 Cr- 10 Ni-Ti pipe	A 409	TP321	8
23 Cr- 12 Ni pipe	A 312	TP309	8
Type 309S A 240	A 358	309S	8
23 Cr- 12 Ni pipe	A 409	TP309	8
18 Cr- 8 Ni	A 451	CPF8	8
18 Cr- 10 Ni-Cb pipe	A 312	TP347	8
Type 347 A 240	A 358	347	8
18 Cr- 10 Ni-Cb pipe	A 376	TP347	8
18 Cr- 10 Ni-Cb pipe	A 409	TP347	8
18 Cr- 10 Ni-Cb pipe	A 312	TP348	8
Type 348 A 240	A 358	348	8
18 Cr- 10 Ni-b pipe	A 376	TP348	8
18 Cr- 10 Ni-Cb pipe	A 409	TP348	8
23 Cr- 13 Ni	A 451	CPH10 or CPH20	8
25 Cr- 20 Ni pipe	A 312	TP310	8

ASTM MATERIAL REFERENCE PER ASME B31.3			
MATERIAL	SPEC.	GRADE	P/S-No.
STAINLESS STEEL PIPES AND TUBES Continued			
Type 310S A 240	A 358	310S	8
18 Cr- 10 Ni-Cb	A 451	CPF8C	8
18 Cr- 10 Ni-Ti pipe smls ≤ 3/8 in. thk; wld	A 312	TP321	8
Type 321 A 240	A 358	321	8
18 Cr- 10 Ni-Ti pipe ≤ 3/8 in. thick	A 376	TP321	8
18 Cr- 10 Ni-Ti pipe	A 409	TP321	8
18 Cr- 10 Ni-Ti pipe ≤ 3/8 in. thick	A 376	TP321H	8
18 Cr- 10 Ni-Ti pipe smls ≤ 3/8 in. thk; wld	A 312	TP321H	8
16 Cr- 12 Ni-Mo tube	A 269	TP316	8
16 Cr- 12 Ni- 2 Mo pipe	A 312	TP316	8
Type 316 A 240	A 358	316	8
16 Cr- 12 Ni- 2 Mo pipe	A 376	TP316	8
16 Cr- 12 Ni- 2 Mo pipe	A 409	TP316	8
18 Cr - 3 Ni- 3 Mo pipe	A 312	TP317	8
18 Cr- 3 Ni- 3 Mo pipe	A 409	TP317	8
16 Cr- 12 Ni- 2 Mo pipe	A 376	TP316H	8
16 Cr- 12 Ni- 2 Mo pipe	A 312	TP316H	8
18 Cr- 10 Ni-Cb pipe	A 376	TP347H	8
18 Cr- 10 Ni-Cb pipe	A 312	TP347	8
Type 347 A 240	A 358	347	8
18 Cr- 10 Ni-Cb pipe	A 376	TP347	8
18 Cr- 10 Ni-b pipe	A 409	TP347	8
18 Cr- 10 Ni-b pipe	A 312	TP348	8
Type 348 A 240	A 358	348	8
18 Cr- 10 Ni-Cb pipe	A 376	TP348	8
18 Cr- 10 Ni-Cb pipe	A 409	TP348	8
18 Cr- 10 Ni-Cb pipe	A 312	TP347H	8
18 Cr- 10 Ni-Cb pipe	A 312	TP348H	8
18 Cr- 8 Ni tube	A 269	TP304	8
18 Cr- 8 Ni pipe	A 312	TP304	8
Type 304 A 240	A 358	304	8
18 Cr- 8 Ni pipe	A 376	TP304	8
18 Cr- 8 Ni pipe	A 376	TP304H	8
18 Cr- 8 Ni pipe	A 409	TP304	8
18 Cr- 8 Ni pipe	A 312	TP304H	8
18 Cr- 10 Ni-Mo	A 451	CPF8M	8

ASTM MATERIAL REFERENCE PER ASME B31.3			
MATERIAL	SPEC.	GRADE	P/S-No.
STAINLESS STEEL PIPES AND TUBES Continued			
20 Cr-Cu tube	A 268	TP443	10
27 Cr tube	A 268	TP446	10I
25 Cr- 10 Ni-N	A 451	CPE20N	8
23 Cr- 4 Ni-N	A 789	S32304	10H
23 Cr- 4 Ni-N	A 790	S32304	10H
12-3/4 Cr	A 426	CPCA-15	6
22 Cr- 5 Ni- 3 Mo	A 789	S31803	10H
22 Cr- 5 Ni- 3 Mo	A 790	S31803	10H
26 Cr- 4 Ni- Mo	A 789	S32900	10H
26 Cr- 4 Ni- Mo	A 790	S32900	10H
25 Cr- 8 Ni- 3 Mo-W-Cu-N	A 789	S32760	S-10H
25 Cr- 8 Ni- 3 Mo-W-Cu-N	A 790	S32760	S-10H
25 Cr- 7 Ni- 4 Mo-N	A 789	S32750	10H
25 Cr- 7 Ni- 4 Mo-N	A 790	S32750	10H
24 Cr- 17 Ni- 6 Mn- 4-1/2 Mo- 1/2 N	A 358	S34565	S8
STAINLESS STEEL PLATES AND SHEETS			
18 Cr- 10 Ni	A 240	305	8
12 Cr-Al	A 240	405	7
18 Cr- 8 Ni	A 240	304L	8
16 Cr- 12 Ni- 2 Mo	A 240	316L	8
18 Cr- Ti- Al	A 240	X8M	...
18 Cr- 8 Ni	A 167	302B	S-8
18 Cr-Ni	A 240	302	8
13 Cr	A 240	410S	7
13 Cr	A 240	410	6
15 Cr	A 240	429	6
17 Cr	A 240	420	7
18 Cr- 13 Ni- 3 Mo	A 240	317L	8
25 Cr- 20 Ni	A 167	310	S-8
25 Cr- 20 Ni	A 240	310S	8
18 Cr- 10 Ni-Ti	A 240	321	8
20 Cr- 10 Ni	A 167	308	S-8
23 Cr- 12 Ni	A 167	309	S-8
23 Cr- 12 Ni	A 240	309S	8
18 Cr- 10 Ni-Cb	A 240	347	8
18 Cr- 10 Ni-Cb	A 240	348	8

ASTM MATERIAL REFERENCE PER ASME B31.3			
MATERIAL	SPEC.	GRADE	P/S-No.
STAINLESS STEEL PLATES AND SHEETS Continued			
25 Cr- 20 Ni	A 167	310	S-8
25 Cr- 20 Ni	A 240	310S	8
18 Cr- 10 Ni-Ti	A 240	321	8
18 Cr- 10 Ni-Ti	A 240	321H	8
16 Cr- 12 Ni- 2 Mo	A 240	316	8
18 Cr-13 Ni- 3 Mo	A 240	317	8
18 Cr- 10 Ni-Cb	A 167	347	8
18 Cr- 10 Ni-Cb	A 240	347	8
18 Cr- 10 Ni-Cb	A 167	348	8
18 Cr- 10 Ni-Cb	A 240	348	8
18 Cr- 8 Ni	A 240	304	8
25 Cr- 8 Ni- 3 Mo-W-Cu-N	A 240	S32760	S-10H
STAINLESS STEEL FORGINGS AND FITTINGS			
18 Cr- 13 Ni- 3 Mo ≤ 5 in. thk.	A 182	F317L	8
18 Cr- 8 Ni	A 182	F304L	8
18 Cr- 8 Ni	A 403	WP316L	8
16 Cr- 12 Ni- 2 Mo	A 182	F316L	8
16 Cr- 12 Ni- 2 Mo	A 403	WP316L	8
20 Ni- 8 Cr	A 182	F10	8
18 Cr- 13 Ni- 3 Mo	A 403	WP317L	8
25 Cr- 20 Ni	A 182	F310	8
25 Cr- 20 Ni	A 403	WP310	8
18 Cr- 10 Ni-Ti	A 182	F321	8
18 Cr- 10 Ni-Ti	A 403	WP321	8
23 Cr- 12 Ni	A 403	WP309	8
25 Cr- 20 Ni	A 182	F310	8
25 Cr- 20 Ni	A 403	WP310	8
18 Cr- 10 Ni-Cb	A 182	F347	8
18 Cr- 10 Ni-Cb	A 403	WP347	8
18 Cr- 10 Ni-Cb	A 182	F348	8
18 Cr- 10 Ni-Cb	A 403	WP348	8
18 Cr- 10 Ni-Ti	A 182	F321	8
18 Cr- 10 Ni-Ti	A 182	F321H	8
18 Cr- 10 Ni-Ti	A 403	WP321	8
18 Cr- 10 Ni-Ti	A 403	WP321H	8
16 Cr- 12 Ni- 2 Mo	A 403	WP316H	8

ASTM MATERIAL REFERENCE PER ASME B31.3			
MATERIAL	SPEC.	GRADE	P/S-No.
STAINLESS STEEL FORGINGS AND FITTINGS Continued			
16 Cr- 12 Ni- 2 Mo	A 182	F316	8
18 Cr- 10 Ni-Cb	A 403	WP347H	8
18 Cr- 10 Ni-Cb	A 182	F347	8
18 Cr- 10 Ni-Cb	A 403	WP347	8
18 Cr- 10 Ni-Cb	A 182	F348	8
18 Cr- 10 Ni-Cb	A 403	WP348	8
18 Cr- 10 Ni-Cb	A 182	F347H	8
18 Cr- 10 Ni-Cb	A 182	F348H	8
16 Cr- 12 Ni- 2 Mo	A 182	F316	8
16 Cr- 12 Ni- 2 Mo	A 403	WP316	8
18 Cr- 13 Ni- 3 Mo	A 403	WP317	8
18 Cr- 8 Ni	A 182	F304	8
18 Cr- 8 Ni	A 403	WP304	8
18 Cr- 8 Ni	A 403	WP304H	8
18 Cr- 8 Ni	A 182	F304H	8
13 Cr	A 182	F6a Cl. 1	6
13 Cr	A 182	F6a Cl. 2	6
25 Cr- 8 Ni-3 Mo-W-Cu-N	A 182	S32760	S-10H
25 Cr- 8 Ni-3 Mo-W-Cu-N	A 815	S32760	S-10H
13 Cr	A 182	F6a Cl.3	S-6
13 Cr- 1/2 Mo	A 182	F6b	
13 Cr	A 182	F6a Cl. 4	S-6
STAINLESS STEEL BAR			
18 Cr- 8 Ni	A 479	304	8
STAINLESS STEEL CASTINGS			
28 Ni- 20 Cr- 2 Mo- 3 Cb	A 351	CN7M	45
35 Ni- 15 Cr-Mo	A 351	HT30	S-45
25 Cr- 13 Ni	A 351	CH8	8
25 Cr- 20 Ni	A 351	CK20	8
15 Cr- 15 Ni- 2 Mo-Cb	A 351	CF10MC	S-8
18 Cr- 8 Ni	A 351	CF3	8
17 Cr- 10 Ni- 2 Mo	A 351	CF3M	8
18 Cr- 8 Ni	A 351	CF8	8
25 Cr- 13 Ni	A 351	CH10	S-8
25 Cr- 13 Ni	A 351	CH20	8
20 Cr- 10 Ni-Cb	A 351	CF8C	8

ASTM MATERIAL REFERENCE PER ASME B31.3			
MATERIAL	SPEC.	GRADE	P/S-No.
STAINLESS STEEL CASTINGS Continued			
18 Cr- 10 Ni- 2 Mo	A 351	CF8M	8
25 Cr- 20 Ni	A 351	HK40	S-8
25 Cr- 20 Ni	A 351	HK30	8
18 Cr- 8 Ni	A 351	CF3A	8
18 Cr- 8 Ni	A 351	CF8A	8
25 Cr- 10 Ni-N	A 351	CE20N	8
12 Cr	A 217	CA15	6
24 Cr- 10 Ni-Mo-N	A 351	CE8MN	10H
25 Cr- 8 Ni- 3 Mo-W-Cu-N	A 351	CD3M-W-Cu-N	S-20H
13 Cr- 4 Ni	A 487	CA6NM Cl.A	6

ASTM BOLTING MATERIALS PER ASME B31.3					
MATERIAL	SPEC. NO.	GRADE	SIZE DIA.In.	TENSILE ksi	YEILD ksi
CARBON STEEL STUDS AND NUTS					
...	A 675	45	...	45	22.5
...	A 675	50	...	50	25
...	A 675	55	...	55	27.5
...	A 307	B	...	60	...
...	A 675	60	...	60	30
...	A 675	65	...	65	32.5
...	A 675	70	...	70	35
...	A 325	...	...	105	81
...	A 675	80	...	80	40
Nuts	A 194	1	...	...	...
Nuts	A 194	2, 2H	...	...	...
...	A 194	2HM	...	...	...
Nuts	A 563	A, Hvy Hex	...	...	...
ALLOY STEEL STUDS AND NUTS					
Cr- 0.2 Mo	A 193	B7M	≤ 4	100	80
Cr- 0.2 Mo	A 320	L7M	$\leq 2\text{-}1/2$	100	80
5 Cr	A 193	B5	≤ 4	100	80
Cr-Mo-V	A 193	B16	$> 2\text{-}1/2, \leq 4$	110	95
...	A 354	BC	...	115	99
Cr-Mo	A 193	B7	$> 2\text{-}1/2, \leq 4$	115	95
Ni-Cr-Mo	A 320	L43	≤ 4	125	105
Cr-Mo	A 320	L7	$\leq 2\text{-}1/2$	125	105
Cr-Mo	A 320	L7A, L7B, L7C	$\leq 2\text{-}1/2$	125	105
Cr-Mo	A 193	B7	$\leq 2\text{-}1/2$	125	105
Cr-Mo-V	A 193	B16	$\leq 2\text{-}1/2$	125	105
...	A 354	BD	$\leq 2\text{-}1/2$	150	130
5Cr nuts	A 194	3	...	...	...
C-Mo nuts	A 194	4	...	...	...
Cr-Mo nuts	A 194	7	...	...	...
Cr-Mo nuts	A 194	7M	...	...	...
STAINLESS STEEL STUDS AND NUTS					
316	A 193	B8M Cl. 2	$> 1\text{-}1/4, \leq 1\text{-}1/2$	90	50
316	A 320	B8M Cl. 2	$> 1\text{-}1/4, \leq 1\text{-}1/2$	90	50
304	A 193	B8 Cl. 2	$> 1\text{-}1/4, \leq 1\text{-}1/2$	100	50
304	A 320	B8 Cl. 2	$> 1\text{-}1/4, \leq 1\text{-}1/2$	100	50
321	A 193	B8C Cl. 2	$> 1\text{-}1/4, \leq 1\text{-}1/4$	100	50
321	A 320	B8C Cl. 2	$> 1\text{-}1/4, \leq 1\text{-}1/4$	100	50

ASTM BOLTING MATERIALS PER ASME B31.3					
MATERIAL	SPEC. NO.	GRADE	SIZE DIA.in.	TENSILE ksi	YEILD ksi
STAINLESS STEEL STUDS AND NUTS Continued					
347	A 193	B8T Cl. 2	$> 1-1/4, \leq 1-1/2$	100	50
347	A 320	B8T Cl. 2	$> 1-1/4, \leq 1-1/2$	100	50
303 sol. trt.	A 320	B8F Cl. 1	...	75	30
19Cr-9Ni	A 453	651B	> 3	95	50
19Cr-9Ni	A 453	651B	≤ 3	95	60
19Cr-9Ni	A 453	651A	> 3	100	60
19Cr-9Ni	A 453	651A	≤ 3	100	70
316	A 193	B8M Cl. 2	$> 1, \leq 1-1/4$	105	65
316	A 320	B8M Cl. 2	$> 1, \leq 1-1/4$	105	65
347	A 193	B8C Cl. 2	$> 1, \leq 1-1/4$	105	65
347	A 320	B8C Cl. 2	$> 1, \leq 1-1/4$	105	65
304	A 193	B8 Cl. 2	$> 1, \leq 1-1/4$	105	65
304	A 320	B8 Cl. 2	$> 1, \leq 1-1/4$	105	65
321	A 193	B8T Cl. 2	$> 1, \leq 1-1/4$	105	65
321	A 320	B8T Cl. 2	$> 1, \leq 1-1/4$	105	65
321	A 193	B8T Cl. 1	...	75	30
304	A 320	B8 Cl. 1	...	75	30
347	A 193	B8C Cl. 1	...	75	30
316	A 193	B8M Cl. 1	...	75	30
316 str. hd	A 193	B8M Cl. 2	$> 3/4, \leq 1$	100	80
316 str. hd	A 320	B8M Cl. 2	$> 3/4, \leq 1$	100	80
347 str. hd	A 193	B8C Cl. 2	$> 3/4, \leq 1$	115	80
347 str. hd	A 320	B8C Cl. 2	$> 3/4, \leq 1$	115	80
304 str. hd.	A 193	B8 Cl. 2	$> 3/4, \leq 1$	115	80
304 str. hd.	A 320	B8 Cl. 2	$> 3/4, \leq 1$	115	80
321 str. hd	A 193	B8T Cl. 2	$> 3/4, \leq 1$	115	80
321 str. hd.	A 320	B8T Cl. 2	$> 3/4, \leq 1$	115	80
12Cr	A 437	B4C	...	115	85
13Cr	A 193	B6	≤ 4	110	85
14Cr-24Ni	A 453	660A/B	...	130	85
316 str. hd.	A 193	B8M Cl. 2	$\leq 3/4$	110	95
316 str. hd.	A 320	B8M Cl. 2	$\leq 3/4$	110	95
347	A 193	B8C Cl.2	$\leq 3/4$	125	100
347	A 320	B8C Cl.2	$\leq 3/4$	125	100
304	A 193	B8 Cl. 2	$\leq 3/4$	125	100
304	A 320	B8 Cl. 2	$\leq 3/4$	125	100
321	A 193	B8T Cl. 2	$\leq 3/4$	125	100

ASTM BOLTING MATERIALS PER ASME B31.3					
MATERIAL	SPEC. NO.	GRADE	SIZE DIA.in.	TENSILE ksi	YEILD ksi
STAINLESS STEEL STUDS AND NUTS Continued					
321	A 320	B8T Cl. 2	≤ 3/4	125	100
12Cr	A 437	B4B	...	145	105
12Cr nuts	A 194	6	...	...	...
303 nuts	A 194	8FA	...	...	...
316 nuts	A 194	8MA	...	...	...
321 nuts	A 194	8TA	...	...	...
304 nuts	A 194	8	...	...	...
304 nuts	A 194	8A	...	...	...
347 nuts	A 194	8CA	...	...	...

EXAMPLE OF MATERIAL GRADE VARIATIONS PER DESIGN TEMPERATURE			
DESIGN TEMPERATURE	FLANGES	STUD GRADE	NUT GRADE
-195° to 102°C	ASTM A182 Gr. F304, F304L, F316, F316L, F321, F347	A320 Gr. B8 Class 2	A194 Gr. 8A
-101° to -47°C	ASTM A350 Gr. LF3	A320 Gr. L7	A194 Gr. 7
-46° to -30° C	ASTM A350 Gr. LF2	A320 Gr. L7	A194 Gr. 7
-29° to 427°C	ASTM A105	A193 Gr. B7	A194 Gr. 2H
428° to 537°C	ASTM A182 Gr. F11, F22	A193 Gr. B16	A194 Gr. 2H
538° to 648°C	ASTM A182 Gr. F11, F22	A193 Gr. B8 Class 1	A194 Gr. 8A
649° to 815°C	ASTM A182 Gr. 304H, 316H	A 193 Gr. B8 Class 1	A194 Gr. 8A

Always consult with the piping spec in conjunction with your Inspections and Quality Control department concerning material grades required. This chart is for reference purposes only showing how design temperatures affect material grade.

CHAPTER 14: RIGGING

The following diagrams, charts, formulas, etc. are gathered from various sources and should be verified and understood before being applied. Never use rigging equipment, chokers, hardware, etc. which does not contain its rated capacity either being stamped on the side such as shackles or tagged as with chokers. The ratings, capacities, charts and dimensions provided within this book are merely for field use in the sense of initiating the search for the required size rigging. ALWAYS verify capacities and dimensions of all rigging by way of the chokers, shackles, links, etc. being used per their stamped or attached tagged ratings and dimensions. THIS SECTION IS FOR REFERENCE PURPOSES ONLY AND TO ADDRESS SOME OF THE CONSIDERATIONS REQUIRED WHEN LIFTING LOADS AND USING RIGGING.

TIPS: One rule of thumb for determining the minimum dimensions for the outrigger pads of a crane is that the tonnage of the machine divided by five equals the square feet of blocking surface area required per outrigger. For example, a 50-ton crane requires 10 square feet of blocking area per outrigger which comes out to approximately a 38" x 38" square padded area per outrigger. Another rule of thumb is that the blocking should cover a minimum of three times the surface area of the crane outrigger's factory installed metal pad.

Crane Operation Near High Voltage Power Line	Minimum Required Clearance in Feet
to 50kV	10
over 50kV to 200kV	15
over 200kV to 350kV	20
over 350kV to 500kV	25
over 500kV to 750kV	35
over 750kV to 1000kV	45

In Transit with no Load and Boom or Mast Lowered	Minimum Required Clearance in Feet
to 0.75kV	4
over 0.75kV to 50kV	6
over 50kV to 345kV	10
over 345kV to 750kV	16
over 750kV to 1000kV	20

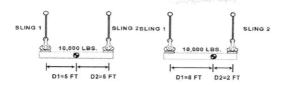

When the center of gravity (CG) is centered between the chokers supporting the load then the load is split equally among the two chokers as with the above image to the left whereby sling 1 and 2 both support 5000 lbs. When the center of gravity is not centered between the chokers supporting the load, then each choker will experience a different stress as each is supporting a different percentage of the load as with an asymmetrical load or two crane lift. This relates to the laws of leverage whereby:

DISTANCE x WEIGHT = DISTANCE x WEIGHT

In the above image to the right the relations are as follows:
Stress at sling 1 = 20% of the total load = 2000 pounds because it is at 80% of the total distance.
Stress at sling 2 = 80% of the total load = 8000 pounds because it is at 20% of the total distance.

8ft x 2000 pounds = 16000
2ft x 8000 pounds = 16000
An alternate way to figure this is:
Sling 1= 10,000 x 2/ (8+2) = 2000 pounds
Sling 2= 10,000 x 8/ (8+2) = 8000 pounds

When sling angles are less than 90 degrees then other considerations apply to selecting the proper choker which is later discussed in terms of the "reduction" and "tension" factor.

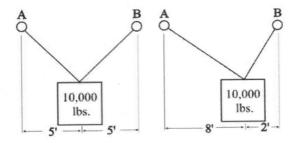

Though I've seen more complex methods, calculating the distribution and transference of weight between two stationary points as with floating or drifting a load from one chainfall to another can be accomplished in the same manner described on the previous page whereby in the image above at the upper left, both points A and B support a load of 5000 lbs. each. In the image above at the upper right however, point A must support 2000 lbs. while point B supports the remaining 8000 lbs. To calculate the stress per chainfall we can simply use the weight distribution we arrived at above and multiply it times the load factor established by the angle of the rigging leg to the load. This load factor per angle can be found in the provided chart on page 177 under the 'tension factor' column. The trigonometry section provides information on how to calculate the angle of the rigging to the load. For the sake of calculation we'll say that the load remains vertically 5' below points A and B throughout the lift. Thus:

Left: A = 45° (1.414 factor)
    A = 5000 x 1.414 = 7070 lbs
    B = 45° (1.414 factor)
    B = 5000 x 1.414 = 7070 lbs

Right: A = 32° (1.887 factor)
    A = 2000 x 1.887 = 3774 lbs
    B = 68.2° (1.079)
    B = 8000 x 1.079 = 8632 lbs

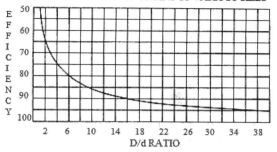

REDUCTION IN STRENGTH OF WIRE ROPE WHEN BENT OVER SHEAVES OR PINS OF VARIOUS SIZES

The D/d Ratio is the ratio of the diameter around which the sling is bent divided by the body diameter of the sling. Example: A 1/2" diameter wire rope is bent around a 10" diameter pipe; the D/d Ratio is 10" divided by 1/2" = D/d Ratio of 20:1. This ratio has an effect on the rated capacity of slings.

When a wire rope is bent around any sheave or other object there is a loss of strength due to this bending action. As the D/d ratio becomes smaller this loss of strength becomes greater and the rope becomes less efficient. The above and below curve and charts relate the efficiency of a rope diameter to different D/d ratios. This curve is based on static loads and applies to 6-strand class 6x19 and 6x37 wire rope.

D/d Ratio	Efficiency	D/d Ratio	Efficiency
40:1	95	8:1	83
30:1	93	6:1	79
20:1	91	4:1	75
15:1	89	2:1	65
10:1	86	1:1	50

D/d CONSIDERATIONS FOR EYE & EYE SLINGS

- The LOOP of an Eye & Eye sling has nearly DOUBLE the strength of it's body. For this reason the D/d ratio in the LOOP is just half as critical as opposed to when the sling is used in a BASKET hitch.
- In most cases the shackle or hook over which the sling is placed will have sufficient D/d Ratio. On the other hand, do not place too LARGE an object into the sling eye as this will result in splitting forces affecting the sling splice and sling safety. The object (a shackle, a crane hook, a steel bar, a piece of pipe, etc.) you place into the sling eye must not be larger than 1/2 of the sling eye length.
- When a sling is used in a BASKET or CHOKER HITCH with D/d Ratios smaller than listed in the capacity tables, the rated capacities (or WLL's) must be decreased.
- For example: The BASKET and CHOKER hitch capacities listed (in all Standard and Regulations) for 6-strand ropes are based on a minimum D/d Ratio of 25:1.
- An object you place into a 1" diameter 6-strand wire rope sling using a BASKET or CHOKER hitch must have a minimum diameter of 25". If the object is smaller than the listed 25:1 D/d Ratio the capacity (or WLL) must be decreased. The Table on the previous page addressing the D/d Ratio reduction aspects illustrates the percentage of decrease to be expected. The following diagrams further illustrate considerations required due to the D/d Ratio of a choker and its connection points.

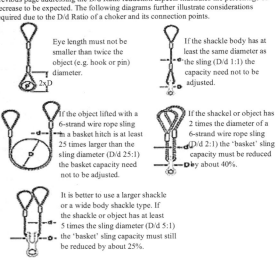

Eye length must not be smaller than twice the object (e.g. hook or pin) diameter. 2xD

If the shackle body has at least the same diameter as the sling (D/d 1:1) the capacity need not to be adjusted.

If the object lifted with a 6-strand wire rope sling in a basket hitch is at least 25 times larger than the sling diameter (D/d 25:1) the basket capacity need not to be adjusted.

If the shackel or object has 2 times the diameter of a 6-strand wire rope sling (D/d 2:1) the 'basket' sling capacity must be reduced by about 40%.

It is better to use a larger shackle or a wide body shackle type. If the shackle or object has at least 5 times the sling diameter (D/d 5:1) the 'basket' sling capacity must still be reduced by about 25%.

REDUCTION OF CHOKER SLING CAPACITY
DUE TO ANGLE OF CHOKE

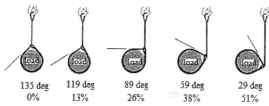

| 135 deg | 119 deg | 89 deg | 59 deg | 29 deg |
| 0% | 13% | 26% | 38% | 51% |

The above diagrams show the related reduction percentages of a chokers rated CHOKE capacity due to the angle by which the choker is rendered upon the load per ASME B30.9.

Angle of Choke Degree	Rated Capacity % (ASME B30.9)
120-180	100
90-119	87
60-89	74
30-59	62
0-29	49

When a load is rigged using a choker hitch, if the choke angle is less than 120° then the rated capacity of the sling must be reduced.
1) Calculate the angle of the choke (see illustration at top of page).
2) Determine the associated reduction factor (see Rated Capacity % above).
3) Multiply the rated capacity for the CHOKER Hitch as indicated on the sling tag by the reduction factor.
4) The result is the safe capacity rating for that sling in that rigging configuration.
EXAMPLE: With a WLL of 1000 pounds at a 89 deg. choke the actual WLL is reduced by 26% as shown in the illustration at the top of the page. Thus, 1000 x 74% (taken from chart) = 740 pound WLL. This is a 260 pound reduction or 26%.

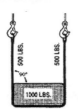

Sling to Load Angle	Method 1: Reduction Factor	Method 2: Tension Factor
90°	1.000	1.000
85°	0.996	1.004
80°	0.985	1.015
75°	0.966	1.035
70°	0.940	1.064
65°	0.906	1.104
60°	0.866	1.155
55°	0.819	1.221
50°	0.766	1.305
45°	0.707	1.414
40°	0.643	1.555
35°	0.574	1.742
30°	0.500	2.000
25°	0.423	2.366
20°	0.342	2.924
15°	0.259	3.863
10°	0.174	5.759

The angle by which a basket or bridal hitch is attached to a load affects the rated capacity and tension per leg. This is discussed further on next page.

FOR BASKET AND BRIDLE HITCHES

Method 1- Determine Reduction to Rated Capacity:
1) Calculate the sling to load angle. Angles below 30° should be avoided.
2) Determine the associated reduction factor (see chart on previous page).
3) Multiply the rated capacity for the basket hitch as indicated on the sling tag by the reduction factor.
4) The result is the safe capacity designation for that sling in that rigging configuration.

Method 2- Determine Increased Tension/Effective Weight of the Load:
1) Calculate the sling to load angle. Angles below 30° should be avoided.
2) Determine the associated tension factor (see chart on previous page).
3) Multiply the load weight by the tension factor.
4) The result is the 'Effective Weight' of the load in that rigging configuration. Be sure to select a sling with adequate capacity. (A longer sling will increase the sling to load angle, thereby reducing the tension factor/effective weight of the load.)

EXAMPLE: A two leg pick of 1000 pounds as seen in the diagram on the previous page has a 500 pound leg tension on each leg at 90 deg. At 60 deg the tension on each leg would be 500 x 1.155 (tension factor from chart) = 577.5 pounds on each leg. If using two chokers, then the working load limit in the vertical position for each choker would have to be rated above 577.5 pounds, which would be the equivalent of lifting a 1155 pound load at 90 deg. If one sling was used in a basket configuration which was rated for 1155 pounds (577.5 x 2) then its actual working load limit at 60 deg would be 1155 x 0.866 (reduction factor from chart) = 1000.23 pounds, which gives the same result as 1155 ÷ 1.155 = 1000 or dividing the rated capacity of the choker by the tension factor. The tension factor is related to trig in that it is the Cosecant of the angle and the reduction factor is the Sin of that angle. Thus, the tension factor can be found for a given length choker whereby it becomes the travel (hypotenuse) and the vertical distance to load becomes the set (side 1) whereby travel/set = cosecant (of angle B) which can be referenced to any trig chart. See the trig section of this book to understand the references in parenthesis.

WIRE ROPE CHOKERS

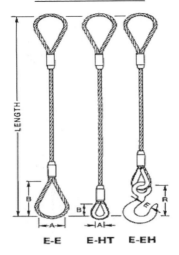

E-E **E-HT** **E-EH**

Environmental Effects:

• Permanently remove from service fiber-core wire rope slings of any grade if they are exposed to temperatures in excess of 180 degrees F (82 degrees C).
• Follow the recommendations of the sling manufacturer when you use metallic-core wire rope slings of any grade at temperatures above 400 degrees F (204 degrees C) or below minus 40 degrees F (minus 40 degrees C).
• Chemically active environments can affect the strength of wire rope slings. Consult the manufacturer before using a sling in such environments.
• Dimensions and capacities for wire rope chokers from single chokers to four part bridals are on pages 180 - 183. Those dimensions and capacities on the following page 180 are for single chokers.

All capacities in tons of 2,000 lbs. All eye and fitting dimensions in inches.

	Rope Dia.	RATED CAPACITY - Tons*						Eye Dimensions		Thimble		Alloy Eye Hoist Hook		
		Vert.	*** Choker Hitch	Basket Hitch				A	B	A	B	WLL** Tons	E	R
				○	60°	45°	30°							
6x19 IWRC	1/4	0.65	0.48	1.3	1.1	0.91	0.65	2	4	7/8	1 5/8	1	.90	3.34
	5/16	1.0	0.74	2.0	1.7	1.4	1.0	2 1/2	5	11/16	1 7/8	1	.90	3.34
	3/8	1.4	1.1	2.9	2.5	2.0	1.4	3	6	1 1/8	2 1/8	1.5	.93	3.81
	7/16	1.9	1.4	3.9	3.4	2.7	1.9	3 1/2	7	1 1/4	2 1/4	2	1	4.14
	1/2	2.5	1.9	5.1	4.4	3.6	2.5	4	8	1 1/2	2 3/4	3	1.13	4.69
	9/16	3.2	2.4	6.4	5.5	4.5	3.2	4 1/2	9	1 1/2	2 3/4	5	1.47	5.77
	5/8	3.9	2.9	7.8	6.8	5.5	3.9	5	10	1 3/4	3 1/4	5	1.47	5.77
	3/4	5.6	4.1	11	9.7	7.9	5.6	6	12	2	3 3/4	7	1.75	7.37
	7/8	7.6	5.6	15	13	11	7.6	7	14	2 1/4	4 1/4	11	2.29	9.07
	1	9.8	7.2	20	17	14	9.8	8	16	2 1/2	4 1/2	11	2.29	9.07
	1 1/8	12	9.1	24	21	17	12	9	18	2 7/8	5 1/8	15	2.50	10.08
	1 1/4	15	11	30	26	21	15	10	20	2 7/8	5 1/8	15	2.50	10.08
	1 3/8	18	13	36	31	25	18	11	22	3 1/2	6 1/4	22	3.3	12.53
	1 1/2	21	16	42	37	30	21	12	24	3 1/2	6 1/4	22	3.3	12.53
	1 5/8	24	18	49	42	35	24	13	26	4	8	30	4	14.06
6x37 IWRC	1 3/4	28	21	57	49	40	28	14	28	4 1/2	9	30	4	14.06
	2	37	28	73	63	52	37	16	32	6	12	37	4.25	18.19
	2 1/4	44	35	89	77	63	44	18	36	7	14	45	4.75	20.12
	2 1/2	54	42	109	94	77	54	20	40	-	-	60	5.75	23.72
	2 3/4	65	51	130	113	92	65	22	44	-	-	-	-	-
	3	77	60	153	133	108	77	24	48	-	-	-	-	-
	3 1/2	102	79	203	176	144	102	28	56	-	-	-	-	-
	4	130	101	259	224	183	130	32	64	-	-	-	-	-

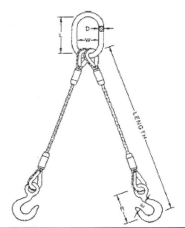

	Rope Dia.	RATED CAPACITY Tons*			Alloy Oblong Link			Alloy Eye Hoist Hook		
		60°	45°	30°	D	L	W	WLL** Tons	E	R
6x19 IWRC	1/4	1.1	0.91	0.65	1/2"	5"	2-1/2"	1	.90	3.34
	5/16	1.7	1.4	1.0	1/2"	5"	2-1/2"	1	.90	3.34
	3/8	2.5	2.0	1.4	1/2"	5"	2-1/2"	1.5	.93	3.81
	7/16	3.4	2.7	1.9	5/8"	6"	3"	2	1	4.14
	1/2	4.4	3.6	2.5	3/4"	5-1/2"	2-3/4"	3	1.13	4.69
	9/16	5.5	4.5	3.2	1"	7"	3-1/2"	5	1.47	5.77
	5/8	6.8	5.5	3.9	1"	7"	3-1/2"	5	1.47	5.77
	3/4	9.7	7.9	5.6	1"	7"	3-1/2"	7	1.75	7.37
	7/8	13	11	7.6	1-1/4"	8-3/4"	4-3/8"	11	2.29	9.07
	1	17	14	9.8	1-1/2"	10-1/2"	5-1/4"	11	2.29	9.07
	1 1/8	21	17	12	1-1/2"	10-1/2"	5-1/4"	15	2.50	10.08
	1 1/4	26	21	15	1-3/4"	12"	6"	15	2.50	10.08
6x37 IWRC	1 3/8	31	25	18	1-3/4"	12"	6"	22	3.3	12.53
	1 1/2	37	30	21	2"	14"	7"	22	3.3	12.53
	1 5/8	42	35	24	2"	14"	7"	30	4	14.06
	1 3/4	49	40	28	2-1/4"	16"	8"	30	4	14.06
	2	63	52	37	2-1/2"	16"	8"	37	4.25	18.19

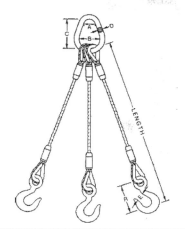

	Rope Dia.	RATED CAPACITY Tons*			Alloy Pear Link				Alloy Eye Hoist Hook		
		60°	45°	30°	A	B	C	D	WLL** Tons	E	R
6x19 IWRC	1/4	1.7	1.4	0.97	1-1/4"	2-1/2"	3-1/2"	5/8"	1	90	3.34
	5/16	2.6	2.1	1.5	1-1/2"	3"	4-1/2"	3/4"	1	90	3.34
	3/8	3.7	3.0	2.2	1-1/2"	3"	4-1/2"	3/4"	1.5	.93	3.81
	7/16	5.0	4.1	2.9	2"	4"	6"	1"	2	1	4.14
	1/2	6.6	5.4	3.8	2"	4"	6"	1"	3	1.13	4.69
	9/16	8.3	6.8	4.8	2"	4"	6"	1"	5	1.47	5.77
	5/8	10	8.3	5.9	2"	4"	6"	1"	5	1.47	5.77
	3/4	15	12	8.4	2-1/2"	5"	7-1/2"	1-1/4"	7	1.75	7.37
	7/8	20	16	11	3"	6"	9"	1-1/2"	11	2.29	9.07
6x37 IWRC	1	26	21	15	3-1/2"	7"	10"	1-3/4"	11	2.29	9.07
	1 1/8	31	26	18	3-1/2"	7"	10"	1-3/4"	15	2.50	10.08
	1 1/4	38	31	22	4"	8"	12"	2"	15	2.50	10.08
	1 3/8	46	38	27	4-1/2"	9"	13-1/2"	2-1/4"	22	3.3	12.53
	1 1/2	55	45	32	4-1/2"	9"	13-1/2"	2-1/4"	22	3.3	12.53
	1 5/8	63	52	37	5"	10"	15"	2-1/2"	30	4	14.06
	1 3/4	74	60	42	5"	10"	15"	2-3/4"	30	4	14.06

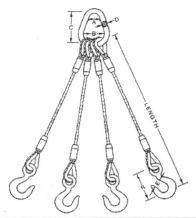

	Rope Dia.	RATED CAPACITY Tons*			Alloy Pear Link				Alloy Eye Hoist Hook		
		60°	45°	30°	A	B	C	D	WLL** Tons	E	R
6x19 IWRC	1/4	2.2	1.8	1.3	1-1/2"	3"	4-1/2"	3/4"	1	.90	3.34
	5/16	3.5	2.8	2.0	1-1/2"	3"	4-1/2"	3/4"	1	.90	3.34
	3/8	5.0	4.1	2.9	1-3/4"	3-1/2"	5-1/4"	7/8"	1.5	.93	3.81
	7/16	6.7	5.5	3.9	2"	4"	6"	1"	2	1	4.14
	1/2	8.8	7.1	5.1	2-1/2"	5"	7-1/2"	1-1/4"	3	1.13	4.69
	9/16	11	9.0	6.4	2-1/2"	5"	7-1/2"	1-1/4"	5	1.47	5.77
	5/8	14	11	7.8	2-1/2"	5"	7-1/2"	1-1/4"	5	1.47	5.77
	3/4	19	16	11	3"	6"	9"	1-1/2"	7	1.75	7.37
	7/8	26	21	15	3-1/2"	7"	10"	1-3/4"	11	2.29	9.07
	1	34	28	20	4"	8"	12"	2"	11	2.29	9.07
	1 1/8	42	34	24	4-1/2"	9"	13-1/2"	2-1/4"	15	2.50	10.08
6x37 IWRC	1 1/4	51	42	30	5"	10"	15"	2-1/2"	15	2.50	10.08
	1 3/8	62	50	36	6"	12"	18"	3"	22	3.3	12.53
	1 1/2	73	60	42	6"	12"	18"	3"	22	3.3	12.53

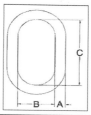

Crosby A-342 Alloy Master Links Reference Chart

Size (in.)	Working Load Limit (lbs.)	Weight Each (lbs.)	Dimensions (in)			Deformation Indicator
			A	B	C	
1/2W	7400	1.3	0.62	2.80	5.00	3.50
5/8	9000	1.5	0.62	3.00	6.00	3.50
3/4W	12300	2.0	0.73	3.20	6.00	4.00
7/8W	15200	3.3	0.88	3.75	6.38	4.50
1W	26000	6.1	1.10	4.30	7.50	5.50
1-1/4W	39100	12.0	1.33	5.50	9.50	7.00
1-1/2W	61100	18.6	1.61	5.90	10.50	7.50
1-3/4	84900	25.2	1.75	6.00	12.00	7.50
2	102600	37.0	2.00	7.00	14.00	9.00
2-1/4	143100	54.1	2.25	8.00	16.00	10.00
2-1/2	160000	68.5	2.50	8.38	16.00	11.00
2-3/4	216900	94.0	2.75	9.88	18.00	12.50
3	228000	115	3.00	9.88	18.00	13.00
3-1/4	262200	145	3.25	10.00	20.00	13.50
3-1/2	279000	200	3.50	12.00	24.00	15.50
3-3/4	336000	198	3.75	10.00	20.00	13.50
4	373000	264	4.00	12.00	24.00	16.00
††4-1/4	354000	302	4.25	12.00	24.00	-
††4-1/2	360000	345	4.50	14.00	28.00	-
††4-3/4	389000	436	4.75	14.00	28.00	-
††5	395000	516	5.00	15.00	30.00	-

Based on single leg sling (in-line load), or resultant load on multiple legs with an included angle less than or equal to 120 degrees.
Ultimate Load is 5 times the Working Load Limit.
†† Welded Link

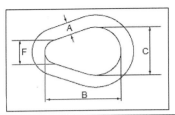

Crosby A-341 Alloy Pear Shaped Links Reference Chart

Size A (in.)	Working Load Limit (lbs.)	Weight Each (lbs.)	Dimensions (in)		
			B	C	F
1/2	7000	.55	3.00	2.00	1.00
5/8	9000	1.10	3.75	2.50	1.25
3/4	12300	1.76	4.50	3.00	1.50
7/8	15000	2.82	5.25	3.50	1.75
1	24360	4.22	6.00	4.00	2.00
†† 1-1/8	30600	6.25	6.50	4.50	2.25
1-1/4	36000	8.25	7.75	5.00	2.50
1-3/8	43000	11.25	8.25	5.50	2.75
†† 1-1/2	54300	14.25	9.00	6.00	3.00
†† 1-5/8	62600	18.50	9.75	6.50	3.25
†† 1-3/4	84900	22.50	10.50	7.00	3.50
†† 1-7/8	95800	29.00	11.25	7.50	3.75
†† 2	102600	34.00	12.00	8.00	4.00
†† 2-1/4	143100	48.00	13.50	9.00	4.50
†† 2-1/2	147300	66.00	15.00	10.00	5.00
†† 2-3/4	216900	88.00	16.50	11.00	5.50
†† 3	228000	114.00	18.00	12.00	6.00
†† 3-1/4	262200	146.00	19.50	13.00	6.50
†† 3-1/2	279000	181.00	21.00	14.00	7.00
†† 4	373000	271.00	24.00	16.00	8.00

Based on single leg sling (in-line load), or resultant load on multiple legs with an included angle less than or equal to 120°.
Minimum Ultimate load is 5 times the Working Load Limit.
†† Welded Link

PLAIN AND SHOULDERED EYE BOLTS

SIZE (in.)	SHANK LENGTH	EYE I.D.	EYE O.D.	TOTAL LENGTH	SAFE LOAD (lbs.)
1/4	1	3/4	1-3/16	2-1/4 2-1/2*	500
5/16	1-1/8	7/8	1-7/16	2-5/8 2-7/8*	900
3/8	1-1/4	1	1-21/32	3 3-9/32*	1300
7/16	1-3/8	1-1/16	1-27/32	3-11/16	1800
1/2	1-1/2	1-3/16	2-1/16	3-9/16 4-1/32*	2400
9/16	1-5/8	1-9/32	2-9/32	4-1/16	3000
5/8	1-3/4	1-3/8	2-1/2	4-1/4 4-25/32*	4000
3/4	2	1-1/2	2-13/16	4-27/32 5-3/8*	5000
7/8	2-1/4	1-11/16	3-1/4	5-5/8 6-1/8*	7000
1	2-1/2	1-13/16	3-9/16	6-7/32 6-13/16*	9000
1-1/8	2-3/4	2	4	6-29/32 7-9/16*	12000
1-1/4	3	2-3/16	4-7/16	7-9/16 8-1/4*	15000
1-1/2	3-1/2	2-9/16 2-1/2*	5-3/16	8-7/8 9-11/16*	21000

*Indicates sizes which pertain to shouldered only when differences in the dimensions between the two arise.

• All eye bolt capacities are for straight pulls. It isn't recommended to pull eyebolts from an angle as capacities decrease greatly as seen by the estimated reduction factors below which only pertain to shouldered versions as plain should never be side loaded:
vertical 0°= good for 100% of rated safe load capacity; 15° from vertical= good for 63% of safe load limit; 30° from vertical= good for 40% of safe load limit; 45° from vertical= good for 25% of safe load limit ; 90° from vertical= avoid

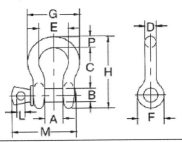

SCREW PIN SHACKLE DIMENSIONS AND CAPACITIES

Size	Cap. tons	Pin Dia. B	A	C	D	E	F	G	H	L	M	P	lbs. Ea.
3/16	1/3	1/4	0.38	0.88	0.19	0.60	0.56	0.98	1.47	0.16	1.12	0.19	0.06
1/4	1/2	5/16	0.47	1.13	0.25	0.78	0.61	1.28	1.84	0.19	1.38	0.25	0.10
5/16	3/4	3/8	0.53	1.22	0.31	0.84	0.75	1.47	2.09	0.22	1.66	0.31	0.18
3/8	1	7/16	0.66	1.44	0.38	1.03	0.91	1.78	2.49	0.25	2.03	0.38	0.31
7/16	1-1/2	1/2	0.75	1.69	0.44	1.16	1.06	2.03	2.91	0.31	2.38	0.44	0.38
1/2	2	5/8	0.81	1.88	0.50	1.31	1.19	2.31	3.28	0.38	2.69	0.50	0.72
5/8	3-1/4	3/4	1.06	2.38	0.63	1.69	1.50	2.94	4.19	0.44	3.34	0.69	1.37
3/4	4-3/4	7/8	1.25	2.81	0.75	2.00	1.81	3.50	4.97	0.50	3.97	0.81	2.35
7/8	6-1/2	1	1.44	3.31	0.88	2.28	2.09	4.03	5.83	0.50	4.50	0.97	3.62
1	8-1/2	1-1/8	1.69	3.75	1.00	2.69	2.38	4.69	6.56	0.56	5.07	1.06	5.03
1-1/8	9-1/2	1-1/4	1.81	4.25	1.16	2.91	2.69	5.16	7.47	0.63	5.59	1.25	7.41
1-1/4	12	1-3/8	2.03	4.69	1.29	3.25	3.00	5.75	8.25	0.69	6.16	1.38	9.50
1-3/8	13-1/2	1-1/2	2.25	5.25	1.42	3.63	3.31	6.38	9.16	0.75	6.84	1.50	13.5
1-1/2	17	1-5/8	2.38	5.75	1.54	3.88	3.63	6.88	10.0	0.81	7.35	1.62	17.2
1-3/4	25	2	2.88	7.00	1.84	5.00	4.19	8.86	12.3	1.00	9.08	2.25	27.7
2	35	2-1/4	3.25	7.75	2.08	5.75	4.81	9.97	13.6	1.22	10.3	2.40	45.0
2-1/2	55	2-3/4	4.13	10.5	2.71	7.25	5.69	12.8	17.8	1.38	13.0	3.13	85.7

A shackles capacity is effected by the angle at which the choker exerts force upon it. The following angles are as measured from verticle and effect the efficiency of the shackles rated capacity per the percentages given:
• 0° verticle = good for 100% of rated capacity
• 45° diagonal = good for 70% of rated capacity
• 90° side load = good for 50% of rated capacity

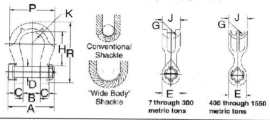

CROSBY WIDE BODY SHACKLE DIMENSIONS AND CAPACITIES

Work Load Limit (t)	Weight Each (lbs.)	A	B	C	D	E	G	H	J	K	P	R
7	4.0	4.14	1.25	.69	.88	1.82	1.25	3.56	1.60	1.25	4.10	5.87
12.5	8.80	5.38	1.69	.92	1.13	2.38	1.37	4.63	2.13	1.63	5.51	7.63
18	14.90	6.69	2.03	1.16	1.38	2.69	1.50	5.81	2.50	2.00	6.76	9.38
30	26.50	7.69	2.37	1.38	1.63	3.50	1.75	6.94	3.13	2.50	8.50	11.38
40	35	9.28	2.88	1.69	2.00	4.00	2.31	8.06	3.75	3.00	10.62	13.62
55	68	10.36	3.25	2.00	2.25	4.63	2.63	9.36	5.00	3.50	12.26	15.63
75	99	14.37	4.13	2.12	2.75	5.00	2.50	11.53	4.75	3.64	12.28	18.41
125	161	16.51	5.12	2.56	3.15	5.71	3.15	14.36	5.91	4.33	14.96	22.65
200	370	20.67	5.91	3.35	4.12	7.28	4.33	18.90	8.63	5.41	19.49	29.82
300	847	24.20	7.38	4.00	5.25	9.25	5.38	23.63	10.38	6.31	23.38	37.26
400	1130	30.27	8.66	5.16	6.30	11.81	6.30	22.64	12.60	7.28	27.17	38.78
500	1440	33.35	9.84	5.73	7.09	13.39	6.69	24.81	13.39	8.86	31.10	42.72
600	1995	36.02	10.83	6.23	7.87	15.50	7.28	27.56	14.57	9.74	34.06	47.24
700	2415	38.91	11.81	6.59	8.46	14.80	7.87	28.94	15.75	10.63	37.01	50.18
800	2880	41.66	12.80	7.30	9.06	16.54	8.27	29.53	16.54	10.92	38.39	52.09
900	3628	43.73	13.78	7.78	9.84	16.93	8.66	29.82	17.32	11.52	40.35	54.04
1000	4155	45.98	14.96	8.33	10.63	17.72	9.06	29.92	18.11	12.11	42.32	55.31
1250	5320	49.86	16.93	9.15	11.81	21.00	10.43	36.61	20.87	12.70	46.26	65.35
1550	8302	54.89	18.31	10.58	12.60	23.82	15.92	42.32	22.82	13.29	49.41	73.43

- Dimension 'B' is +/- 0.02. Dimension 'D' is +/- 0.02.
- Forged alloy steel from 7 through 300 metric tons.
- Cast alloy steel from 400 through 1,550 metric tons.
- All ratings are in metric tons, embossed on side of bow.

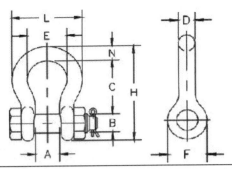

| BOLT TYPE SHACKLE DIMENSIONS AND CAPACITIES ||||||||||||
Size	Capacity (tons)	A	B	C	D	E	F	H	L	N	lbs. Each
3/16	1/3	0.38	0.25	0.88	0.19	0.60	0.56	1.47	0.98	0.19	0.06
1/4	1/2	0.47	0.31	1.13	0.25	0.78	0.61	1.84	1.28	0.25	0.11
5/16	3/4	0.53	0.38	1.22	0.31	0.84	0.75	2.09	1.47	0.31	0.22
3/8	1	0.66	0.44	1.44	0.38	1.03	0.91	2.49	1.78	0.38	0.33
7/16	1-1/2	0.75	0.50	1.69	0.44	1.16	1.06	2.91	2.03	0.44	0.49
1/2	2	0.81	0.63	1.88	0.50	1.31	1.19	3.28	2.31	0.50	0.79
5/8	3-1/4	1.06	.75	2.38	0.63	1.69	1.50	4.19	2.94	0.69	1.68
3/4	4-3/4	1.25	.88	2.81	0.75	2.00	1.81	4.97	3.50	0.81	2.72
7/8	6-1/2	1.44	1.00	3.31	0.88	2.28	2.09	5.83	4.03	0.97	3.95
1	8-1/2	1.69	1.13	3.75	1.00	2.69	2.38	6.56	4.69	1.06	5.66
1-1/8	9-1/2	1.81	1.25	4.25	1.13	2.91	2.69	7.47	5.16	1.25	8.27
1-1/4	12	2.03	1.38	4.69	1.25	3.25	3.00	8.25	5.75	1.38	11.71
1-3/8	13-1/2	2.25	1.50	5.25	1.38	3.63	3.31	9.16	6.38	1.50	15.83
1-1/2	17	2.38	1.63	5.75	1.50	3.88	3.63	10.00	6.88	1.62	19.00
1-3/4	25	2.88	2.00	7.00	1.75	5.00	4.19	12.34	8.86	2.25	33.91
2	35	3.25	2.25	7.75	2.00	5.75	4.81	13.68	9.97	2.40	52.25
2-1/2	55	4.13	2.75	10.50	2.62	7.25	5.69	17.84	12.87	3.13	98.25
3	85	5.00	3.25	13.00	3.00	7.88	6.50	21.50	14.36	3.62	154
3-1/2	120	5.25	3.75	14.63	3.62	9.00	8.00	24.63	16.50	4.12	265
4	150	5.50	4.25	14.50	4.10	10.00	9.00	25.69	18.42	4.56	338

A shackles capacity is effected by the angle at which the choker exerts force upon it. The following angles are as measured from verticle and effect the efficiency of the shackles rated capacity per the percentages given: • 0°=100% of rated capacity
• 45°=70% of rated capacity
• 90°=50% of rated capacity

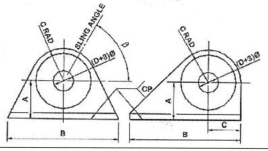

PADEYES/LIFTING LUGS GOOD FOR ALL VALUES OF β								
Work Load Limit (t)				PIN-HOLE Pin Dia. +1/8" (3mm)	NO Chk.Pls.	WITH Chk.Pls	CHEEK PLATES		
							THICK	DIA.	Weld.
	A	B	C		T	T	t	E	F
3-1/4	1-3/4	4-1/2	1-3/8	7/8	13/16	1/2	1/4	1-15/16	1/4
4-3/4	2-3/16	5-5/16	1-9/16	1	1	5/8	1/4	2-3/8	1/4
6-1/2	2-3/16	5-7/8	1-3/4	1-1/8	1-1/4	13/16	1/4	2-3/4	1/4
8-1/2	2-3/8	6-5/16	1-15/16	1-1/4		1	1/4	3-1/8	1/4
9-1/2	2-9/16	7-5/16	2-3/16	1-3/8		1	5/16	3-9/16	1/4
12	2-3/4	7-7/8	2-3/8	1-1/2		1	3/8	3-15/16	1/4
13	2-15/16	8-11/16	2-9/16	1-5/8		1	3/8	4-5/16	1/4
17	3-3/8	9-1/16	2-3/4	1-3/4		1-1/4	3/8	4-3/4	1/4
25	4-1/8	11	3-3/8	2-1/8		1-9/16	1/2	5-7/8	5/16
35	4-3/4	11-5/8	4-1/8	2-3/8		1-15/16	3/8	6-11/16	5/16
45	5-1/8	13-3/8	4-1/2	2-5/8		1-15/16	5/8	7-1/2	5/16
55	5-7/8	14-3/16	5-1/8	2-7/8		1-15/16	13/16	8-11/16	3/8

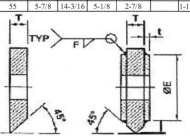

The dimensions and working load limit of the lifting lugs are designed to work with shackles of the same working load limit in metric tons (which is the actual stamped capacity of most shackles). Thus, considerations were made for proper clearances.

NYLON FLAT & TWISTED EYE CHOKER CAPACITY								
Width	Ply	Vertical	Choke	Basket	Width	Ply	Vertical	Choke	Basket
1	1	1600	1300	3200	6	1	9600	7700	19200
	2	3200	2600	6400		2	16300	13100	32600
	3	4100	3300	8200		3	22900	18300	45900
	4	5500	4400	11000		4	30600	24500	61200
2	1	3200	2600	6400	8	1	12800	10200	25600
	2	6400	5100	12800		2	20500	16400	41000
	3	8200	6600	16500		3	30700	24600	61400
	4	11000	8800	22000		4	41000	32800	81900
3	1	4800	3800	9600	10	1	16000	12800	32000
	2	8900	7100	17800		2	24000	19200	48000
	3	12300	9900	24700		3	36000	28800	72000
	4	16500	13200	32900		4	48000	38400	96000
4	1	6400	5100	12800	12	1	19200	15400	38400
	2	11500	9200	23000		2	26900	21500	53700
	3	15300	12200	30600		3	40300	32200	80600
	4	20400	16300	40800		4	53700	43000	107400

Environmental Effects:

• Temperature - Do not allow nylon and polyester slings to be used in contact with objects or at temperatures in excess of 194 degrees F (90 degrees C), or below minus 40 degrees F (minus 40 degrees C).

• Sunlight & Ultraviolet - Long-term exposure to sunlight or ultraviolet radiation can affect the strength of synthetic webbing slings. Consult the sling manufacturer for proper retirement criteria for synthetic webbing slings subjected to long-term storage or use in sunlight.

• Chemical - The strength of synthetic webbing slings can be degraded by chemically active environments. This includes exposure to chemicals in the form of solids, liquids, vapors or fumes. Consult the sling manufacturer before using slings in chemically active environments.

POLYESTER ROUND SLING CAPACITY AND COLOR CODE

COLOR	Vertical	Choke	Basket	Dia.	Wt. per Ft.	Model
Purple	2600	2100	5200	.60	.30	BLR1
Green	5300	4200	10,600	.80	.40	BLR2
Yellow	8400	6700	16,800	1.00	.50	BLR3
Tan	10,600	8500	21,200	1.20	.65	BLR4
Red	13,200	10,600	26,400	1.30	.80	BLR5
White	16,800	13,400	33,600	1.45	1.00	BLR6
Blue	21,200	17,000	42,400	1.55	1.20	BLR7
Orange	25,000	20,000	50,000	1.75	1.50	BLR8
Grey	31,000	24,800	62,000	1.95	2.00	BLR9
Orange	40,000	32,000	80,000	2.35	2.80	BLR10
Brown	53,000	42,400	106,000	3.15	3.60	BLR11
Olive	66,000	52,800	132,000	3.95	4.60	BLR12
Black	90,000	72,000	180,000	4.50	5.60	BLR13
Black	103,200	82,650	206,400	5.00	6.00	BLR14

Environmental Effects:

• Temperature - Do not allow polyester round slings to be used in contact with objects or at temperatures in excess of 194 degrees F (90 degrees C), or below minus 40 degrees F (minus 40 degrees C).
• Some synthetic yarns do not retain their breaking strength during long-term exposure above 140 degrees (60 degrees C). Consult the sling manufacturer for the effects of long-term heat exposure.
• Sunlight & Ultraviolet - Long-term exposure to sunlight or ultraviolet radiation can affect the strength of polyester round slings. Consult the sling manufacturer for proper retirement criteria for polyester round slings subjected to long-term storage or use in sunlight.
• Chemical - Chemically active environments can affect the strength of synthetic round slings. Consult the manufacturer before using a sling in such environments. Ensure that in chemically active environments the cover is the same yarn as the load-bearing core.

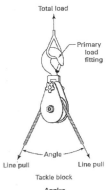

Angles

When lifting or pulling with a snatch block, the line pull force applied is increased or decreased to equal the total load at the hook by a factor determined by the angle between the line pulls. The multiplication factor of any angle can be arrived at by dividing the angle by 2 and looking up the COS for that angle in the trig chart provided in the trig section and then multiplying it times 2.

MULTIPLICATION FACTORS FOR SNATCH BLOCK LOADS				
Angle	Multiplication Factor	Angle	Multiplication Factor
0°	2.00	100°	1.29
10°	1.99	110°	1.15
20°	1.97	120°	1.00
30°	1.93	130°	0.84
40°	1.87	135°	0.76
45°	1.84	140°	0.68
50°	1.81	150°	0.52
60°	1.73	160°	0.35
70°	1.64	170°	0.17
80°	1.53	180°	0.00
90°	1.41		

Example: 1000 lbs. (line pull) and angle is 130° (x 0.84) then total load = 840 lbs. Solving for line pull: 840 lbs. (load) ÷ 0.84 (130° angle) = 1000 lbs. line pull

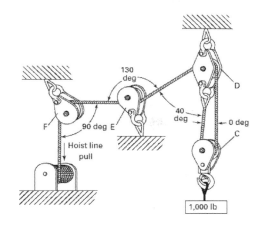

CALCULATING LOADS ON BLOCK AND TACKLE

Example: Load = 1,000 lbs.
Line Pull: 1,000 lbs./ 2 = 500 lbs.
Load Block "C" = 500 lbs. x 2 = 1,000 lbs.
           (Line pull x factor for 0 deg. angle)
Load Block "D" = 500 lbs. x 1.87 + 500 lbs. = 1,435 lbs.
           (Line pull x factor for 40 deg. angle + dead-end load)
Load Block "E" = 500 lbs. x 0.84 = 420 lbs.
           (Line pull x factor for 130 deg. angle)
Load Block "F" = 500 lbs. x 1.41 = 705 lbs.
           (Line pull x factor for 90 deg. angle)

CALCULATING LINE PARTS FOR REEVED BLOCKS

Ratio A Bronze Bushed Sheaves	Ratio B Anti-Friction Bearing Sheaves	Number of Line Parts	Ratio A Bronze Bushed Sheaves	Ratio B Anti-Friction Bearing Sheaves	Number of Line Parts
.96	.98	1	8.52	9.79	11
1.87	1.94	2	9.11	10.60	12
2.75	2.88	3	9.68	11.40	13
3.59	3.81	4	10.20	12.10	14
4.39	4.71	5	10.70	12.90	15
5.16	5.60	6	11.20	13.60	16
5.90	6.47	7	11.70	14.30	17
6.60	7.32	8	12.20	15.00	18
7.27	8.16	9	12.60	15.70	19
7.91	8.98	10	13.00	16.40	20

Ratio A or B = $\frac{Total\ Load\ To\ Be\ Lifted}{Single\ Line\ Pull\ (lbs.)}$

After calculating Ratio A or B, consult table to determine number of parts of line.

Examples

• To find the number of parts of line needed when weight of load and single line pull are known, and using Bronze Bushed Sheaves.

Ratio A = $\frac{72{,}180\ lbs.(load\ to\ be\ lifted)}{8{,}000\ lbs.(single\ line\ pull)} = \frac{9.02}{(Ratio\ A)}$

Refer to ratio 9.02 in table or number nearest to it, then check column under heading "Number of Line Parts" = 12 parts of line to be used for this load.

• To find the single line pull needed when weight of load and number of parts of line are known, and using antifriction bearing sheaves.

Single Line Pull = $\frac{68{,}000\ lbs.(load\ to\ be\ lifted)}{7.32\ (Ratio\ B\ of\ 8\ part\ line)}$ = 9,290 lbs.

9,290 lbs. single line pull required to lift this load on 8 parts of line.

• To find the lift capacity when the parts of line and single line pull are known, and using anti-friction bearing sheaves.

  10,000 lbs. (single line pull)
  x 4.71   (Ratio B of 5 parts of line)
= 47,100 lbs. (lift capacity)

10,000 lbs. single line pull with 5 parts of line will accommodate 47,100 lbs. lift capacity.

NOMINAL STRENGTH AND WEIGHT OF WIRE ROPE 6×19 CLASS – 6×37 CLASS

DIA.	NOMINAL STRENGTH (TONS)			APPROX. Wt/Ft (lbs)	
	IPS		EIPS		
	Fiber Core	IWRC	IWRC	Fiber Core	IWRC
3/16	1.55	1.67	–	0.059	0.065
1/4	2.74	2.94	3.40	0.105	0.116
5/16	4.26	4.58	5.27	0.164	0.18
3/8	6.10	6.56	7.55	0.236	0.26
7/16	8.27	8.89	10.2	0.32	0.35
1/2	10.7	11.5	13.3	0.42	0.46
9/16	13.5	14.5	16.8	0.53	0.59
5/8	16.7	17.9	20.6	0.66	0.72
3/4	23.8	25.6	29.4	0.95	1.04
7/8	32.2	34.6	39.8	1.29	1.42
1	41.8	44.9	51.7	1.68	1.85
1-1/8	52.6	56.5	65.0	2.13	2.34
1-1/4	64.6	69.4	79.9	2.63	2.89
1-3/8	77.7	83.5	96	3.18	3.50
1-1/2	92	98.9	114	3.78	4.16
1-5/8	107	115	132	4.44	4.88
1-3/4	124	133	153	5.15	5.67
1-7/8	141	152	174	5.91	6.50
2	160	172	198	6.72	7.39
2-1/8	179	192	221	7.59	8.35
2-1/4	200	215	247	8.51	9.36
2-3/8	222	239	274	9.48	10.4
2-1/2	244	262	302	10.5	11.6
2-5/8	268	288	331	11.6	12.8
2-3/4	292	314	361	12.7	14.0
2-7/8	317	341	393	13.9	15.3
3	–	370	425	–	16.6
3-1/8	–	399	458	–	18.0
3-1/4	–	429	492	–	19.5
3-3/8	–	459	529	–	21.0
3-1/2	–	491	564	–	22.6

Note: The above "strength" values are NOT wire rope choker ratings as they do not contain the critical safety factor associated with wire rope chokers.

IPS- Improved Plow Steel
EIPS- Extra Improved Plow Steel
IWRC- Independent Wire Rope Core

| WIRE ROPE CLIPS ||||
Wire Rope and Clip Size (in.)	Minimum Number of Clips	Amount of Rope to turn back (in.)	Torque in Ft. Lbs.
1/8	2	3 1/4	4.5
3/16	2	3 3/4	7.5
1/4	2	4 3/4	15
5/16	2	5 1/4	30
3/8	2	6 1/2	45
7/16	2	7	65
1/2	3	11 1/2	65
9/16	3	12	95
5/8	3	12	95
3/4	4	18	130
7/8	4	19	225
1	5	26	225
1 1/8	6	34	225
1 1/4	7	44	360
1 3/8	7	44	360
1 1/2	8	54	360
1 5/8	8	58	430
1 3/4	8	61	590
2	8	71	750
2 1/4	8	73	750
2 1/2	9	84	750
2 3/4	10	100	750
3	10	106	1,200
3-1/2	12	149	1,200

If a pulley (sheave) is used for turning back the wire rope, add one additional clip.

If using more clips than shown, the amount of turnback should be increased proportionately.

The torque values are based upon the threads being clean, dry, and free of lubrication.

Efficiency ratings for wire rope end terminations are based upon the catalog breaking strength of wire rope. The efficiency rating of a properly prepared loop or thimble eye termination for clip sizes 1/8" through 7/8" is 80%. For sizes 1" thru 3-1/2" it is 90%. The number of clips shown is based upon using RRL or RLL wire rope, 6 x 19 or 6 x 37 Class, FC or IWRC; IPS or XIP. If Seale construction or similar large outer wire type construction in the 6 x 19 Class is to be used for sizes 1 inch and larger, add one additional clip. If a pulley (sheave) is used for turning back the wire rope, add one additional clip. Always put the clip u-bolt on the 'dead' side and the saddle on the 'live' side of the wire rope loop. A Flemish Eye (Molly Hogan) can be spliced in the cable in conjunction with cable clips.

LOAD CAPACITY OF THREADED HANGER RODS ASTM A36, A575 AND A576 HOT ROLLED CARBON STEEL PER ASME B31.1-2007 TABLE 121.7.2(A)

Nominal Rod Diameter (inches)	Root Area of Thread (in^2)	Maximum Safe Load (lbs.)	Maximum Safe Load (kg.)
3/8	0.068	730	3.23
1/2	0.126	1,350	5.98
5/8	0.202	2,160	9.61
3/4	0.302	3,230	14.4
7/8	0.419	4,480	19.9
1	0.552	5,900	26.2
1-1/4	0.889	9,500	42.4
1-1/2	1.293	13,800	61.6
1-3/4	1.744	18,600	82.8
2	2.292	24,600	109
2-1/4	3.021	32,300	144
2-1/2	3.716	39,800	177
2-3/4	4.619	49,400	220
3	5.621	60,100	267
3-1/4	6.720	71,900	320
3-1/2	7.918	84,700	377
3-3/4	9.214	98,500	438
4	10.608	114,000	505
4-1/4	12.100	129,000	576
4-1/2	13.690	146,000	652
4-3/4	15.379	165,000	733
5	17.165	184,000	819

SYNTHETIC AND MANILLA ROPE CAPACITIES

DIA. IN.	POLYPROPYLENE Break Strength	POLYPROPYLENE Lbs./100ft.	NYLON Break Strength	NYLON Lbs./100ft.	MANILLA Break Strength	MANILLA Lbs./100ft.	Safe Load Ratio
1/4	1250	1.2	1650	1.5	540	2.0	10:1
3/8	2700	2.8	3700	3.5	1220	4.1	10:1
1/2	4200	4.7	6400	6.5	2380	7.5	9:1
3/4	8500	10.7	14200	14.5	4860	16.7	7:1
13/16	9900	12.7	17000	17.0	5850	19.5	7:1
1	14000	18.0	25000	26.4	8100	27.0	7:1
1-1/4	21000	27.0	37500	40.0	12200	41.6	7:1
1-1/2	29700	38.5	53000	55.0	16700	60.0	7:1
1-3/4	43000	59.0	78000	83.0	23800	89.5	7:1
2	52000	69.0	92000	95.0	28000	108.0	7:1

Always factor in the safe load ratio into the breaking strength to determine the safe working load limit.

CHAPTER 15: MAKING CALCULATIONS

- There are many calculations that can be made by using the information within this guide. Let's start with exchanger heads and their associated weights. By using the provided table on steel plate weights per square foot, we can calculate the weight of any geometric shape simply by converting such to a total square foot value. The fact that the steel plate chart has accounted for thickness thus effectively making it a volume representation prevents us from having to calculate in terms of volume whereby allowing only a square foot value to be sufficient. Simply by using the charts and information herein such as the geometric math, weight charts, etc. we can easily break an exchanger head down to its fundamental components for correct calculation of its total weight. For instance, a dollar plate (channel cover) can be converted to a square foot value allowing its thickness to be matched to that of the steel plate chart which further allows for an approximate weight, while a channel head can be broken down to its fundamental components of a pipe, flanges and nozzles thus allowing for those components to be calculated individually and added together for a total weight value.

- The following pages will outline the methods used to calculate the weights of such components thus allowing for another reference source when rigging on such heads and components. Although it would be nice to have an engineered or stamped weight on everything that requires rigging, more often the only reference source is the ability to calculate such on one's own. Even when an outside source is provided, it's always a good practice to have another means of verification. It should also be noted that when using the steel plate chart that values can be added to achieve the desired thickness. For instance, 1"= 40.8 pounds per square foot and 2"= 81.6 pounds per square foot or twice the weight per square foot of 1". We could easily figure the weight of any thickness by the proper addition of those provided. One must also pay close attention to the proper conversion of values and units thereof when making such calculations as with properly converting values to the same unit parameters such as making sure that when dealing in square feet that all values are properly converted from square inches to square feet. Incorporating varying dimensional units into the same calculation yields drastically inaccurate outputs and should be avoided. Many of the following formulas and methods should be practiced on the sections herein whereby such calculations have already been done as with verifying the weight per linear foot of pipe by way of the methods further discussed to establish that one is performing the calculations correctly. Blind flange calculations are also comparable to dollar plates and have values herein which have already been calculated thus allowing a method of practice. Knowledge is a good thing, but a little knowledge can be more dangerous than none at all. Always go the extra steps to verify all information that is critical to performing a task safely and efficiently. That includes all information provided herein.

DOLLAR PLATE

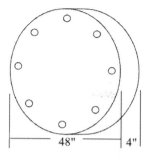

Surface area= πr^2
4" Steel Plate= 163.36 pounds per square foot

3.14159 x 24"x 24"= 1809.556 sq. in.
1809.556 sq. in. = 12.566 sq. ft.
12.566 sq. ft. x 163.36 = 2052.78 pounds

Blind Flange dimensions and weights can be found in other sections of this book in a range of sizes and thicknesses which could give a close approximation of the weights of dollar plates if one is unable to perform the correct calculations. I would suggest a calculation to be made if possible along with a cross reference of the previous mentioned resources to supply at least two sources of confirmation.

CHANNEL HEAD

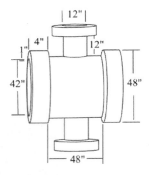

12" sch. 80 pipe x 12" long = 88.51 x 2= 177.02 pounds
12" 300# weld neck flange = 142 x 2= 284 pounds
48" x 40"x 4"flange = 626.525 x 2= 1253.05 pounds
42"OD x 48" long x 1"wall thickness pipe = 1751.75 pounds

177.02 + 284 + 1253.05 + 1751.75 = 3465.82 total pounds

The flange and small bore pipe weights were taken from the provided charts within this book, but can ultimately be estimated similar to the methods used to calculate the large bore flanges at each end along with the channel head body which is often a common piping size. To calculate piping weights simply use the circumference at the center of the pipe which is half way between the OD and ID which is equal to the OD minus one wall thickness or the ID plus one wall thickness.

Multiply this circumference times the length to get the square inches which can be converted to square feet and multiplied times the weight of steel plate at that wall thickness per square foot to yield the weight of the pipe. If one linear foot is used then you effectively have pipe weight per linear foot.

Example:

36"OD- XS pipe has a wall thickness of 1/2" and linear weight per foot of 189.57 pounds per the charts in this book.

36"- 1/2" = 35 1/2" center working diameter
35 1/2 x 3.14159 = 111.5264 x 12" (linear foot) = 1338.317 square inches
x .006944 = 9.2933 square feet x 20.4 (pounds per square foot) = 189.58
(with the slight difference being merely due to a rounding factor)

To estimate the square footage of a flange simply subtract the inside diameter square footage from the outside diameter square footage to give the remaining square footage of the flange. Example:

48" OD x 40" ID
24 x 24 x 3.14159 = 1809.556 sq. In. = 12.566 sq. Ft.
20 x 20 x 3.14159 = 1256.636sq. In. = 8.727 sq. Ft.
12.566 – 8.727 = 3.839 sq. Ft. of metal within the flange which could now be multiplied by a weight per square foot per thickness from the steel plate chart to give a total estimated weight of the flange. The metal lost due to the bolt holes is negligible and adds to the safety factor if they are not deducted.

Bell heads could be roughly estimated by the surface area formulas of half a sphere or closed end cylinder provided in the geometry formulas section which can be further converted to a weight by the before shown processes.

Bundle weights can be estimated by finding the weight per linear foot for the tube size of which it is constructed in the <u>Plate and Tubing</u> section and multiplying that value by the total number of tubes which will establish a collective bundled tube weight per linear foot which can be multiplied times the total length of the bundle to establish an estimated overall tube weight. The tube sheet weight can be factored per its thickness and square feet measure by referencing the plate weight chart. Considerations must also be given for the extra length of tube in the bends of a u-tube which can be accomplished by multiplying half the diameter of the bundle by the bundled weight per linear foot being as there are various radius tube bends comprising the bundle. Further considerations must also be given to any pull through floating heads which can be estimated per its thickness and square feet measure also.

CG'S AND THE LAWS OF LEVERAGE

Much of the methodology I'm fixing to discuss was a result of information from various sources throughout my studies along with some personal applications of various aspects which I've learned and used throughout the years. Rigging is one of the most immediately dangerous tasks amongst the construction industry so I would urge anyone involved to verify this method externally along with becoming familiar with it if it is found to be useful whereby assuring it is applied correctly which should in turn limit the potential for accidents due to improper rigging. I am not an engineer and only offer this method as a tool of investigation of the many dynamic aspects involved with finding and rigging to the center of gravity of a rigid system to be lifted.

Gravity acts upon a system in a predictable manner which can be calculated if certain parameters are known. It isn't acting across the universe in some random fashion but rather adheres to the structural relationship of material structured systems. When rigging, the crane hook will always find its way over the center of gravity of the load which it is attached by way of rigging which means the further you've rigged away from such, the more unstable the load when lifted. Therefore, to prevent unaccounted for stresses upon the rigging at certain points which may result in rigging failure it is best to try to calculate the center of gravity for a rigid system and rig to that point whereby individual angles and loads per connection point can then be factored in the equation. This in turn assures a more stable load which doesn't shift once fully supported by the rigging whereby causing a potential for instability and safety issues. But...finding a CG is something which very few rigging manuals and classes will address, though some good ones do. They insist that one is required but often leave out the actual methods for doing so, and we all know that an engineer provided CG might be an option for a critical or non-routine lift, but is never an option for the day to day piping, valve, exchanger bundle and heads, etc. lifts which represent the greatest immediate threat to day to day safety amongst the rigging department.

A symmetrical straight run of pipe of any length will balance at its center as most of us know. Thus, one choker can be placed at five feet upon a ten foot long pipe and it will balance. Two chokers can be centered upon this five foot mark whereby receiving a more stable load while still being concentrated upon the same CG. Move the two choker centerline over a foot in either direction and you'll find an un-level load upon lifting with the angle of deflection relative to the amount of motion required for the actual CG to align itself with the hook of the crane. It's pretty easy to find such a CG concerning a straight run of pipe, but attach another run with a 90° fitting and the problem becomes more complicated, but not unsolvable.

The reason the before mentioned pipe balances at the exact position that it does is because of the same laws which govern leverage and the forces acting over distances, which with further investigation also relate to the very relationship by which the planets orbit the sun in terms of the force by which gravity acts over vast distances as two equally massive bodies interacting at a distance in space will have a barycenter of mass at a centralized distance between them of which they both orbit. Change the ratio of mass to mass while maintaining the distance of separation and the barycenter moves accordingly towards the more massive body whereby its effects upon the less massive body can be seen to a greater degree than can the less massive bodies effects upon the more massive body in terms of each affecting the trajectory of the other. In the case of large differences in mass as with the sun and planets, the earth and moon, etc. the barycenter is often positioned within the structure of the larger body as the larger body simply wobbles about this point. Otherwise it's just somewhere within the space between the two bodies. We see these same dynamics being expressed in various ways within the parameters we must consider when placing rigging upon a load to be lifted.

The laws of leverage establish that distance x weight = distance x weight which means that the fulcrum of a balanced system is at a point whereby the product of the distance and weight upon each side of it are canceling each other out. With a symmetrical straight run of pipe with a choker acting as the fulcrum, this will take place at the linear center of measure or five feet along a ten foot run. Being able to establish the CG for one run allows us to work from it to the next run whereby another ten foot section connected by a 90 ° fitting establishes that we have a travel distance separating the two individual CG's which can be easily calculated using simple trig:

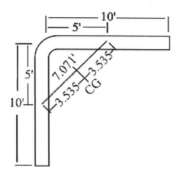

What most people fail to realize is that despite the two individual sections being connected by a fitting, they are still acting upon each other within a relationship of the distance between their individual constituent CG's relative to their individual weights which are acting over these distance. Their ratio of weight is equal to their ratio of length when dealing with the same size and schedule pipe.

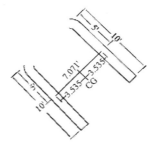

Notice in the diagram on the previous page that we're still merely balancing two constituent systems across a distance with the fulcrum being positioned and determined by the ratio of one's weight to the other as seen in the above diagram. These measurements will also work for any size and schedule as long as they are symmetrical throughout. If lifting this section of pipe horizontally, then the hook would be directly over the CG between the two pieces of pipe. However, if lifting vertically, the hook will still be directly above the CG, but it will also be above the top run of pipe. Being as we are dealing with a right angle triangle, simple trig will determine the exact position along the other axis as the same ratio can be used across the diagonal as can be used across the horizontal. Here's how the calculations were arrived at after the initial simple trig was done to calculate the distance from CG to CG:

5' + 5' = 10' ..... 5' ÷ 10' = .50 ..... 7.071' x .50 = 3.535'

To satisfy that the product of distance and weight be the same on each side of the CG it must be located at center of the diagonal due to each side having the exact same weight (also length in this example). To find the distance from the center of the vertical run as rigging the pipe upright:

5' x .50 = 2.5'

This distance from the center of the vertical run down the horizontal run will position the hook directly over the CG. It's as if you were dropping a plumb bob from the hook of the crane down through the intersection of the CG. What this formula is capturing is how to determine the percentage across a separation length to travel to establish a CG relative to the ratio of weight upon each side of the separation length. Simply put, weights establish ratios which establish percentages which establish distances to a CG. When dealing with two constituent systems to establish a composite CG the formula requires the addition of both weights to be divided into the larger weight which will give the percentage of linear travel from the lighter side, whereby the remaining travel will reflect the remaining percentage which is established by dividing the sum of both of the weights into the lesser weight.

For example, if we replace the diagram with a 6' x 8' configuration of pipe, then the resulting centralized triangle will be the famous 3' x 4' x 5'. The CG to such a configuration would be established by:

3' + 4' = 7' .... 4' ÷ 7' = .5714 .... 3' ÷ 7' = .4285
.5714 + .4285 = 1(these two added together will always equal 1)
5' x .5714 = 2' 10-5/16" from the lighter side towards the heavier
5' x .4285 = 2' 1-11/16" from the heavier side towards the lighter

Notice how the CG favors the heavier side which should be common sense as with moving a choker towards an end that picks up unevenly heavy. The CG will always be offset closer to the heavier side to be balanced. Sometimes the combined composite CG will be somewhere within the system but sometimes the geometry demands that the CG be found as a hypothetical point in space to which one must rig to establish a secure and balanced load. No matter the geometry, all systems have a hypothetical point to which all gravitational forces balance or equalize which is the very place to which the rigging must position the hook over while establishing proper tension upon each leg.

When considering the same size pipe throughout a system, one can factor using only lengths as the weight per unit of length is symmetrical. However, if there exists a size or schedule change to the pipe, then the actual weight of each size pipe in conjunction with the distances must be considered. For instance, change the schedule of either pipe in the diagram and the CG must be moved towards the heavier side to account for the increased weight. This means that the length relationship of the two is no longer the only parameter needed but we must also know the difference in weight of the two to properly calculate the composite CG from the constituent components.

Now one can also consider how this relates to the required force needed to be applied to a crowbar on one end with a fulcrum positioned at a distance from a known weight being leveraged at the other end to balance or move the load. If you have a 5:1 ratio established by the pivot position of the fulcrum, then your one moves five times its load at the other end whereby the distance times weight requirement is maintained. You are effectively putting in 1/5 the force due to your force acting over a greater distance. Example:

A six foot bar is pivoting at one foot from its end with a load of 500 pounds at that end. This leaves five foot on your end whereby you must only supply approximately 100 pounds to satisfy the equation: 1 x 500 = 500; 5 x 100 = 500

One thing this will tell you is that if you have a long pry bar checking the downward force of a load as the crane comes up as with sticking it between two flanges which establishes a big mechanical advantage and you place your entire body weight on the bar and nothing moves, then there's obviously a lot of weight still pushing down at this point. You basically can now figure your output per mechanical advantage. This also relates to chain falls, cum-a-longs block and tackle, etc.

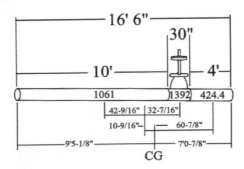

14" pipe schedule 80 @ 106.1 pounds per foot
14" 300# butt weld gate valve @ 1392 pounds

Always remember that when figuring a CG of a composite system that you'll be solving for one group which gives its composite results which will be used to solve out to the next group.

Here we have three constituent systems which we must find a composite CG for. First we'll solve for the long joint of pipe and the valve. The distance relationship between the two will be the distance between their constituent CG's, which is the sum of half of their distances. Next we'll solve from their composite system to the remaining constituent system of the short run of pipe. Working in inches eases the calculation efforts.

60"+ 15" = 75"... 1061 + 1392 = 2453 ... 1392 ÷ 2453 = .5675 ... 75" x .5675 = 42-9/16" ... 75"- 42-9/16" = 32-7/16" ... 32-7/16" + 15" + 24" = 71-7/16" ... 2453 + 424.4 = 2877.4 ... 2453 ÷ 2877.4 = .8525 ... 71-7/16" x .8525 = 60-7/8" ... 71-7/16" – 60-7/8" = 10-9/16" ... 60-7/8" + 24" = 7' 0-7/8" ... 16' 6" – 7' 0-7/8" = 9' 5-1/8"

Notice how we are merely using the weights to find percentages of the distances. This is the key to finding CG's as we merely want to know the effects of weight acting over distances relative to each other whereby we understand how the system leverages itself to form a rigid composite system which can be balanced from a single point. The addition of the weights followed by the division of the greater weight by the result of the previous addition is the simple way to find the percentage by which to multiply to the length between the two constituent CG's to determine the exact location by which distance and weight will be equal to distance and weight, which is how we arrive back at the laws of leverage. Here we'll go back to the first composite CG and verify this result as follows. I'll be converting the fractions to decimals for ease of calculation:

42.5625 x 1061 = 45158.81
32.4375 x 1392 = 45153

The difference you see here is negligible but will often be present as a product of rounding a decimal place or a calculator resolving to the nearest 1/16". If you work the problem with a construction calculator which does round as such you'll get:

42-9/16" x 1061 = 45158-13/16 ÷ 1392 = 32-7/16"

Here we can clearly see that the distance and weight products are equal on both sides of the composite CG. Now we'll check the next composite CG to verify it. Remember that here we are working as though the valve and the long run of pipe are a combined weight working from their composite CG distance. This is critical to remember.

10-9/16" x 2453 = 25909-13/16
60-7/8" x 424.4 = 25835-3/8

At first look you might think that the CG should be adjusted, but I'll move the equation by adding 1/16 to the long end and taking it away from the short end and show the results below.

10-1/2" x 2453 = 25756-1/2
60-15/16 x 424.4 = 25861-7/8

As you can plainly see, the amplification of even 1/16" of an inch when multiplying by such a large number exaggerates the slightest of differences greatly. The first set of equations show that the closest we can get to the nearest 1/16" is the original CG. It's important to understand such concepts when factoring such complex equations. Confidence in your calculations means a world of difference when you find yourself in certain situations. That is why I am spending so much time on this section and also encourage you to understand these methods and their inner workings and possible limitations.

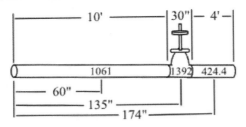

Another method used to calculate a composite CG from various constituent CGs is to divide the total moment of the system by its total weight. The total moment is the sum of all of the individual moments from each constituent system. These two methods should always be used in conjunction with each other to allow a means of double checking each other. The calculation for this method is as follows:

1061	60 × 1061 = 63660
1392	135 × 1392 = 187920
<u>424.4</u>	174 × 424.4 = <u>73845.6</u>
2877.4 lbs. total	325425.6 total moment

325425.6 / 2877.4 = 113.097" = 9'5-1/8" from left to CG

Now we see that once we've rounded up to the nearest sixteenth we arrive at the very same value for the composite CG from the left side of the system as we did by using the other method outlined on the previous pages. Thus, we can be a little more certain that our calculations were performed correctly.

The image on the top left of the following page represents the geometry and trig involved with the process of determining ever larger composite CG's from ever more constituent systems. The key is to be able to figure each systems CG and then be able to figure the composite relationship of their combined CG's. This is a representation as if we were to be lifting an entire metal floor with two pieces of equipment having to be factored into the lift. The factoring of the floors CG is done in the same way in terms of figuring the distribution of the steel beams beneath and their pounds per foot which is generally given in the beams discription (an I-beam which is labeled W27 x 161 has a flange to flange or depth measurement of 27" and wieghs 161 pounds per foot). Once the composite CG and total weight of the floor is known, it can be factored against the vessel on the left whereby receiving a composite CG for those two whose total weight and CG can now be factored against the cylindrical vessel on the right allowing for an overall composite CG which must be rigged to for a controlled and stable load. The tension of each corner choker could also be factored at this point using the methods discussed in the rigging section.

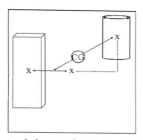

The image to the bottom left is a three dimensional isometric representation of a piping system with two 90° angles. Here we see the two upper runs being factored to a composite CG which is then transferred to the lower run of pipe per their weight ratios having determined distance to be moved along the various axes. Transferring from the upper composite system to the lower constituent system requires some 3d trigonometry much the same as figuring rolling offsets in piping fabrication. The black lines represent the transference axis of the CG while the dotted lines outline the hypothetical 3d cube required to correctly transfer from one axis to another allowing the trig relationships to be easily visualized. Piping systems with 90° fittings is pretty straight forward to calculate while systems which contain 30°, 45°, etc. fittings is a bit more complex in determining the distances between the CG axis of one constituent system relative to another whereby the weights will then determine the composite CG. It takes a bit of practice to be able to apply the complex trig which allows for such calculations but it is possible by simply finding where to apply the right angle calulations which yeild these various distances by solving for one triangle to effectively solve another. For instance, many times you will find that rather than creating the run and set of the trig function, fittings other than 90° allow the pipe to actually be factored as the travel of another right angle triangle which sometimes must be formed by a hypothetical centerline extension of the other run connected to the same fitting.

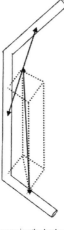

A detailed calculation isn't always required, but being intimately familiar with the dynamics involved in doing one allows an even better visual approximation when merely 'eyeballing' a CG as we all do. Once familiar with these methods, you'll find yourself looking along the hypothetical axis from constituent CG to constituent CG while simultaneously factoring the weight of one system to the other which helps you to decide on the approximate place to establish the hook over once proper choker tension is achieved. Though it's always recommended to use sufficient chain falls for needed adjustment on a complex three point pick, I have in the past simply positioned the crane hook over the composite CG with some sufficiently long equal length chokers and began by wrapping the long leg first and raising the hook to remove all the slack. After which, I would wrap the other two legs an extra wrap or two until the hook was properly tensioned from all directions while remaining over the CG as I would add a shackle if needed to make up a little length here or there. I don't recommend this practice in the field, but it does save some time offloading a trailer or simply rearranging the laydown yard.

Always practice such calculations as outlined in the previous pages on the smallest and least dangerous scenarios of piping and such as with unloading a trailer of prefabricated pipe or pulling small spools from the unit to become as familiar as you can with the dynamics at play here. This helps to build proficiency in performing the calculations and also builds confidence that you may need someday when making a critical lift which holds potential dangers to property and personnel. Double check my calculations and instructions elsewhere. Never be satisfied with your level of intelligence when putting yourself or others in a potentially dangerous situation pertaining to such things as rigging, which always has some degree of danger to it. I used to measure and calculate the most meaningless of lifts which would often get me laughed at because what they didn't understand was that even though it might not have mattered then, when it did matter I would have all of the small victories behind me which would increase my confidence enough to take on the larger and more dangerous tasks. These methods may very well be in other manuals, but I have seen very little of the actual calculations to finding complex composite CG's and actually learned much of this through various other avenues of investigation such as the application of the leverage laws. For this reason I debated upon sharing this information but I do so not to take the chance of getting someone injured, but to provide a reference of the many dynamics at play concerning how a composite system rigidly distributes its forces to establish a center of gravity, which must be known to perform any lift properly and safely to prevent unforeseen distributions of weight which results in unstable loads and potential damage to rigging.

Once understood and verified properly, I have attempted to outline the means to determine nearly every aspect of a lift from finding weights and a resulting CG to determining angles of rigging and the resulting tension factors which would allow the proper selection of rigging. It's the lack of information to many of these very processes in our line of work that urges me to provide this book. It's not meant to be the last word on the information it provides, but rather an eye opener to the many aspects to doing a job safely and efficiently with the highest quality possible. There's always the potential that information herein could contribute to an unsafe situation, which is why I urge everyone to verify and check the data being used. I simply overcome this concern by providing information as accurately as possible and by knowing that this very information might also prevent many unsafe situations which I know exist in the field every day by simply establishing a starting point which might lead some to wanting to better understand the many aspects of doing certain jobs safely and efficiently. One example is that most people aren't aware of how often they get into the 5:1 safety factor of rigging when rendering chokers and such while bull rigging. A rating on a choker is just a starting point. There are many situations which one can put that choker in whereby that rating must be properly adjusted to maintain its designed limitations and safety factor. I hope I have done a good job at capturing important information pertaining to your daily tasks. If this book has helped you then drop me an email and let me know. Be safe and work smarter rather than harder.